The New Republic

THE LONGMAN HISTORY OF AMERICA
General Editor: Mark White

Forthcoming titles in the Series

THE NEW REPUBLIC

The United States of America 1789–1815

Reginald Horsman

 LONGMAN

An imprint of PEARSON EDUCATION

Harlow, England · London · New York · Reading, Massachusetts · San Francisco · Toronto · Don Mills, Ontario · Sydney
Tokyo · Singapore · Hong Kong · Seoul · Taipei · Cape Town · Madrid · Mexico City · Amsterdam · Munich · Paris · Milan

Pearson Education Ltd
Edinburgh Gate
Harlow
Essex CM20 2JE
England

and Associated Companies around the World.

Visit us on the World Wide Web at:
www.pearsoneduc.com

First published 2000

ISBN 0582-29287-5 PPR
    0582-29288-3 CSD

British Library Cataloguing-in-Publication Data
A catalogue record for this book can be obtained from the British Library

Library of Congress Cataloging-in-Publication Data
Horsman, Reginald.
    The new republic : the United States of America, 1789–1815 /
Reginald Horsman.
        p.   cm. — (The Longman history of the United States of
America)
    Includes bibliographical references and index.
    ISBN 0–582–29288–3. — ISBN 0–582–29287–5 (pbk.)
    1. United States—History—Constitutional period, 1789–1809.
    2. United States—History—1809–1817.   3. United States—Politics
and government—1789–1815. I. Title. II. Series.
    E310.H67   1999
    973—dc21   99–40529
                                                    CIP

10 9 8 7 6 5 4 3 2 1
04 03 02 01 00

Typeset in 11/13½pt Columbus by 35

The publishers wish to extend special thanks to Peter Newark of Peter Newark's
American Pictures for permission to reproduce the images in the plate section.

SERIES EDITOR'S PREFACE

This series on American history has a number of objectives. One is to provide a multi-faceted treatment of consecutive periods in American history. Textbooks on America have tended to be either political or socio-cultural in focus. Rarely has the gap between traditional history and the 'New History' been bridged. This series seeks to do that. Naturally, the balance between political and socio-cultural history will vary from volume to volume, depending on the period covered and, to some extent, the author's speciality. Nevertheless, the commitment is to the writing of genuinely eclectic works.

A second objective is for the authors to present both their own and recent scholarship in an accessible manner. While the structure and analytical emphasis will be different in each volume, authors will try to introduce readers to the diversity of recent work in the periods they are covering.

Thirdly, this series is aimed at generating a degree of Anglo-American collaboration that, it seems to be me, is unusual in the field of American history. As someone who has studied and taught in both the United States and the United Kingdom, my impression is that there is a lack of connection between American Americanists and British Americanists. Certainly, British scholars are well aware of what their American counterparts are writing, but the work of British Americanists is probably less recognized in the United States. Yet American history has become an ever more significant field in Britain, with active professional organizations and increasing numbers of talented academicians. This is a series conceived in the United Kingdom, but involving American as well as British historians, and aimed at both American and British students and scholars, as well as those in other countries. It is a truly Anglo-American series.

The series will ultimately comprise ten works on consecutive periods, from pre-colonial times to the recent years of American history. Beyond all the objectives enumerated above, the aim is to provide what all series of this sort should – namely, lucid and engaging works.

Mark J. White
Queen Mary and Westfield College
University of London

CONTENTS

ABBREVIATIONS

AC	*Annals of the Congress of the United States, 1789–1824* 42 vols (Washington, DC, 1834–56)
ADM	Admiralty Records, Public Record Office, London
ASP, F	*American State Papers, Finance*, II (Washington, DC, 1832)
ASP, FR	*American State Papers, Foreign Relations*, II, III (Washington, DC, 1832)
ASP, IA	*American State Papers, Indian Affairs*, I (Washington, DC, 1832)
ASP, MA	*American State Papers, Military Affairs*, I (Washington, DC, 1832)
ASP, MI	*American State Papers, Miscellaneous*, I (Washington, DC, 1834)
CO	Colonial Office Records, Public Record Office, London
FO	Foreign Office Records, Public Record Office, London
IBM	Bernard Mayo (ed.), *Instructions to the British Ministers to the United States, 1791–1812* (*American Historical Association, Annual Report*, 1936, vol. 3, Washington, DC, 1941)
JER	*Journal of the Early Republic*
JP	Jefferson Papers, Library of Congress
LC	Library of Congress, Washington, DC
M&P	James Richardson (ed.), *A Compilation of the Messages and Papers of the Presidents, 1789–1897*, 1 (Washington, 1900)
MADP	Madison Papers, Library of Congress
MONP	Monroe Papers, Library of Congress
NYCA	Howard B. Rock (ed.), *The New York City Artisan, 1789–1825: A Documentary History* (Albany, NY, 1989)

PAH Harold C. Syrett *et al.* (eds), *The Papers of Alexander*   [ix]
       Hamilton 27 vols (New York, 1961–81)
PJM Herbert A. Johnson *et al.* (eds), *The Papers of John*
       Marshall (Chapel Hill, NC, 1974–)
PTJ Julian Boyd *et al.* (eds), *The Papers of Thomas*
       Jefferson (Princeton, NJ, 1950–)
S&I   Arthur H. Schlesinger and Fred L. Israel (eds), *History*
       of American Presidential Elections, 1789–1968 4 vols
       (New York, 1971)
WJM Gaillard Hunt (ed.), *The Writings of James Madison*
       9 vols (New York, 1900–10)
WMQ *William and Mary Quarterly*
WO   War Office Records, Public Record Office, London
WOTJ Paul Ford (ed.), *The Works of Thomas Jefferson*
       12 vols (New York, 1904–5)

INTRODUCTION

The years from 1789 to 1815 were critical in the history of the United States. In these years the federal government had to prove that the Constitution drafted in 1787 would work, and that republicanism was capable of existing over a vast area. In the past 200 years new nations have often written elaborate constitutions, but frequently they have proved unworkable in practice. In 1789 many Americans feared that federal control over a nation that stretched from Maine to Georgia, and from the eastern seaboard to the Mississippi River, would mean either disintegration or an ever-increasing concentration of power at the center. There was no guarantee in 1789 that the states could be persuaded to combine at the expense of diminution of their own powers. Also, while there was a general trust that George Washington would preserve the revolutionary legacy, there were doubts about how well a lesser figure would be accepted in the office of president.

The new nation had to face this central task of achieving a successful union under the new Constitution while coping with pressing foreign problems and far-reaching internal changes. In 1789 the territorial integrity of the nation was being challenged in the Northwest by England and in the Southwest by Spain. Since the Revolution neither of these nations had respected American boundaries in the Mississippi Valley. The British in Canada still occupied posts within American territory, and exerted a strong influence among the Indian tribes to the south of the Great Lakes. The Spanish along the Gulf of Mexico refused to allow the United States free use of the rivers running into the Gulf, operated far to the north of the line that the United States claimed was the boundary, and also kept close contact with the Indians. A decade later, western problems were compounded when France renewed its ambitions in the Mississippi Valley. Only state and individual acceptance of the new federal powers would give the nation the ability to deal effectively with these problems in the West.

The internal changes of these years reached most facets of American life. The social and economic structures of colonial America were in the process

[2] of transformation. Patterns of deference and an ordered sense of community were challenged by a new individualism that ranged through all aspects of life. New evangelical religions – particularly the Baptists and Methodists – made huge inroads against older denominations, stressing individual religious experience rather than doctrine, and challenging the older, learned clergy. In politics, ordinary white males were gaining a larger role in government. The Founding Fathers' hope that a national government unified behind one set of leaders would maintain a general sense of civic responsibility collapsed as leaders disagreed on policy and offered the electorate different interpretations of how America's future greatness could best be achieved. Political parties developed in the 1790s, and they disagreed strongly about major questions in both domestic and foreign policy. Leaders of each party were convinced that the policies of the other party threatened the success of the republican experiment.

In these decades a new individualism also began to permeate American economic life. While agriculture remained the main pursuit of most Americans, a new commercialism became a pervading feature of American society. The market-place became of dominant importance. Farmers sought to expand their markets both internally and externally, artisans and craftsmen looked beyond their immediate vicinities for sales, entrepreneurs began more extensive speculation in land and commodities, numerous banks and other companies were founded, and in the Northeast there was even the tentative beginning of a factory system.

Opportunities for sales abroad soared after 1793 when Europe erupted into general warfare that lasted until 1815. There was increased demand for American agricultural produce, and the chance to make great profits re-exporting the products of European colonies from the West Indies to Europe. Yet, the desire of the United States to benefit economically from the wars in Europe brought with it great dangers; dangers similar to those that were later encountered in 1914 and 1939. The European belligerents were unwilling to allow their enemies to benefit freely from American neutral trade, and American shipping and seamen encountered constant dangers. Ultimately, the American reaction to European efforts to restrict American commerce led to a declaration of war against England in 1812. This war came near to ruining much of what had been achieved since 1789.

For many Americans these issues of federal power, war, markets, and profits were only of peripheral concern, for the Revolution had not changed some basic aspects of the society. In 1789 politics and public life were still the domain of white males; the Revolution did not transform the position of

women or of African Americans. The attack on slavery that had been incorporated in revolutionary rhetoric weakened in the post-revolutionary years.
In 1790 the population of approximately four million people included some
700,000 slaves. Even the 60,000 African Americans who were free did not
exist as equal citizens in the new republican society.

The American Indians were also within the territory of the United States
without sharing the advantages of the new republic. In 1789 nearly all of the
land northwest of the Ohio River was in the possession of Indian tribes, and
though settlers from the East were advancing into Kentucky and Tennessee
most of the territory south of those regions was in Indian hands. The leaders
of the revolutionary generation had hopes that the Indians might be brought
within the republic as individuals, but greed for land and animosities generated in border areas led to extensive warfare and Indian expulsion.

The early republic was a time of great achievements, but it was also a time
in which it became fully apparent that the revolutionary gains were not to be
shared equally by all Americans.

CHAPTER 1

THE UNITED STATES IN 1789

The old Confederation Congress had decided that the government under the new Constitution would begin in New York on the first Wednesday in March, 1789. When that day arrived, neither House of Congress had the quorum that was needed. It was 6 April before a sufficient number of representatives and senators assembled to fulfill their constitutional duty of opening and counting the ballots for the office of president. There had never been any doubt about the result of the presidential vote. All 69 presidential electors who voted had given their vote to George Washington. In leading the armies to victory in the War of Independence, Washington had achieved a legendary status. When the delegates at Philadelphia had created a powerful presidency, they had no other candidate in mind. In a time of crisis, they expected him to preserve the republic that he had made possible.

Although there was a desperate need for the new government to begin governing, there was still further delay. This was an America with means of communication inferior to that of the Roman Empire. It took a week for the news of the election result to be carried to Mount Vernon, and another week for Washington to reach New York for his inauguration. Finally on 30 April Washington was inaugurated. The world was now to discover whether the dream of a federal republic over an extensive area could succeed.

From 1781 the Articles of Confederation had set in place a formal national government, but much of the power had been left in the hands of the individual states. With no power of direct taxation and no control over commerce, the Confederation government had become bankrupt. It could not pay its debts, or even the interest on the debts, and did not have the means to raise the military forces necessary to achieve its ambitions in the Mississippi Valley. It dealt with foreign powers from a position of weakness. By the late 1780s many of the leaders who had led the United States to independence believed that the new republic was in danger of collapse, and thought that only a new and more powerful central government would enable the new nation to reach its full potential.

At Philadelphia in the summer of 1787, delegates to the Constitutional [5] Convention had attempted to write a constitution that would give the new federal government the powers that the Confederation government had lacked; powers that would enable it to tackle the host of problems that faced the new nation both at home and abroad. Unlike its predecessor, this new federal government could tax and control commerce, and had a potentially powerful chief executive, but it was uncertain whether those who had ardently resisted the yielding of such powers to a central authority would cooperate in making the new system work. Ratification had been a contentious process, and the convention votes had been extremely close in Virginia and New York. Members of state conventions had suggested constitutional amendments that they thought essential, particularly the incorporation of a bill of rights. If the new government was to gain acceptance, these concerns would have to be addressed.

The choosing of a vice-president had also demonstrated that the hopes that all would rally behind a unified national government were likely to be disappointed. The Constitution had provided that there would be no separate vote for vice-president; whoever finished second to the presidential choice would serve in that position. Alexander Hamilton had used his influence to have John Adams of Massachusetts put forward as the choice of the Federalist supporters of the new Constitution, but Adams had received the vote of only 34 electors. State and local interests flourished to the extent that over 20 other men received votes.[1]

In the discussions surrounding the writing and ratification of the Constitution, there had been fear that a stronger centralized government would mean the arbitrary use of power, and a loss of both state and individual rights. Many had argued that creating a centralized government over a great area would mean that the nation would follow the path of Rome and move from republic to empire. They said that extensive, diverse areas, with a variety of different interests, could only be held together by a force that was incompatible with republican freedom. Montesquieu's statement that 'It is natural for a republic to have only a small territory; otherwise it cannot long subsist,' carried great weight for many in the revolutionary generation.[2]

---

1 Marcus Cunliffe, 'The elections of 1789 and 1792,' in S&I, pp.3–19; Richard McCormick, *The Presidential Game: The Origins of American Presidential Politics* (New York, 1982), pp.16–40.

2 Baron de Montesquieu (Charles de Secondat), *The Spirit of the Laws*, trans. Thomas Nugent, rev. edn, 2 vols (New York, 1899), 1, p.120. See also Gordon Wood, *The Creation of the American Republic, 1776–1787* (Chapel Hill, NC, 1969), pp.499–505; J. G. A. Pocock, *The Machiavellian Moment: Florentine Political Thought and the Atlantic Republic Tradition* (Princeton, 1975), pp.506–52.

[6]   The Federalists who had supported the Constitution had pointed out that Montesquieu had also said that a confederated republic could help solve the problem of size, and James Madison had argued that the creation of a representative rather than a direct democracy had made possible what had never been achieved before. A direct democracy, Madison argued, was confined to a small area because all of its citizens had to assemble to transact the business of government. The new American republic could extend over a vast area because the people had delegated governmental powers to their representatives.[3] This argument was particularly necessary because the United States had already devised plans to advance government into the trans-Allegheny West. The Northwest Ordinance of 1787 had provided for a future three to five states between the Ohio and the Mississippi Rivers, and it had been agreed that these states would be admitted to the Union on full equality with the original thirteen.

The fear that the combination of size and power at the center would transform the republic into an empire arose again in the state debates over ratification. Those who dissented from the approval to the Constitution given in the Pennsylvania ratifying convention argued that 'nothing short of the supremacy of despotic sway could connect and govern these United States under one government'. A Boston newspaper thundered in November 1787 that this new Constitution was 'nothing less than a hasty stride to Universal Empire in this Western World, flattering, very flattering, to young ambitious minds, but fatal to the liberties of the people'.[4] Fears of loss of state power were very great, and when the new government began its operations North Carolina and Rhode Island had still not agreed to enter the Union. North Carolina entered in November 1789, Rhode Island in May 1790.

The regional jealousies that had often near-paralysed the Confederation Congress had also emerged strongly in the debates on ratification. Throughout the 1780s the Northeast had shown concern cover the rapid advance of southern settlement into Kentucky and Tennessee; it feared a diversion of American interests away from Atlantic commerce. The author of the Massachusetts *Letters of Agrippa* argued that commerce, not power, was the true

---

3   Wilbourn E. Benton (ed.), *1787: Drafting the US Constitution*, 2 vols (College Station, Texas, 1986), 2, p.1225 (James Wilson, 1 June 1787); *The Federalist*, ed. by Jacob E. Cooke (Middletown, Conn, 1961), pp.52–3 (Federalist 9, Alexander Hamilton). For Madison see ibid., pp.61–5 (Federalist 10), pp.83–6 (Federalist 14).

4   Merrill Jensen (ed.), *The Documentary History of the Ratification of the Constitution*, 2, *Ratification of the Constitution by the States, Pennsylvania* (Madison, Wis, 1976), p.626; *American Herald* (Boston), quoted in Samuel B. Harding, *The Contest Over the Ratification of the Federal Constitution in the State of Massachusetts* (1896; rpr, New York, 1970), p.26.

bond of union, and that people were better governed by local laws and institutions. 'The idle and dissolute inhabitants of the south,' he wrote, 'require a
different regimen from the sober and active people of the north.'[5] Northeastern fears of southern influence in the new government were increased by
southern spokesmen like David Ramsay of South Carolina, who argued in a
published address on the new Constitution that those in his state who feared
the new document should remember that southern influence was constantly
increasing because of their western lands. The Southern states, he wrote, had
extensive areas of land in process of settlement, while northeastern land was
small in area and so poor in quality that residents were constantly leaving. 'In
fifty years,' he prophesied, 'it is probable that the southern states will have a
great ascendency over the Eastern.'[6] Those who governed under the new Constitution had to satisfy many who still thought locally rather than nationally.

The territory of the United States in 1789 was indeed great by European
standards. It stretched from the Atlantic in the east to the Mississippi in the
west, from the Great Lakes in the north to a disputed boundary north of the
Gulf of Mexico in the south. The region west of the Mississippi, and the land
along the Gulf belonged to Spain. To the north was British Canada. There
was an intense American interest in the region beyond the Alleghenies. The
inability of the old Confederation government to protect those settlers who
had advanced beyond the mountains had helped to destroy it, and in the
spring of 1789, when the new government was beginning its operations in
New York, settlers were laying the foundations of new states in Kentucky
and Tennessee, and trying to move beyond the Ohio River into what was to
become the state of Ohio. The Indian tribes of the Mississippi Valley were
making every effort to protect their lands from the intrusion of the Europeans.

The embattled areas west of the Alleghenies by no means represented the
limits of America's ambitions. When Jedidiah Morse issued his *American
Geography* in 1789 he wrote that 'we cannot but anticipate the period, as not
far distant, when the AMERICAN EMPIRE will comprehend millions of
souls, west of the Mississippi.'[7] The Americans of the revolutionary generation had ardently defended localism while dreaming of continental empire.
Even the disappointments and confusions of the post-1783 years had not
crushed a belief in American destiny on the North American continent.

---

5 'Letters of Agrippa', in Paul Leicester Ford (ed.), *Essays on the Constitution of the United States*
(Brooklyn, NY, 1892), p.91.
6 'An Address to the People of South Carolina', in Paul Leicester Ford (ed.), *Pamphlets on the
Constitution of the United States* (1888; rpr. New York, 1968), p.375.
7 Jedidiah Morse, *The American Geography* (1789; rpr, New York, 1970), p.469.

[8]   In the post-revolutionary years these dreams of continental republican empire had been confronted with the reality of an impotent central government that could not achieve even limited objectives across the Alleghenies. The central government had wanted to ensure the safety of settlers moving into the Mississippi Valley, and to ease its financial problems by selling the public lands that had been ceded to it by the states. Lands had been sold, but settlers had been under constant attack. In 1789 Indian resistance west of the mountains remained unbroken.

Problems of settlement in the Mississippi Valley were compounded because the United States had failed to establish its territorial sovereignty over the boundaries given to it at the end of the Revolution. In the North, the national boundary was supposed to run through the Great Lakes, but the British had retained posts within American territory at a number of key spots including Niagara, Detroit, and Mackinac. The Great Lakes were a British preserve and, from their posts within American territory, the British influenced the Indians of the region, supplying them and encouraging them to resist the advancing American pioneers. Prevented by lack of money from raising more than pitifully few troops, the old Confederation government had failed totally in asserting its authority in the Northwest.

In the Southwest, a similar situation existed, but one which was even more destructive to American interests. At the end of the Revolution separate British treaties with the Americans and the Spanish had caused boundary confusion. The United States claimed that their boundary in the south was the 31st parallel, but the Spanish on the Gulf sent ships up the Mississippi far to the north of that line, had troops on what the Americans considered their territory and, like the British in the north, encouraged the Indians within American territory to resist the American advance. The Spanish territories of East and West Florida stretched along the Gulf beyond the modern limits of Florida to the Mississippi River. The Spanish control over the lower Mississippi and the port of New Orleans created a critical problem for the United States. The new American settlers in the trans-Allegheny West could not send their produce to market eastwards over the mountains; the difficult terrain and lack of roads made the cost prohibitive. Their way to market was by water. Pioneers settled on the tributaries of the Mississippi, and sent their goods down that river through New Orleans to the sea. This trade had been irregular since 1783, because the Spanish had refused to sign a commercial treaty with the United States. American dreams of a republican empire in the Mississippi Valley depended on markets, and the markets could only be reached by way of the Gulf of Mexico.

When Jedidiah Morse wrote of his expectation that millions of Americans [9] would cross the Mississippi River, he was anticipating the removal of Spanish power on the North American continent. 'The God of nature,' he wrote, 'never intended that some of the best part of the earth should be inhabited by the subjects of a monarch, 4,000 miles from them.'[8] Many now hoped that the new government with greatly enhanced powers would ensure that a Mississippi Valley dominated by the British and the Spanish would be a futile European dream.

The Confederation government's inability to ensure commercial advantages for its citizens in the Southwest was only a symptom of a larger problem. As the Confederation had no power over commerce, it had been unable to control the individual commercial aims of the states and unable to command the respect of the European powers. The Confederation government had been unable to negotiate commercial treaties with either Great Britain or Spain. American overseas commerce was flourishing, but American ambitions far exceeded what had been achieved.

In 1790 the first national census listed a total American population of 3,929,214. The American Indians, who were numerous over much of the western region of the nation, were not included in this tally, but the 700,000 African American slaves were. There were also some 60,000 free blacks. Africans and their descendants thus composed about one-sixth of the total population. Estimates based on family names indicate that nearly 90 per cent of the free white population was from the British Isles, mostly from England but with substantial numbers from Scotland and Ireland. The next largest group was of German origin. Immigration was not to have any striking effect on this mix in the next 30 years. Until 1819 no accurate records were kept, but estimates place the number of European immigrants in the years from 1783 to 1815 at no more than 250,000. The most important single immigrant group in these years – exceeding any single European nationality – were Africans. Over 200,000 new slaves arrived in the United States between 1790 and 1810. The official ending of the foreign slave trade in January 1808 slowed this African increase to a trickle.[9]

---

8 Ibid.

9 *A Century of Population Growth: From the First Census of the United States to the Twelfth, 1790–1900* (Washington, DC, 1909), pp.47, 116–24; 'Report of the Committee on Linguistic and National Stocks in the Population of the United States,' in *American Historical Association, Annual Report*, 1931, vol. 1 (Washington, DC, 1932), pp.103–408; Roger Daniels, *Coming to America: A History of Immigration and Ethnicity in American Life* (New York, 1990), p.117; Curtis B. Nettels, *The Emergence of a National Economy, 1775–1815* (New York, 1962), p.131; Roger Anstey, 'The volume of the North American slave carrying trade from Africa, 1761–1810,' in *Société Française D'Histoire D'Outre Mer* 62 (1975), pp.47–66.

[1 0]   The impact of immigration was minor, but the natural population increase was dramatic – over 5,300,000 in 1800, more than 7,230,000 in 1810, and an estimated 8,500,000 in 1815. For much of the eighteenth century, the pattern was for an American wife to become pregnant within a year of her marriage, and to bear a child every two or three years until she was dead or beyond her years of fertility. Colonial American birth rates were much higher than those of Western Europe. American women married young, and brides were in high demand.

The birth rate gradually declined in the late eighteenth and early nineteenth centuries, but in the years following the Revolution brides were frequently pregnant before they were married; in rural New England almost one-third. There were frequent deaths of babies and young children. In 1790 those white men and women who survived until they were 20 had a life expectancy of 45; that of African Americans was as much as ten years lower. Medical care offered few solutions. Hampered by a lack of knowledge of the specific causes of disease, physicians frequently adopted general theories of the causation in the hope that one course of treatment would be successful. In these years many physicians put their confidence in 'heroic medicine,' in which extremely heavy doses of purges and emetics were combined with blood-letting in the hope of achieving rapid cures. Without anesthetics, and with no knowledge of the need for antiseptic procedures, even the most minor surgery was fraught with great dangers. But for all the deaths, and even with a slow decline in the birth rate, the population soared in the decades after the Revolution.[10]

In 1790 the vast majority of the American population still lived on the Atlantic coast. Western Pennsylvania was gaining settlers, but Pittsburgh was still a frontier outpost, a jumping-off point for those making the dangerous journey down the Ohio to reach new American settlements. Kentucky and Tennessee had first received settlers from the East before the Revolution, but in 1790 these settlers were still engaged in conflict with the Indians of the region. North of the Ohio River, Indians still dominated. A few American pioneers were desperately clinging to the north bank of the river, and there were isolated old French-Canadian communities at Mackinac, Detroit, Green Bay, and Prairie du Chien. These settlements had far more contact

10   Jack Larkin, *The Reshaping of Everyday Life, 1790–1840* (New York, 1988), pp.63, 67–8, 193–4, 199; Mary Beth Norton, *Liberty's Daughters: The Revolutionary Experience of American Women, 1750–1800* (Boston, 1980), pp.71–91; Maris A. Vinovskis, *Fertility in Massachusetts from the Revolution to the Civil War* (New York, 1981), pp.3–23; Joyce Appleby (ed.), *Recollections of the Early Republic: Selected Autobiographies* (Boston, Mass, 1997), p.xviii.

through the Great Lakes to British Canada than they did with the Americans who nominally ruled them.

For the most part the American Indians had disappeared from the eastern seaboard. Disease and warfare had killed most of them, and the remnant had moved west to mingle with other tribes. The Indians of the eastern half of the Mississippi Valley, who occupied much of the land from the Great Lakes and the Canadian border in the north to the Spanish possessions on the Gulf, were still hopeful that they could retain their lands. In the years since the Revolution they had made determined efforts to stop the advance of settlers, and aided by the British and the Spanish had been able to offer effective resistance. For the new government, which was determined to settle the lands beyond the Alleghenies, an effective policy for the West was essential. For the Indians, the new government threatened their lands and their way of life.

The original 13 states varied widely in population. The most populous, Virginia, which included the region that was later to become West Virginia, had nearly 750,000 inhabitants (over 292,000 of these were slaves). This far exceeded the next most populous state, Pennsylvania, which had less than 440,000. The South Atlantic states (Maryland, Virginia, North and South Carolina, and Georgia), boosted by their large slave populations, outnumbered the other two main regions – New England (New Hampshire, Massachusetts, Rhode Island, and Connecticut), and the Middle states (New York, New Jersey, Pennsylvania, and Delaware). The South Atlantic states had a population of nearly 1,800,000, while New England and the Middle states each had a population of a little over 1,000,000. Kentucky and Tennessee increased the political weight of the southern slave states.

In 1790 slavery still existed in much of the North as well as the South, but the great majority of slaves lived in the southern states. Slaves comprised over 40 per cent of the population in South Carolina and almost 40 per cent in Virginia. In the Constitutional Convention in 1787 the influence of those from the lower South who wanted to continue to import slaves had been used to ensure a constitutional provision that the federal government would not interfere with the importation of slaves for 20 years. As the revolutionary attack on slavery weakened, the flurry of slave manumissions that had followed the Revolution was lessening. Those African Americans who were free were encountering severe difficulties in trying to enjoy the liberties that had been won in the American Revolution.

Pioneering was not confined to the trans-Allegheny West. Northern New England was still a frontier region. Vermont was soon to enter the Union,

[1 2] but there was little settlement in Maine except along the coast. In the Middle states, northern and western New York and western Pennsylvania were yielding to the axe as pioneers sought regions that were safer than those down the Ohio. In the South, what was to become West Virginia was a raw, frontier country. Parts of western North Carolina were still in the hands of the Cherokee, and Georgia was largely in the hands of the Creek Indians.

In those areas in which the 1790 census was carried out (this excluded extensive areas north of the Ohio River) the population density was only about 10 to the square mile. Rhode Island, the most densely populated state, had 63.4 to the square mile, and Georgia, the least densely populated, had a density in the few counties that had been created and enumerated of only 4.6.

The American population was overwhelmingly rural. In 1790 little more than 3 per cent of the population lived in places of 8,000 or more; only five cities had a population of more than 8,000. The largest city, Philadelphia, including its suburbs, had some 42,000 residents, and the next largest, New York, just over 33,000. Neither Boston nor Charleston had reached 20,000, and Baltimore had only 13,500.

In the next 25 years there was to be very little movement into the cities. New York, which in the 1790s passed Philadelphia as the most populous city, had just over 60,000 residents in 1800. By 1810 it was approaching 100,000. By far the most dramatic growth was in expansion westward. Kentucky had surpassed 400,000 by 1810, and by 1820 the combined population of Kentucky and Tennessee was almost 1,000,000. The extensive region between the Ohio and Mississippi Rivers, with a non-Indian population of only about 4,000 in 1790, had over 250,000 by 1810. The state of Ohio reached 581,000 by 1820. Dynamic population growth and movement was a striking feature of the early republic.[11]

Opportunities for many Americans arose dramatically in the three decades after the Revolution, but independence had not created an egalitarian society. Free white males had a variety of political and personal rights denied to those in Europe, but already there were considerable differences in wealth and these were to increase with the economic transformations of the next decades. Women labored under severe restrictions. Free blacks had many fewer rights than free whites, slaves were excluded from the very idea of the republic, and Indians were regarded either as 'savage' enemies to be removed or destroyed, or as hindrances to republican progress who had to be transformed to survive.

11 *Century of Population Growth*, pp.11–15, 47, 57, 135; Larkin, *Reshaping*, p.6, *NYCA*, p.xix.

In 1798 the federal government assessed a general tax based on the value [1 3] of American houses. Leo Soltow has argued from his sampling of this data that there were considerable inequalities of wealth in the United States – the top 10 per cent of adult males had houses that amounted to almost half of the total wealth in housing. Only one in ten lived in a house worth $700, and the great majority of houses were valued at between $99 and $500. The poorest dwellings, particularly in frontier regions, were valued at $10 or less, and this was also the type of dwelling lived in by the numerous slaves. Yet, the inequalities were far less than those in Europe, and the extent of individual land ownership much greater. A majority of adult white males could expect to own land in their lifetime.[12]

The continuing and expanding gulfs in wealth that separated Americans were often reflected in their beliefs. Many of the leaders who were shaping the new American government had brought the rational ideas of the Enlightenment into their views of society and religion. They looked less to heavenly reward and more to the fashioning of a perfected society on the North American continent. But many of their ordinary fellow citizens, and many who were not allowed citizenship, found solace in religious enthusiasm. The popular participation in government that had arisen in the revolutionary era was matched by new and popular enthusiasm for evangelical religion. Nathan Hatch has demonstrated that the democratization of American religion was a striking feature of the decades following the Revolution, and a way in which masses of Americans challenged old authorities and old beliefs.

Although this new religious enthusiasm affected older denominations, its most obvious success was in the growth of the Methodists and Baptists among poorer Americans, both black and white. The Methodist Episcopal Church had some 14,000 members in 1784; it had 250,000 by 1820. In the 30 years after the Revolution the number of Baptist churches increased from 500 to over 2,500. In the South the new religions swept through the African Americans as well as the whites. At first, in religious and revolutionary egalitarianism, the different races even mingled in congregations. By the 1790s, however, white attitudes were forcing the African Americans to leave and form their own churches.

The new churches avoided strict doctrines, a highly educated clergy, and patterns of deference, and replaced them with fiery enthusiasm, promises of

---

12   Lee Soltow, *Distribution of Wealth and Income in the United States in 1798* (Pittsburgh, Pa, 1989), pp.3–8, 35–6, 48, 233–7, 244–6, 252; Lee Soltow, 'Egalitarian America and its inegalitarian housing in the federal period', *Social Science History* 9 (1985), pp.199–213; Larkin, *Reshaping*, pp.105–14.

[1 4] salvation, and new charismatic ministers. In this second Great Awakening, revivals swept through the back country. By 1800 camp meetings were attracting great crowds to hear a variety of preachers thunder of heaven and hell in a highly charged emotional atmosphere. Orthodox beliefs were looked upon as hindrances to true religious commitment, and traditionally educated, establishment ministers were deserted in favor of the new charismatic preachers.[13]

While women participated vigorously in the religious enthusiasm, the new egalitarianism did not mean that they could aspire to leadership positions. In religion, as in other human endeavors, deference to men was still paramount. Women were given no specific mention in the Constitution, and those who drafted it expected women to confine themselves to the domestic sphere. A whole generation of historians has written on the status of women in this tumultuous post-revolutionary society. There has been a particular expansion of knowledge about middle- and upper-class women in New England, and about the nature of women's work, both rural and urban.[14]

For the articulate women of the Northeast, this was a period when exclusion from the public sphere was to some extent compensated for by the development of their roles as republican mothers; it was stressed that mothers had the responsibility of raising males for a nation of virtuous republicanism. Separate male and female spheres became more clearly defined. There was never any question of women participating in the public arena. A quirk in the way in which the revolutionary New Jersey Constitution was drafted, and the exigencies of politics, temporarily gave adult single women the vote in that state, but this was an odd exception that ended in 1807.[15]

Yet, in these years, women became much more active in developing their own ties and enhancing the idea of their essential domestic role in a republican society. This, in turn, gave a great impetus to education for women. If women were to raise men fitted to participate in the new republican society,

---

13 Nathan O. Hatch, *The Democratization of American Christianity* (New Haven, Conn, 1989), pp.3–14, 49–55, 220; Albert J. Raboteau, 'The slave church in the era of the American Revolution,' in Ira Berlin and Ronald Hoffman (eds), *Slavery and Freedom in the Age of the American Revolution* (Charlottesville, Va, 1983), pp.193–213.

14 Norton, *Liberty's Daughters*; Linda Kerber, *Women of the Republic: Intellect and Ideology in Revolutionary America* (Chapel Hill, NC, 1980); Joan Hoff, *Law, Gender, and Injustice: A Legal History of US Women* (New York, 1991); Nancy Cott, *The Bonds of Womanhood: 'Women's Sphere' in New England, 1780–1835* (New Haven, Conn, 1977); Jeanne Boydston, 'The woman who wasn't there: woman's market labor and the transition to capitalism in the United States,' *JER* 16 (1996), pp.183–206.

15 Judith Apter Klinghoffer and Lois Elkins, ' "The Petticoat Electors": women's suffrage in New Jersey, 1776–1807,' *JER* 12 (1992), pp.159–93.

it could be argued that they needed more education than had previously [15] been available to them. Educational opportunities were enhanced in these years. It seems likely that women's literacy had been half that of men in the years immediately following the Revolution. This gap closed significantly in the years between 1790 and 1830, although the South lagged behind the North. Education for women also changed in content. The traditional emphasis on dress and physical deportment was lessened in an age when frivolity and fashion was frowned on, and republican virtue and service were stressed as ideals for a responsible citizenry. In New England it was expected that well-informed, virtuous women would help inculcate the spirit of service that would protect the republican nation. In these years elementary public education began to be opened to women, and female private academies expanded both in numbers and in their curriculum, which began to include history, geography, and composition. In the 1790s in New York charity schools even began to provide education for girls from families of artisans and unskilled laborers. In the South there was comparatively little development of the new education for women in the years before 1815.[16]

In the years of the American Revolution, with its disruption of the normal patterns of life, women had been thrown into unaccustomed roles. With their husbands away, women had assumed responsibilities that would have been impossible in more normal times. This in turn helped raise the status of their domestic roles. Increasing educational opportunities, and a new sense of their worth, however restricted, meant that women soon were able to assume a quasi-public role in voluntary organizations. By the beginning of the nineteenth century, women in northeastern cities were meeting in organizations formed to relieve social problems: a New York society formed in 1797 eventually devoted its efforts to poor widows with small children; another, formed in 1814, was to help respectable, aged, indigent females; the Boston Female Asylum (1800) was to aid female orphans. Women from 'good' families, in a limited manner, began to assume roles outside of their homes.[17]

Much of the first research on women concentrated on the better-off and articulate of the Northeast, but there has also been a considerable interest in women's work beyond its simply domestic function; on the part played by women in the household and wider economy, whether in spinning and weaving in a rural setting, helping in the tasks of an artisan's household, or

16 Kerber, *Women of the Republic*, pp.235–46; Norton, *Liberty's Daughters*, pp.256–99.
17 Norton, *Liberty's Daughters*, pp.155–94, 224–5, 228–38; Anne M. Boylan, 'Women and politics in the era before Seneca Falls,' *JER* 10 (1990), pp.363–82.

[1 6]   in helping to run a southern plantation. Women's domestic work was largely unpaid – managing a household, child-rearing, preparing a variety of household products and clothing – but, beyond this, women often contributed to the household income, particularly by spinning and weaving. Most of the cloth produced in the United States in the early nineteenth century was still woven at home by women, and when the first textile factories appeared in these years women were an essential part of the labor force. As the older household economies began to yield to the new forces of commercialism and a market economy, class divisions became more important for American women. As more men became entrepreneurs, using investment and management skills to earn their living, more women had to find a role other than that of helping supplement the household income, while in a growing class of wage-earners women's earnings often became essential.[18]

The vital role of women in the economy of many families, and the new stress on women as republican mothers, did not in these years bring any marked improvement in their legal status. Indeed, as the political and civic rights of most white males had been enhanced by the Revolution, it could well be argued that relatively the status of women had declined. It was not simply that women had no political rights, by marriage they lost most of their other rights as well – they could not own property, could not sue or be sued. Any money a wife earned belonged to her husband, and she had no legal rights over her children. Divorces were very difficult to obtain, although separation and divorce became a little more common after the Revolution. For the most part Sir William Blackstone's English legal dictum that the husband and wife were one person in law still prevailed. In some respects the legal position of women deteriorated during the early republic. Dower rights, by which a woman was assured about one-third of her deceased husband's estate, were weakened, and it was to be the middle of the nineteenth century before married women's property acts began to be common in American states.[19]

While lacking many of the rights enjoyed by males, free white women could at least share in the remarkable prosperity of the new nation. Unlike most of the colonial areas that achieved their independence in the twentieth

18   Linda Gordon, 'US women's history,' in Eric Foner (ed.), *The New American History* (Philadelphia, 1990), pp.193–5; Carol Lasser, 'Gender, ideology, and class in the early republic,' *JER* 10 (1990), pp.331–7; Boydston, 'The woman who wasn't there,' pp.183–206; *NYCA*, p.59.

19   Hoff, *Law, Gender, and Injustice*, pp.49–50, 89–90, 103–4, 106–11, 116, 120, 188; Kerber, *Women of the Republic*, pp.9–10, 119–55.

century, the American colonies came to independence already prosperous, [17] and poised for momentous growth. If internal unity and foreign safety could be achieved, the economic possibilities were limitless. As President Washington took office the national government was bankrupt, but it was bankrupt because the Confederation government had lacked the means to tap America's wealth, not because the country was impoverished.

Historians have differed sharply on the time of the arrival of a liberal, commercial, capitalistic America. Some have stressed the ways in which community-oriented, civic values of classic republicanism persisted well into the early nineteenth century, while others have traced a liberal, individualistic, capitalistic society back into colonial America. It is clear, however, that whatever had existed before, a new, driving spirit of commercial enterprise flourished in the United States in the first decades of the new republic.[20] It was not simply anti-Americanism that caused Englishman Leigh Hunt to write in 1808 about 'the noisy and vulgar money-changers of America.' Americans and foreigners alike were aware of and commented upon the pervasive spirit of enterprise that permeated the new American republic.[21]

The opportunities for making money rose dramatically after 1789. Large investors expanded their investments in shipping, construction, banking, and a variety of other activities. Entrepreneurs sprang up in the larger seaport towns, and extended their activities to numerous smaller locations. Even Americans with more modest means could share in the flourishing commercialism. Howard Rock has written that for American artisans the American Revolution meant not only the chance to live in a republican government but also the opportunity to pursue entrepreneurial ambitions.[22] Local craftsmen saw the opportunity to expand beyond their local market, and began the process of moving from household and shop production to larger-scale activities in which wage labor began to replace the traditional forms of work by masters and journeymen. In cities such as New York and Philadelphia these ambitions were to create tensions in the first decades of the nineteenth century. In 1789 many supported the new government because they thought that this would facilitate economic development. American leaders agreed that the prospects for economic growth were limitless, but they were to divide bitterly on how this growth could best be achieved.

---

20 See Paul A. Gilje, 'The rise of capitalism in the early republic,' *JER* 16 (1996), pp.159–81, and Michael Merrill, 'Putting "Capitalism" in its place: a review of recent literature,' *WMQ* 3rd Ser., 52 (1995), pp.315–26.
21 *Examiner* (London), 13 Nov. 1808.
22 *NYCA*, p.111.

[1 8]   At the base of America's prosperity in 1789 was its agriculture, and in the South prosperity leaned heavily on foreign exports. The slave-based economy had prospered in colonial times on the growth and export of tobacco. Tobacco became less profitable in the years after the Revolution, although it was still the most important American export. In the older areas of the Chesapeake planters were beginning to shift their production to grain and general farming, and expanding into a variety of European markets. In the lower South, rice continued to be important, and new direct markets in southern Europe appeared, but cotton was of no importance at the time the new Constitution went into effect. The 1790s, however, was to see a dramatic change, and by 1820 cotton was to supersede tobacco as the great southern export. These shifts in southern production were to have major effects on slavery and on the slaves. The lower South wanted slaves, and the upper South had a surplus it could sell. Slave lives were to be totally disrupted, and their working conditions often deteriorated as cotton growing expanded.[23]

The new nation had inherited from its colonial past one of the great merchant marines in the world. No sooner was the United States independent than her merchant shipping was ready to challenge the British in the carrying of goods. From Savannah, Charleston, and Baltimore in the South, to Philadelphia, New York, and the ports of New England, ships sailed to every ocean of the world.

American commerce could achieve new heights if European powers could be persuaded to allow the Americans to trade within their imperial systems. Both the British and Spanish empires were closed to direct American trade, and the commercial treaty signed in 1778 with France had not produced the expansion of French trade that had been expected. Direct trade to France was nothing like as lucrative as that to Great Britain, and after the Revolution France had opened only a few of her West Indian ports to American shipping. The British refusal to sign a commercial treaty was particularly galling to many Americans because before the Revolution American trade had flourished within the British system. Americans could send their products to Great Britain in American ships, but were now officially excluded from the British colonies. This had brought disruption to the farmers of the Middle states and the North. The lucrative British West

---

23   Allan Kulikoff, *Tobacco and Slaves: The Development of Southern Cultures in the Chesapeake, 1680–1800* (Chapel Hill, NC, 1986), pp.118–61; Joyce E. Chaplin, *An Anxious Pursuit: Agricultural Innovation and Modernity in the Lower South, 1730–1815* (Chapel Hill, NC, 1993), pp.227–329; John S. Otto, *The Southern Frontiers, 1607–1860: The Agricultural Evolution of the Colonial and Antebellum South* (Westport, Conn, 1989), pp.82–127.

Indies market for the grain of Pennsylvania and New York, and for the dried [1 9] fish and provisions of New England, was officially closed to the Americans, although there was considerable smuggling.[24] As the United States was the most important purchaser of British manufactured goods, America could seemingly hope for commercial concessions from the British. How to use a new and more powerful government to achieve these concessions was to be a source of considerable political disagreement.

The situation changed dramatically after 1793 when war broke out between England and France. For most of the years from 1789 to 1815 Europe was at war, and demands for American ships and American goods soared. But though it was now possible to engage in extensive West Indian trade without formal restrictions, wartime blockades brought dangers to all American shipping. From 1807, when the United States turned to economic coercion as a means of retaliation against European powers, American over-seas trade was put under severe restrictions by the American government.

Problems of commercial regulation and war abroad were matched at home by difficulties of internal communications and transportation. The new efforts to expand internal markets were severely restricted by the inability to ship goods cheaply and efficiently. Primitive roads were often impassable in spring and autumn, and bulk produce could only be moved by water. In an age before America had built canals, and before steam navigation, this placed severe limitations on what could be moved profitably for any distance, and on the possible directions of traffic. On the Atlantic coast, east–west trade was constrained by the fall line; the point at which the rivers running from the mountains to the sea dropped through rapids and became unnavigable. For those in the up-country of the South, the sale of their products beyond a local market meant laboriously moving the items by wagon around the fall line, shipping them downriver to the coast, and transhipping them on coastal or ocean-going vessels to the North or to Europe.

Even greater problems blocked economic links between the Atlantic coast and the rapidly expanding settlements in the Mississippi Valley. It was pro-hibitively expensive to haul produce across the Alleghenies by wagon. The farmers of the Mississippi Valley could drive livestock eastward over the mountains, but their grain and other products had to be shipped south by water to New Orleans. It was not possible, however, to use that route to import goods because it was unfeasible before the steamboat to bring goods

24 Lowell Ragatz, *The Fall of the Planter Class in the British Caribbean, 1763–1833* (New York, 1928), pp.173–83.

[2 0]   north against the flow of the river. It was difficult to imagine that state resources and planning could solve the basic problems of internal communication, yet in 1789 most Americans believed that this was a state not a federal responsibility.

The snail-like pace of communications made it extremely difficult for those wanting to expand their markets to obtain information on prices or business conditions with any speed. The mail service was abysmal. At the beginning of the War of 1812 Fort Mackinac, in the distant northern lakes country, was to fall to the British because news of the American declaration of war reached the Canadians before it reached the edges of the American frontier. In 1789 contracts for carrying the mail were given to individual stagecoach lines. Some areas had no official service, and in practically all areas mail was erratic.[25]

Banking was in its infancy. In 1789, the United States had only three banks – in Philadelphia, Boston, and New York. They had been recently created, and they had limited capital. Since the Revolution there had been only minor ways in which the government could shape or influence financial policies. Currency was in a chaotic state. The United States had no mint. In 1785 the Confederation had officially adopted a decimal system, but the grossly inadequate gold and silver coins in circulation were Spanish, British, French, and Portuguese. Values differed from region to region, and from state to state. One of the first major achievements of the new government under the Constitution was the creation of the First Bank of the United States. This inaugurated a period of dramatic growth in banks and banking.[26]

The great question in 1789 was whether the new Constitution would prove workable. Economic growth, safety, and the territorial integrity of the nation depended on an efficient federal government. There was no danger of the United States again falling under foreign rule, but there was a danger of a fragmented nation failing to retain the allegiance of distant areas beyond the Alleghenies, and of England and Spain keeping strategic areas under their own control. American safety, the ability of the country to reach its economic potential, and territorial expansion on the American continent depended upon the success of the new government.

25   Nettels, *Emergence*, pp.308–10.
26   Bray Hammond, *Banks and Politics in America: From the Revolution to the Civil War* (Princeton, NJ, 1957), pp.40–67; Margaret G. Myers, *A Financial History of the United States* (New York, 1970), pp.38–40.

CHAPTER 2

THE SHAPING OF GOVERNMENT

At Philadelphia in the summer of 1787 the delegates to the Constitutional Convention had created the framework of a new government. In the spring and summer of 1789 that theoretical structure came to life. The initial success of this experiment in republicanism depended to a great extent on President Washington. It was Washington who provided the unity to retain the allegiance of those who feared federal power. As the hero of the Revolution, he could command support that was available to no other politician. Though a revolutionary, his political instincts were conservative.

In the two terms he was to serve as president, Washington provided the dignity and respect for a balanced government that was desperately needed at this moment of the consolidation of the Revolution. For Americans, Washington had become the symbol of independence. Many distrusted the new constitution with its provision for a strong executive branch, but they could accept it with Washington as president. While other leaders were still thought of as representatives of their regions or states, Washington was a truly national figure. He was not the supreme Virginian, he was the supreme American.

Washington himself acted in a manner that befitted the elevated status granted to him by his contemporaries. Although he had spent much of his life as a soldier, he was no military adventurer, ready to parlay a legendary reputation into ostentatious personal power. While others thought of him as the great national hero, he thought of himself as a Virginia planter called upon to serve his nation in time of crisis. At the end of the Revolution he had returned to his plantation. When called upon to serve as president he attempted to stay above the fray, leaning on his main advisors for the shaping of policy while giving them the national authority they needed for their policies to be effective.

The tone that Washington set was that of dignified simplicity. In its first weeks the Senate debated the possibility of granting him some exalted title. The Senate's decision, made with some disagreement, coincided with that of

[2 2] the President himself. There would be no exalted title, no splendid show. Steeped in classical history, and beset by fears of another republic assuming the trappings and excesses of empire, America's leaders hoped for the grave demeanour and public virtue of a citizen leader of the Roman republic. They were not disappointed.[1]

The two matters that Congress knew it had to take up in this first session in the spring and summer of 1789 were the concern that no bill of rights had been included in the Constitution and the creation of executive departments. From the time the Constitution had been written, the lack of a bill of rights had been one of the major criticisms leveled at the document. This had been a major theme of the discussions at the state ratifying conventions, and it was assumed that action on this question would help still the fears of those who had opposed the new national government. The debate on a bill of rights was taken up in June but the question was not resolved until September. The main problem was not opposition to the idea, but sorting through the variety of state amendments to decide which should be included and in what form.

The assertions of individual rights that became the first ten amendments to the Constitution reflected the degree to which leaders of the revolutionary generation were steeped in the ideas of the Enlightenment, their sense of what was needed to protect classical republicanism, and their resentment at the arbitrary actions of Great Britain in the years preceding the Revolution. Freedom of religion, freedom of speech, freedom of assembly were at the heart of what those who had shaped a revolution thought of as their achievements. Their reading told them that standing armies and powerful navies were a threat to a republic, and they hoped that the right to bear arms would ensure that a militia, not regular troops, would form the military arm of the republic. A long list of individual rights culminated in another attempt to reassure the states that their powers were not to be consumed by the new national government; what was to become the tenth amendment stated that those powers that were not specifically given to the federal government by the Constitution were reserved to the states or the people.[2]

The bill of rights was to ensure that the individual rights won in the Revolution would not be lost by the creation of a new, distant federal

1   Stanley Elkins and Eric McKitrick, *The Age of Federalism* (New York, 1993), pp.34–50. For the importance of Washington as the symbol of the new nation, see David Waldstreicher, *In the Midst of Perpetual Fetes: The Making of American Nationalism, 1776–1820* (Chapel Hill, NC, 1997), pp.117–26.

2   Robert A. Rutland, *The Birth of the Bill of Rights, 1776–1791* (Chapel Hill, NC, 1955), pp.190–217; David P. Currie, *The Constitution in Congress, 1789–1801* (Chicago, 1997), pp.110–15, 190–217.

government, but to make that government effective it was essential that [2 3] Congress should act quickly to create executive departments. With the federal government bankrupt, Indian war in the West, and hostile powers abroad, the last vestiges of the old system had to be removed as soon as possible. In the course of the summer Congress created Departments of State, Treasury, and War. There was not complete agreement on the details of these actions. Concerned at the possibility of individual corruption, some wanted a treasury board rather than a Secretary of the Treasury, but as this had been the system in the years of chaotic Confederation finance their arguments were rejected.

A more difficult question concerned the constitutional provision that appointments should be made with the 'advice and consent' of the Senate. Did this mean that Washington would also have to obtain the permission of the Senate to remove these officials? James Madison, who had been at the heart of the shaping of the Constitution in Philadelphia, took the lead in giving the president the power of removal. In the Senate this decision needed the casting vote of the vice-president.[3]

The question of advice and consent was also unclear in another respect. In August 1789 Washington went in person to the Senate to seek the advice and approval of the senators regarding a treaty with the southern Indians. The senators found it difficult to speak with candor in the presence of Washington, the meeting did not go as easily as he had hoped, and he was not to return. In the following years the leaders of the new departments would gradually assume the function of a cabinet, an institution not mentioned in the Constitution. At first Washington sought individual written advice, but gradually the pattern of cabinet meetings developed.[4]

Article 111 of the Constitution had simply stated that 'The judicial power of the United States, shall be vested in one supreme Court, and in such inferior Courts as the Congress may from time to time ordain and establish,' and had provided direction regarding the tenure of the justices and the courts' jurisdiction. The details regarding the number of courts and justices, and their territorial areas, had been left to the new government. The Judiciary Act, passed in September, established a Supreme Court with a Chief Justice and five Associated Justices, 13 district courts, with one judge each, and three circuit courts, whose membership would be the district judges in that

3 Leonard D. White, *The Federalists: A Study in Administrative History* (New York, 1948), pp.20–5.
4 William Maclay, *Sketches of Debate in the First Senate of the United States in 1789–90–91*, ed. by George W. Harris (Harrisburg, Pa, 1880), pp.120–6.

[2 4]   circuit together with two justices from the Supreme Court. The Act also contained detailed provisions regarding the powers of the various courts. John Jay of New York became the first Chief Justice.[5]

The debates on the executive departments, the bill of rights, and the judiciary department took much of the summer, but few Congresses ever again achieved so much. There had been arguments, but those who had opposed the Constitution had not attempted to sabotage the new government. Disagreements about how the new government should exercise its powers were emerging, but there was a general effort to rally behind Washington to make the new government work. Mindful of regional jealousies, Washington in October and November went on a tour into New England. His importance to national unity and the success of the government was emphasized by the joy with which he was greeted.[6]

Before he left on his tour, Washington made his appointments to the executive departments. He wanted men of the highest caliber, and he was fortunate enough to have them available. Alexander Hamilton had become close to Washington as his wartime aide-de-camp. A self-made man, Hamilton had risen with remarkable speed. The illegitimate son of a West Indies merchant, he had come to New York in his teens, attended King's College (later Columbia), and joined the revolutionary army. He had enhanced his already splendid prospects when he married into the influential Schuyler family of New York. In the 1780s he had made his voice heard in support of a stronger government, and had shown a particular interest in ways of achieving financial stability. Hamilton was interested in a powerful, successful, prosperous America, but distrustful of popular government. He admired the way in which England had risen to world commercial supremacy, and thought that the United States could learn from her old enemy.

For Secretary of State, Washington turned to his fellow Virginian Thomas Jefferson, who at the time of his appointment was American minister in France. He did not assume his duties in America until March 1790. A large-scale slave owner who passionately believed in individual human freedom, Jefferson brought to the position of Secretary of State an ingrained distrust of Great Britain, and a hatred of the way in which she used her maritime power. Like Hamilton, he wanted a prosperous and powerful America, but he very much wanted to achieve it as far from English connections and influence

5   Erwin S. Surrency, *History of the Federal Courts* (New York, 1987), pp.14–17; Currie, *Constitution*, pp.47–54.

6   Douglas S. Freeman, *George Washington: A Biography* 7 vols (New York, 1948–57), 6, pp.240–5.

as possible. In an age in which so much of American trade and finance was [2 5] channeled through Great Britain this was to prove extremely difficult.

For his other appointments Washington could hardly expect men of the stature of Hamilton and Jefferson, but he had confidence in his choices. As Secretary of War he retained Henry Knox, a pre-war Boston bookseller who had commanded Washington's artillery in the Revolution. The president knew him well, and Knox had extensive experience to prepare him for service in the new government. From 1785 he had led the old Confederation War Department, and had seen the chaos brought about by the inability of the federal government to provide the money to raise effective military forces. Knox was particularly concerned that the United States should create a rational Indian policy to provide for the advance of American settlers and the ending of chronic warfare.

As the cabinet gradually evolved, Hamilton, Jefferson, and Knox were Washington's key advisors. They were joined by Virginian Edmund Randolph, who became Attorney-General. In these years before parties, and before party patronage assumed a major role in political life, the Postmaster-General did not have cabinet status. Samuel Osgood, the man who presided over the inefficient American mail service, made no mark on the national political scene.

The issue that was to provide the greatest area of disagreement in the political discussions of the new government, and was ultimately to set the scene for the emergence of political parties, was Hamilton's scheme for achieving the financial solvency and prosperity of the federal government and of the country. As Secretary of the Treasury Hamilton was confronted by a critical situation: dependent upon the states for its revenue, the Confederation government had failed to repay American revolutionary debts. It had even stopped paying the interest on these obligations.

Primarily by making use of a modest tariff on imports, Hamilton believed that he could quickly raise enough money to fund the national debt. He saw trade with Great Britain as vital to the success of his scheme. Tariffs on British manufactured goods would raise the money he needed, while American exporters could still keep their traditional links with British importers and British capital. The old government securities would be called in and replaced by new ones, on which the federal government would now have the means to meet the interest payments, and eventually repay the principal.

But financial solvency was only one of Hamilton's objectives. He believed that the government should use its resources to stimulate investment and boost the economy. To further these ends, he wished to tie the moneyed

[26] class to the new government by their investment in government securities. Hamilton also wished to establish a national bank, partially owned by the government, to further the link between public and private credit. He wanted the government to be actively involved in making available the capital that would promote private economic growth. In the immediate future he was not interested in eliminating the national debt. He believed that if the government's financial policies regained public confidence then the securities that secured the debt would provide a means of stimulating the economy. Businessmen who bought public securities would be able to use them to invest in private business growth. Merchant capitalists, he believed, would be a vital element in the future success and prosperity of the nation.[7]

Even before Hamilton's appointment in September 1789 Congress had addressed some of the questions that would be involved in Hamilton's scheme. From its early weeks it became apparent that some of its members, led by James Madison, had an agenda that included more than raising the money needed for solvency. Madison, like Jefferson, thought that the United States was still tied far too closely to Great Britain. They both believed that British trade brought English influence and English corruption, and that Great Britain would like nothing better than to use its power to sap at the vitals of the young republic.

In Congress, Madison took the lead in proposing the legislation that would establish tariff policies and raise revenue. Although he knew that economic ties to Great Britain were at the heart of American foreign trade, he wanted to use commercial policies to lessen American dependence on British manufactured goods, and to weaken the intricate financial ties between the two nations. At the same time he wanted to force the British to allow American ships into the British West Indies. He believed that this could be achieved by commercial discrimination against Great Britain. His plan for tariffs and tonnage duties on foreign ships in American ports called for advantages for those nations that had signed commercial treaties with the United States and discrimination against others. This discrimination was aimed primarily at Great Britain.[8]

Congress agreed to a tariff on imports and a tax on shipping tonnage. Advantage was given to American shipping, but Congress did not accept the idea of discrimination against the British. All foreign ships would have

---

7 Drew McCoy, *The Elusive Republic: Political Economy in Jeffersonian America* (Chapel Hill, NC, 1980), pp.146–52; Forrest McDonald, *Alexander Hamilton: A Biography* (New York, 1979), pp.117–88.
8 McCoy, *Elusive Republic*, pp.136–46; Elkins and McKitrick, *Age*, pp.77–92.

to pay a 50 cents tonnage tax. The tariff duties were very low and were [2 7] intended to bring in revenue. Madison had failed in his effort to have special discrimination against Great Britain, although this legislation very much boosted the use of American ships for imports.[9] He was to keep reintroducing the issue in the following years, but did not get what he wanted.

When Jefferson returned from France in March 1790 he joined Madison in urging policies that would free the United States from dependence on British trade. Like Madison, he was convinced that British trade meant British influence, and British influence would lead to the corruption of the republic. Opposition to close British ties brought both men into direct conflict with Hamilton, for Hamilton's policies were premised on the assumption that close ties to Great Britain, and the emulation of large parts of her economic system, were essential for American economic growth. Moreover, Hamilton specifically designed his policies to benefit the merchant entrepreneurs, a group that Madison and Jefferson believed were most prone to English influence.

By January 1790 Hamilton was ready to introduce the first stage of his financial scheme. In his report on public credit he announced his plan for funding the public debt. Hamilton calculated that the federal government had a debt of some $54,000,000; over $42,000,000 of this was owed domestically, and under $12,000,000 abroad. The state debts that he wished to assume were not precisely known, but they eventually came to some $18,000,000, which was less than Hamilton thought. There was general agreement that the foreign bankers would have to be repaid, but there was a major controversy about the domestic debt. In the bankrupt days of the 1780s many of the original purchasers of government securities, who had helped the government in the Revolution, had sold them at a very large discount. They had been bought by speculators who had the money to invest in the possibility of an eventual government repayment of its obligations. In the late 1780s the well-informed could have expected the funding of the debt by a new government. Hamilton's plan called for no discrimination between original holders and speculators, for these speculators were the merchant capitalists that he wanted to encourage in his pursuit of American economic growth. They were also the merchant capitalists feared by Madison and Jefferson.

The plan for the assumption of state debts aroused different fears – that of an all-powerful federal government ignoring the Constitution to encroach on the powers of the states. If individual states were helped, what about

9   John C. Miller, *The Federalist Era, 1789–1801* (New York, 1960), pp.15–19.

[2 8] those who had no debts? The issue was also complicated by the different degree to which states had suffered, and had been obliged to borrow, during the Revolution.[10]

Hamilton and Madison had allied in support of the Constitution, but their estrangement began with their differences regarding policies towards Great Britain. It was completed by Madison's attack on Hamilton's funding and assumption plans in the early months of 1790. Hamilton, however, held the advantage. The members of Congress were eager for the new government to work. It was a government headed by Washington, and Hamilton had been his choice to handle the financial affairs of the nation. Madison's various attempts to change the proposals – by discriminating in the amount of repayment between the original and later purchasers in the refunding of the national debt, and by denying federal money for state repayment of debts – were defeated in Congress.

The assumption issue was even more contentious than the funding of the national debt, and in April 1790 it was defeated in the House by two votes. Its ultimate passage became entwined with an argument about the location of a new federal capital. This issue had concerned Congress from the beginning of its operations. The controversy involved regional competition because it was expected that proximity to the capital would bring regional influence, and it was also expected that the capital would attract trade to the area in which it was located. There was agreement that the location would have to be fairly central. The Virginians – Washington, Jefferson, and Madison – who wanted a capital on the banks of the Potomac, contended with northerners who were hoping for a location in Pennsylvania, and who at least wanted New York to remain as the capital until a new one was constructed.[11]

Jefferson and Madison ultimately proved willing to modify their bitter opposition to the assumption plan in return for Hamilton's willingness to use his influence to reduce the northeastern opposition to a capital on the Potomac. In July 1790 the House, in close votes, passed bills funding the national debt, assuming state debts, and locating a federal capital. It was agreed that the new capital would be built on the banks of the Potomac; in the meantime the capital would move from New York to Philadelphia.[12]

10 *PAH*, 6, pp.51–168 (9 Jan. 1790).
11 Elkins and McKitrick, *Age*, pp.133–4, 150–1.
12 Elkins and McKitrick, *Age*, pp.136–60; James Rogers Sharp, *American Politics in the Early Republic: The New Nation in Crisis* (New Haven, Conn, 1993), pp.33–8; Wilhelmus D. Bryan, *A History of the National Capital* 2 vols (New York, 1914), 1, pp.27–43; *PTJ*, 17, pp.452–71; 19, pp.3–73.

Hamilton's plans had split Congress, and laid the basis for the future [29] rise of political parties, but he had achieved his objectives. Entrepreneurs now had reason to back the new national government, and he had pumped capital into the nation's economy. The government securities that Hamilton issued were used to invest in new private enterprises. There was now faith in the government's abilities to pay its debts.

The next major portion of Hamilton's plan for national economic progress came in two reports submitted to the House in December 1790 – a second report on public credit, and a report proposing the establishment of a national bank. The second report on public credit ultimately raised a storm of protest. To help pay for his plans Hamilton proposed increasing the tariff and levying an excise tax on the manufacture of distilled liquors.[13] This was a relatively minor revenue measure, as by far the largest part of the government's income would still come from the tariff, but for many ordinary Americans, particularly in frontier regions, it helped confirm them in the view that Hamilton was designing a government to line the pockets of the moneyed interests of New York, Philadelphia, and Boston, while laying burdens on hard-working farmers.

In the early years of the republic there was no large-scale liquor industry engaged in the manufacture of distilled liquors. The main 'manufacturers' were farmers who distilled barrels of bourbon from corn. With roads often in an impassable state, and the necessity of shipping goods circuitously by water, it was impossible to ship bulk corn and make a profit. Barrels of whisky gave a far higher return for weight. This was particularly the case in the new frontier regions. The settlers of western Pennsylvania, or those farther down the Ohio River, in Ohio or Kentucky, shipped whisky long distances down local rivers to the Ohio and the Mississippi, and then to Natchez or New Orleans.

In Congress, the excise tax aroused less opposition than funding or assumption, but to some it brought back memories of the hated British 'internal taxes' that had aroused such resistance in the years before the Revolution. It seemed part and parcel of a Hamiltonian plan to institute a 'British' system. When it gained approval, early in 1791, Congressman John Steele of North Carolina announced in a letter to his constituents that 'assuming, funding and excising have taken root in America. How these foreign plants will flourish in free soils, time must determine.' To him the excise tax was 'so new, and so odious'.[14]

---

13   *PAH*, 7, pp.225–56, 305–42 (13 Dec. 1790).
14   Noble E. Cunningham, Jr (ed.), *Circular Letters of Congressmen to their Constituents, 1789–1829* 3 vols (Chapel Hill, NC, 1978), 1, p.4 (27 Jan.).

[3 0]   In Congress in late 1790 the strongest passions were stirred not by the excise tax but by Hamilton's proposal to establish a national bank. His report recommended a bank that would be owned partially by the government and partially by private interests. It would be capitalized at $10,000,000, and one-fifth of this capital would be provided by the federal government, which would appoint one-fifth of the directors. Private individuals would provide the rest of the capital, but in buying bank stock they would only have to pay one-fourth in specie. The rest of the payment could be government securities, which would mean that the value of government securities would be enhanced. The government would use the institution as its bank of deposit, and branch offices could be established. The bank's notes could be used for all debts due to the United States. Hamilton was about to bring those investors who had benefited from funding and assumption even more closely into cooperation with the federal government.

The economic advantages to be gained from the bank were obvious: a nation with totally insufficient banking resources would, with one measure, have an institution that could provide credit both to the government and to private enterprise; a nation chronically short of a circulating currency would have an infusion of soundly backed bank notes; and in depositing its own revenue the federal government would materially help provide the credit for an expanding American economy. But when the bank bill was introduced into Congress early in 1791 the political objections were equally obvious: fears that Hamilton was tilting the government in favor of the moneyed class; fears that British influence was prevailing in an institution so clearly inspired by the Bank of England; and, above all, fears that Hamilton was leading the federal government to violate the Constitution.

In January the bank bill proceeded through Congress. In the House, Madison led the attack on the bank's constitutionality, arguing that the establishment of a bank was not among the enumerated powers that had been given to the federal government in the Constitution. His resistance, and the fears of his followers that Hamilton was changing the nature of the republic, were not enough to defeat the bill. By 20 January it passed, and was given to Washington for his decision. The vote in the House of Representatives revealed strong sectional differences on the measure; northern representatives were almost unanimously in favor, while a majority of southern representatives opposed it.[15]

15   Bray Hammond, *Banks and Politics in Early America: From the Revolution to the Civil War* (Princeton, NJ, 1957), pp.114–22; Elkins and McKitrick, *Age*, pp.226–32; Sharp, *American Politics*, pp.38–9.

For Washington his decision on the bank bill was a decisive step in aligning him with the Hamilton forces in the developing political division. Fully aware of the widely divergent views on the constitutionality of the measure, Washington asked his heads of departments to give him written opinions. Jefferson argued that the bank bill was unconstitutional, and made much use of the tenth amendment to the Constitution, which had not yet been adopted. This amendment stated that powers not delegated to the United States were reserved to the states or to the people. As the power to establish a bank was not among the enumerated powers, it was unconstitutional. Jefferson also dealt with that part of article 1 section 8 of the Constitution that, after listing the enumerated powers, states that Congress has the power 'to make all the Laws which shall be necessary and proper to carrying into Execution the foregoing Powers.' He argued that the bill was not 'necessary,' it was merely 'convenient'. Jefferson was supported by the Attorney-General, fellow Virginian Edmund Randolph.[16]

Hamilton, of course, strongly defended the bank's constitutionality. He argued that the framers of the Constitution intended the 'necessary and proper' clause to be applied liberally. More importantly, he emphasized the sovereign power of the federal government. As the laws of the federal government were the supreme law of the land, it was intended that all the powers given to the federal government were sovereign in their nature and that the means necessary to carry them out could be employed. Washington had given Hamilton responsibility for the finances of the nation, and he was convinced by his arguments. On 25 February he signed the bank bill.[17]

When the subscription books for the bank were opened on 4 July 1791 the $8,000,000 in private capital was subscribed in the first hour. The bank certificates that the subscribers obtained soared in value. The investors Hamilton wished to encourage now had even more reason to throw their backing behind the new government and his policies. The bank itself opened in Philadelphia in December. Although Jefferson, and those who thought like him, distrusted it for encouraging the speculative, 'British', tendencies that they feared would corrupt the republic, it was a great success, and in 1792 branches were opened in New York, Boston, Baltimore, and Charleston. By 1805 there were also branches in Norfolk, Washington, Savannah, and New Orleans.[18]

---

16   *PTJ*, 19, pp.275–82 (15 Feb. 1792).
17   *PAH*, 8, pp.97–134 (23 Feb. 1791); Forrest McDonald, *The Presidency of George Washington* (Lawrence, Kans, 1974), pp.76–8.
18   Hammond, *Banks and Politics*, pp.123–7; Elkins and McKitrick, *Age*, pp.242–3.

[3 2]   While Hamilton had great success in persuading the president and Congress to adopt most of his financial plans, he was unable to convince Congress that the federal government should use its powers to promote the growth of manufacturing. In December 1791 Hamilton gave Congress a Report on the Subject of Manufactures, arguing that tariffs and some government bounties would help redress the imbalance between agricultural and manufacturing in the United States. Congress did not respond favorably to his suggestions, but his efforts to encourage large-scale manufacturing further disturbed the emerging opposition. Both Madison and Jefferson wanted manufacturing to remain at the domestic level.[19]

In the fall of 1791 Madison and Jefferson encouraged the poet Philip Freneau to establish a newspaper in Philadelphia, with the object of countering Hamilton's influence. He agreed, and the first issue of the *National Gazette* came out at the end of October. Before this time the main newspaper providing news on government policies was John Fenno's *Gazette of the United States*. Fenno was a strong supporter of Hamilton. In the winter of 1791–2 Madison began to write a series of articles in Freneau's paper. The *National Gazette* took the lead in attacking the idea that there had to be general support for the policies of a government led by Washington. In a republic, Madison argued, dissent was appropriate, and anti-republican tendencies had to be attacked. He criticized Hamilton's financial program as a moneyed system promoting English aristocratic tendencies. In the summer Hamilton lashed back (anonymously) in the *Gazette of the United States*, and criticized Jefferson for his support of Freneau. Jefferson had given Freneau a post as translator in the State Department.[20]

Jefferson was convinced that Hamilton's policies were leading the republic away from republicanism, and in May 1792 he wrote a long letter to Washington attacking funding, the excise tax, and the bank. He argued that the debt had been raised to a level that could not be paid, and that Hamilton's financial policies had ensured that moneyed speculators would control Congress. The object of all this, he claimed, was to attack republicanism, and bring back monarchy. Washington passed on the gist of Jefferson's criticisms to Hamilton, and the breach between the two men became irreparable.[21]

---

19   *PAH*, 10, pp.230–340 (5 Dec. 1791).
20   Elkins and McKitrick, *Age*, pp.266–9, 282–8; McCoy, *Elusive Republic*, pp.155–9; Sharp, *American Politics*, pp.43–7; James Axelrad, *Philip Freneau: Champion of Democracy* (Austin, Tex, 1967), pp.200–13.
21   *PTJ*, 23, pp.535–41 (23 May 1792); Elkins and McKitrick, *Age*, pp.287–8.

By the spring and summer of 1792 the original concept of a national [3 3] government without parties had been severely weakened. The unity that still existed very much depended on Washington himself. Although there were still no organized political parties, Congressmen increasingly were committing themselves to Hamiltonian or Jeffersonian positions. There was also a strident newspaper battle. The newspapers that were coming into existence rapidly throughout the United States followed Hamiltonian or Jeffersonian points of view, and reprinted articles from the *National Gazette* or from the *Gazette of the United States*. In Philadelphia, as the divisions between the Hamiltonian and the Jefferson/Madison factions increased, both sides became convinced that for the good of the country it was essential that Washington should continue as president after the fall election.

As late as May, however, Washington was so serious about retiring that he began to consider announcing this to the public. Hamilton, Jefferson, and Madison urged him to stay. It was known that if Washington was the candidate he would be re-elected. The manner in which presidential elections were conducted in these early years of the new nation complicated the question of Washington's possible candidacy. Candidates did not campaign openly for the office of president. The ideal was that of the public-spirited citizen of the Roman republic who felt obliged to serve if his country needed him. Washington never announced he was running in 1792, but his silence was taken to mean that he had reluctantly decided to stay if he was needed.

As there was no presidential campaign, the discussions about who should be supported went on in letters and in private meetings between the most prominent politicians in the various states. The new divisions that were entering national life were reflected not in the election of the president, but in the discussions about the vice-president and in the congressional races. The system that had been set up in the Constitution had not yet been changed. President and vice-president were elected on the same ticket. Hamilton and his friends did not find Vice-President John Adams particularly compatible, but were willing to support him. Some of the anti-Hamiltonians, including those from Virginia and New York, hoped that they could persuade enough electors to vote for George Clinton of New York. There was also some support for Clinton's fellow New Yorker Aaron Burr, but Madison threw his weight behind Clinton.

At the end of the year, the election was held at different times in different states. As yet there was no one day set aside for federal elections; the states could name their electors at any time within 34 days, and they varied in their methods. In some, electors were chosen by popular vote, but over half left

[3 4] the decision to their state legislatures. There were 15 states participating because Vermont and Kentucky had become states during the first Washington administration. The results showed both the elevated status of Washington and the increasing divisions on the national political scene. Washington was unanimously re-elected, receiving 132 electoral votes, but the vice-presidential vote was divided: Adams received 77 and Clinton 50 (Jefferson received 4, and Aaron Burr 1). The 50 votes given to Clinton reflected the degree to which an opposition was beginning to coalesce, and the degree to which the South was disturbed by Hamilton's policies. The electors from Virginia, North Carolina, and Georgia gave all of their 37 votes to Washington and Clinton.

The development of an opposition was helped by the congressional races. There would be more anti-Hamiltonians in the Congress that would assemble late in 1793. Jefferson believed that his supporters would now have a majority. Candidates had frequently made known their position regarding the Hamiltonian financial policies, but while there were obvious divisions there were no formal parties.[22] The existing factions were not to emerge as full-blown parties until the deep divisions regarding the course of the government's domestic policies were widened by similar arguments concerning the course of the government's foreign policy.

22   Richard P. McCormick, *The Presidential Game: The Origins of American Presidential Politics* (New York, 1982), pp.43–9; Marcus Cunliffe, 'The Elections of 1789 and 1792', in S&I, 1, pp.19–29.

CHAPTER 3

NEUTRAL RIGHTS

When the new government began operations in the spring of 1789 the most pressing problems in foreign policy were related to the advance of settlement in the Mississippi Valley. Indian resistance was proving a severe obstacle to settlement in both the Northwest and the Southwest, and this resistance was being aided by the British and the Spanish. The new government urgently needed a more effective military force to combat Indian hostility north of the Ohio. It also needed diplomatic negotiations that would secure British and Spanish withdrawal from American territory, and their promise to stop backing the Indians. Settlers in the rapidly expanding settlements of Kentucky and Tennessee were also urging governmental efforts to secure their right to ship goods through Spanish New Orleans to the sea. Their need for this export route was so great that in the 1780s they had shown a willingness to deal separately with the Spanish, raising fears in the East that the new western settlements would be lost to the Union.

American merchants were also extremely anxious that better arrangements should be made for American foreign trade, particularly by means of commercial treaties with England or Spain. Neither of those powers had been willing to sign a commercial treaty with the United States. With Britain, there were also various difficulties that had arisen in regard to the carrying out of the 1783 Treaty of Paris: the failure of the British to evacuate their posts on American territory along the Great Lakes; the debts that southern planters still owed to British commercial houses; the American treatment of British Loyalists in the United States; American protests about the slaves that the British had carried off with their retreating armies; and the exact location of the northeastern boundary between Maine and Canada were problems that showed no sign of being resolved.

In the 1780s American efforts at opening a diplomatic dialogue with the British had encountered an icy resistance. Although John Adams had been received (without enthusiasm) in England, the British had sent no minister to the United States. In 1789 chances for some agreement seemed better.

[3 6] The federal government was now in a position to command at least moderate respect, and in Hamilton, who had the greatest influence in shaping the policies of the new government, the British had a good friend. Secretary of State Jefferson, however, totally distrusted the British government, and was wary of any arrangement that might benefit the British or give them additional influence in the United States.

The initial British reaction to the new government was as unyielding as ever. Even before Jefferson arrived to begin his service as Secretary of State, Washington sent envoy Gouverneur Morris, who was in France, across the Channel to find out if the British government would now be willing to enter into formal diplomatic negotiations. It was not, but a temporary British/Spanish crisis in 1790 made the British somewhat more amenable to American overtures. In 1789 British traders had begun to trade in Nootka Sound off Vancouver Island on the Pacific coast of North America. The expansion of British activities in the Pacific was worrying the Spanish, and an expedition from Mexico seized British vessels. In 1790 the British delivered an ultimatum to the Spanish, demanding release of the ships and men taken and the right to settle and trade on the unoccupied areas of the American coast. Spain yielded, and the affair petered out, but in the meantime the British, who for a time had faced the possibility of needing to cross American territory to attack the Spanish on the Gulf, began to rethink aspects of their American policy.[1]

For the Americans, the Nootka crisis brought new fears about access to the Gulf of Mexico. Concern was expressed by Adams in England and by Jefferson and Madison in the United States that if Britain declared war on Spain she might fight it by conquering Spanish Louisiana and the Floridas. Jefferson believed that, if necessary, every possible step should be taken to prevent this happening, even if it meant war.[2]

In the early 1790s Jefferson and Hamilton were working at cross-purposes in regard to Great Britain. Jefferson, along with Madison in Congress, wanted to convince the British that their intransigence was likely to lead to American commercial retaliation. Hamilton, however, in private talks with Major George Beckwith, who acted for the British in the United States, tried to assure the British that the intentions of the American government were friendly and that there would be no commercial discrimination against

---

1 Charles R. Ritcheson, *Aftermath of Revolution: British Policy Toward the United States, 1783–1795* (Dallas, Tex, 1969), pp.95, 99–104.
2 John A. Logan, *No Transfer: An American Security Principle* (New Haven, Conn, 1961), pp.39–47.

them. Yet, though Hamilton was indiscreet, a combination of his far-reaching [3 7] financial policies and the talk in Congress of possible action to force a change in British policies helped convince the British government that the new federal government had to be taken more seriously than that of the Confederation. At last a minister was sent to the United States. George Hammond arrived in October 1791. The British hoped that by at least talking to the Americans they could head off any actions that might injure trade. Any hope that Hammond's arrival might produce a real settlement of outstanding issues was hampered not only by the British refusal to make any concessions but also by Jefferson. He showed no willingness to cooperate in any general discussion of issues. Suspicious of every step the British took, he emphasized America's specific grievances.[3]

A major problem faced by Jefferson in attempting to deal with the pressing problem of British presence on American territory in the Old Northwest, and her backing of the Indians in that region, was that the first attempts of the new United States to use military force north of the Ohio were an abysmal failure. Desperate to provide for the sale and settlement of lands in that region, the War Department acted before there was time for the new government to organize effective military forces. The first attempt to move north from Fort Washington (Cincinnati) in an attempt to crush the center of Indian resistance in what is now northeastern Indiana was made by a force led by General Josiah Harmar in the fall of 1790. Harmar had to return without carrying out the objects of his expedition, and suffered minor defeats. In the following year a second effort, led by Arthur St Clair, was a disaster. His force was ambushed by the Indians, and over 600 of his men were killed. There would be no rapid military solution in the Old Northwest. General Anthony Wayne was given the task of training an army to accomplish what Harmar and St Clair had failed to do. In the meantime, the British remained in Detroit and other posts along the Great Lakes, confident that the United States lacked the force to control the region. Washington expressed the opinion in the fall of 1792 that the western tribes would not be brought 'to a quiescent state so long as they may be under an influence which is hostile to the rising greatness of these States.'[4]

---

3 Ritcheson, *Aftermath*, pp.112–19, 231–42; Stanley Elkins and Eric McKitrick, *The Age of Federalism* (New York, 1993), pp.244–56.
4 Washington to Gouverneur Morris, 20 Oct. 1792, in William R. Manning (ed.), *Diplomatic Correspondence of the United States: Canadian Relations, 1784–1860* 4 vols (Washington, DC, 1940–5), 1, pp.53–4; James R. Jacobs, *The Beginning of the US Army, 1783–1812* (Princeton, NJ, 1947), pp.52–128.

[3 8]   The existing log-jam in foreign affairs was broken less by the increasing strength of the American government than by the outbreak of general European wars. These wars created a host of new problems at sea, but they also brought the possibility of the solution of some of the existing difficulties on the American continent, and a dramatic expansion in American commercial opportunities. Although the European wars involved a continuation of the struggle between Great Britain and France that had gone on for the past century, they were complicated for the United States by their emergence out of the French Revolution.

When the French Revolution broke out in 1789 the news was greeted with general joy in the United States. Only a few Americans feared where it might lead. It appeared to many that America's own Revolution had inspired the French to emulate American reforms. Delight and approval remained general into 1792. News that the French had declared a republic was looked upon as a triumph for American principles of liberty. By the end of 1792 doubts were emerging, and in the following year the unanimity of the American response vanished. Violence, extremism, and the French declaration of war on Britain alienated a large segment of American opinion. Existing divisions in American political life were dramatically reinforced, and in the spring of 1793 Washington's second administration began in an atmosphere of crisis.

The strongest reaction to the changing nature of the French Revolution came from Hamilton and his supporters. Hamilton was imaginative and forward-looking in his economic policies, but looked to the past in his belief in rule by the few. He distrusted the mass of the people, thought men of property and wealth should control political affairs, and saw much to like in monarchy. When first Louis XVI and then his queen, Marie Antoinette, were guillotined, and as the guillotining of the old aristocracy became general, a shudder went through many American men of property.

While many substantial and respectable American citizens condemned French violence and extremism, Virginia planter and slave owner Thomas Jefferson and many of his supporters continued to argue that developments in France would ultimately be beneficial for the French and the world. As a rationalist and a man of intellect, Jefferson admired the advance of liberty, and he was willing to accept that blood might have to be shed on its behalf. His reading had convinced him that monarchy should vanish and that republicanism should triumph, and had even persuaded him that the slavery by which he was surrounded, and in which he participated, was wrong. Yet, he was able to compartmentalize his thinking. Although slavery was wrong, he convinced himself that the Southern chaos that would be created by ending it justified its retention in the immediate future. In regard to Europe, he had no qualms about chaos. Republicanism and freedom were destined to succeed monarchy and despotism, and bloodshed and temporary disruptions were a small price to pay. He thought that the United States should encourage what was happening in France.

In practical terms individual reactions to the events in France were less important for American foreign policy than the war between France and Great Britain. France was still the ally of the United States – the two treaties of 1778 (one political, one commercial) were still in effect. If France was again at war with Britain, did the United States owe her the support that France had given the United States during the American Revolution? Even if the United States did not fight on the French side should she offer the French a friendly neutrality, and favor her in the war? This latter course appealed to Jefferson. A friendly neutrality towards France would be a way of weakening the English, and weakening the English was for Jefferson a way to help the United States.

For Hamilton the outbreak of war between Britain and France, and the possibility of the United States helping the French, was a potential disaster. His whole financial system was based on close commercial ties with Britain. The income of the national government largely depended on the tariffs levied on British goods, American exports still were sent in great amounts to British ports, and American shippers arranged most of their European financial transactions through British commercial houses. If American relations with Britain collapsed then all this was threatened. By instinct Hamilton hated what was happening in France, but his major fear was estrangement from Great Britain.

News that France had declared war on Britain reached Philadelphia in April 1793. Although there was much support for continuing the French alliance, none of Washington's main advisors wanted any military commitment to support France. Jefferson, however, who disputed Hamilton's view that the French alliance should be suspended until the situation became clearer, had to be persuaded that an immediate neutrality proclamation should be issued. He hoped to use the war to force concessions from Britain. On 22 April Washington proclaimed American neutrality.[5]

---

5   Albert H. Bowman, *The Struggle for Neutrality: Franco-American Diplomacy During the Federalist Era* (Knoxville, Tenn, 1974), pp.49–55; Alexander DeConde, *Entangling Alliance: Politics and Diplomacy under George Washington* (Durham, NC, 1958), pp.186–97.

[4 0]   Although the alliance of 1778 committed the United States to protecting France's West Indian possessions, and allowed her to bring naval prizes into American ports, France was not concerned at this proclamation of neutrality. The United States could be a lot more use to the French as a strong, friendly commercial neutral than as a weak military ally. Facing the powerful British navy, the French would have major difficulty in carrying on trade with their West Indian colonies. They hoped that American ships would take the place of the French. The Franco-American commercial treaty of 1778 had agreed on the principle of extensive rights for neutrals in time of war; the assertion that 'free ships make free goods' had been supported, and contraband narrowly defined. The United States already had limited concessions in the French West Indies. They would now be allowed to trade there as they wished.

The question of what constituted neutral rights in time of war was to be a vital element in American participation in Europe's wars. From the very first American statements of the principles of United States foreign policy in 1776, the United States tried to defend the position that neutral shipping should be able to trade with few restrictions in wartime. The American government acknowledged that a neutral could not trade with belligerents in specific items of contraband, such as armaments, but they wanted this list to be narrow. It was willing to acknowledge that belligerents could blockade the ports of an enemy, but they maintained that this blockade had to be strictly carried out by a cordon of ships, sealing access in the same manner that a besieging army blocked entry to a town. It could not be a 'paper blockade' in which a government declared a whole long coastline of the enemy blockaded, and then stopped neutral ships far out at sea to examine the papers and the cargo. The very stopping of ships caused problems. The Americans said that this should simply involve an examination of the ship's papers, not a long, delaying search.[6]

While the Americans took the position that this was an abstract question of neutral rights, in reality it was a very practical question of defending the American right to export goods, and to expand the carrying trade to European ports in time of war. Great Britain, with a major dependence on naval power, took the position that in time of war neutrals could not be allowed to help the enemy. If Great Britain could sweep French ships from the seas, she was certainly not prepared to allow neutrals to replace them.

6   See W. Alison Phillips and Arthur H. Reede, *Neutrality: Its History, Economics, and Law*, 2, *The Napoleonic Period* (New York, 1936), pp.10–17.

The arguments about the way in which the United States should react [4 1] to the European war very much deepened the gulf that separated the Hamiltonians from their opponents. Hamiltonians wholeheartedly supported the neutrality proclamation, but Jefferson thought that the neutrality should be combined with a friendliness towards the French. Hamilton believed that continued trade with Great Britain was far more important than any abstract defense of neutral rights. The French for their part thought that they had every reason to expect the friendly cooperation of the Americans, and this belief was reflected in the actions of their minister Edmond Genêt who landed in Charleston in April 1793 just before the neutrality proclamation was issued.

South Carolina gave Genêt a tumultuous welcome, and this enthusiastic greeting continued along Genêt's route to Philadelphia. For ordinary Americans Genêt was the representative of the new republican France, the enemy of England. Genêt was an able and enthusiastic young man, and his popular reception convinced him that the United States was a country wholeheartedly behind France. He had been instructed to use the United States as a base for privateering against English shipping, to encourage popular uprisings in British and Spanish possessions, and to attack the Spanish possessions on the Gulf of Mexico. At the beginning of the war Spain had reversed her traditional stance and had joined the British in an effort to stop the contagion of the French Revolution. This reversal was not to last – traditional Spanish aims were to reassert themselves – but temporarily Spain was Britain's ally against France.

Genêt's general reception, and Jefferson's initial greeting in Philadelphia, gave him no reason to believe that the French could not use the United States as a base for anti-British activities. But it was not popular opinion, or even Jefferson, that was ultimately most important in shaping the domestic and foreign policy of the Washington administrations. Genêt was soon to be disillusioned. Hamilton was able to convince Washington of the importance of the ties to Great Britain.

From the time of his arrival in Philadelphia in mid-May, Genêt acted as though the United States was a French satellite. To help in the French sea war against the British, he commissioned American ships as French privateers. They were to sail from American ports, and bring their prizes back to be dealt with by French consuls. To help in a land war, he began to make arrangements to use American territory and recruits to attack Spanish territory. He advertised openly in the *Kentucky Gazette* for volunteers to be used down the Mississippi against New Orleans, and gave a commission for this endeavor to the revolutionary hero, George Rogers Clark. More reasonably he urged the American government to defend those parts of the French commercial treaty of 1778 that related to neutral rights in time of war.

In less than a month even the pro-French Jefferson was becoming impatient at Genêt's actions, and he tried to restrain him from acts that would clearly violate the United States position as a neutral. On meeting resistance to his plans, Genêt threatened to appeal to the people over the heads of government officials. By August he had completely alienated the American government. New rules were issued to control the activities of belligerents while in the United States, and foreign governments were specifically prohibited from enlisting Americans on American soil. The French government was asked to recall Genêt, but he never went back. France was entering a period of purges and constant executions. The United States was far more tolerant. Genêt married the daughter of Governor George Clinton of New York, farmed on Long Island, eventually became an American citizen, and stayed in the United States for the rest of his life.[7]

There was no advantage to France in reacting too strongly to the Genêt affair, for the problems caused in America by the Genêt mission were minor compared to the *furor* brought about by Britain's maritime actions. In June 1793 the British issued an Order in Council stating that neutrals carrying corn, flour, or meal to French ports were to be seized and brought to British ports, where they would have to sell their cargoes. This seemed moderate compared to the Order in Council issued in November, by which all ships carrying goods from France to her colonies or from the colonies to France were liable for seizure. In issuing this order the British had gone beyond their usual policy towards neutrals in time of war. Their position as established by the so-called Rule of 1756 had been that no trade closed to neutrals in time of peace could be opened in time of war. The November order went beyond this in condemning all trade with the French colonies, even those parts of it that had been open in peacetime. It was to bring Great Britain and the United States to the brink of war.

Particular anger was caused in the United States by the way the British chose to enforce the new order. Rather than giving advance warning, the British did not announce the measure until British ships had begun extensive seizures in the Caribbean. With great speed, the British seized some 250

7   See Harry Ammon, *The Genêt Mission* (New York, 1973); Simon P. Newman, *Parades and Politics of the Street: Festive Culture in the Early American Republic* (Philadelphia, 1997), pp. 120–40.

American vessels that were taking advantage of France's opening of all her [4 3] West Indian trade to neutral ships. By the time the news of these seizures reached Philadelphia in March 1794 Britain had already modified the November order to bring it more in line with traditional policies.[8]

In the winter of 1793–4 the process by which the national government was becoming a Hamiltonian government had accelerated. In the summer Jefferson had decided that this was not an administration he could continue to serve – his resignation as Secretary of State took effect at the end of December. In his last month in office, in a report on the condition of American commerce, he recommended commercial discrimination against the British.[9]

In January, Madison made use of Jefferson's report to revive his earlier proposals for discrimination. Hamilton no longer had a clear majority in Congress, and the debate was ardent. Hamilton gave advice to those who opposed Madison's proposals. He feared that a course of commercial retaliation against Great Britain would thrust the United States closer to France, and might eventually lead to war. Writing anonymously, Hamilton pointed out that any war with Britain would be disastrous to American prosperity. American commerce would be swept from the seas, agriculture would suffer, and in a nation that obtained nine-tenths of its revenue from duties, the financial situation would be ruinous.[10]

In March the atmosphere of the discussion was transformed. First, news came of the extreme Order in Council of November 1793, and, later in the month, word of the numerous British seizures of American ships in the Caribbean.[11] Hamilton's hope of resisting commercial retaliation, or even sterner measures, against Great Britain was lessened by additional news from the Old Northwest. The British authorities in Canada were concerned that the outbreak of war in Europe and problems at sea might bring aggressive action by the Americans on the North American continent. Their reaction was to increase their activities among the Indians. In February 1794 the Governor in Chief of Canada, Lord Dorchester, told an Indian delegation that war with the United States was likely, and if it occurred the warriors would have to act.[12]

---

8   Ritcheson, *Aftermath*, pp.278–87, 299–304; Samuel F. Bemis, *Jay's Treaty: A Study in Commerce and Diplomacy* rev. edn (New Haven, Conn, 1962), pp.210–17.
9   *PTJ*, 27, pp.567–79 (16 Dec. 1793).
10 *PAH*, 15, pp.669–78 (31 Jan. 1794), 16, pp.12–19 (7 Feb. 1794).
11 Elkins and McKitrick, *Age*, pp.388–93.
12 Reginald Horsman, *Matthew Elliott: British Indian Agent* (Detroit, Mich, 1964), pp.93–5.

[44]   The Congressional debates of the early months of 1794 revealed a dilemma for those who wished to take a stronger line against Britain, reduce the dependence on British trade, and move the United States closer to France. Jefferson, Madison, and their anti-Hamiltonian supporters wished to assert American independence, but they also opposed increased taxes, and thought that large military forces were a threat to the republic. On land, they wanted to depend on the militia for protection, and they objected to the creation of a fighting navy. Unlike the opposition, the Hamiltonians did not fear standing military forces. Hamilton's own response to the crisis in Europe had been to suggest an enlarged army, and a strengthening of the main ports. In Congress the Hamiltonians took up the cause of a stronger United States. They wanted a small fighting navy, an army of 15,000 men, 80,000 militia in reserve, and higher taxes. Both the general plans for national defense and Madison's proposal of commercial retaliation against Great Britain were ultimately abandoned, but the proposal for a small navy received the approval of Congress, against strong resistance from Madison and many of his supporters. The discussion on the navy involved more than the immediate crisis.[13]

The United States had disbanded its fighting navy at the end of the Revolution, and in 1789 Congress had not provided for a navy department. The Jeffersonians distrusted a fighting navy. They evoked the memory of the role of Pompey and the Roman navy in arguing that a navy could act with a regular army to bring down the republic. But, even before the crisis in European affairs, the Hamiltonians had been able to argue that a naval force was essential because of the depredations that American shipping was suffering in the Mediterranean. The States of North Africa – particularly Algiers and Tripoli – had for centuries used their fleets to prey on merchant shipping. These 'Barbary Pirates' seized ships, enslaved crews, and demanded ransom from those they thought might be able to pay it. European powers had long paid 'protection money' as the cheapest way of dealing with a pernicious maritime problem. After the Revolution, the United States was on her own. Bankrupt in the 1780s, and trying to maintain that a republican nation did not stoop to bribery, the United States could not prevent her ships from being taken and her seamen from being enslaved. Hamiltonian commercial interests supported a fighting navy for more than resisting the Barbary powers, but seizures gave the Hamiltonians a strong debating point. In February 1794 Congress authorized six frigates. It was

13   John C. Miller, *The Federalist Era, 1789–1801* (New York, 1960), pp.150–1.

later agreed to reduce this number to three, but the United States would [45] begin to build a tiny navy.[14]

In late March and April 1794 the talk in Philadelphia was of severing commercial relations with Britain or even of war. Hamilton knew that his system was in danger of collapse. His opponents in Congress were urging strong measures against the British. In late March Congress passed a 30-day embargo on American shipping in order to give time for a decision on what action to take. In April the embargo was renewed, and the House also passed a measure to suspend all trade with Great Britain beginning on 1 November. The opponents of this action needed the casting vote of the vice-president to defeat the measure in the Senate.[15]

While Congress moved towards retaliation, Hamilton used all his influence to persuade Congress and the president that a settlement was essential. In March he was helped by a delegation of his Senate supporters, who urged the president to send a special envoy to Great Britain. Washington agreed, and decided his envoy would be the Chief Justice of the Supreme Court, John Jay, a supporter of Hamilton and an admirer of England. Jay had helped negotiate American independence and had served as Secretary of Foreign Affairs in the 1780s. The Senate confirmed him, and in May Jay sailed for England.[16]

Although Jay's instructions were sent by Secretary of State Edmund Randolph, Hamilton had the greatest influence in shaping them. Jay was to ask only for those items that Britain might be able to give – the transfer of the Northwest posts to the United States, compensation for seizures of American ships and for the slaves taken at the end of the Revolution, a limited opening of the West Indies to American ships, and British help in securing navigation rights on the Mississippi from Spain. Jay was also to try to sign a commercial treaty. He was not ordered to make a vigorous defense of American neutral rights, or to demand that Great Britain renounce her maritime pretensions. The comment of John Adams in a letter to Jefferson was that the president had sent Jay 'to try if he can find any Way to reconcile our honour with Peace.'[17]

---

14 See Marshall Smelser, *The Congress Founds the Navy, 1787–1798* (Notre Dame, Ind, 1959), pp.35–59.

15 DeConde, *Entangling Alliance*, pp.95–7; Miller, *Federalist Era*, p.154; Elkins and McKitrick, *Age*, pp.391–4.

16 Bemis, *Jay's Treaty*, pp.265–70.

17 Adams to Jefferson, 11 May 1794, Lester J. Cappon (ed.), *The Adams–Jefferson Letters: The Complete Correspondence between Thomas Jefferson and Abigail and John Adams* 2 vols (Chapel Hill, NC, 1959), 1, p.255; Bemis, *Jay's Treaty*, pp.289–98.

[4 6] Hamilton did all he could to ensure that the British would be prepared to deal with Jay. In private conversation with British minister George Hammond, Hamilton assured him that the United States was anxious to retain her friendship with Great Britain. He also assured him that the United States would not be joining the so-called 'Armed Neutrality' that had been set up by Sweden and Denmark to resist British maritime pretensions. The United States had been invited to join, but the decision that had been taken to decline had not yet been made public. Hamilton saw no problem in these private conversations with British envoys; he believed that American interest demanded that friendly relations with Great Britain be maintained.[18]

Jay spent a difficult summer and autumn in England. If possible, the British wished to prevent the Americans severing commercial relations or going to war, but they were not prepared to make any substantial concessions to achieve these aims. The rights that the British Admiralty claimed at sea were untouchable. Britain believed that its power and greatness depended upon supremacy on the ocean. Neutrals would not be allowed to threaten this. British manufacturers would certainly suffer if they lost the American market for their manufactured goods, but the British government would let them suffer rather than do anything that they thought would jeopardize British maritime supremacy.

The British felt confident of their power, and had no respect for a United States that had practically no military forces. There was also among the British ruling classes a surviving resentment against the country that had waged a successful war of independence in alliance with the old British enemy, France. This alliance was thrust before the British in these months by the actions of James Monroe, the American minister in Paris. Monroe, who was extremely friendly towards France, had been appointed minister there in the spring of 1794 on the recommendation of his fellow Virginian, Secretary of State Randolph. When Monroe arrived in France he acted most undiplomatically, by making speeches leaving no doubt that he supported France in its struggle against Britain.[19] With Jay in London trying to assure the British that the United States was anxious to maintain close ties, the British and French governments were receiving mixed signals. These mixed signals resulted from a sharp division in American political and diplomatic thinking.

18 John C. Miller, *Alexander Hamilton: Portrait in Paradox* (New York, 1959), pp.418–20; Julian P. Boyd, *Number 7: Alexander Hamilton's Secret Attempts to Control American Foreign Policy, with Supporting Documents* (Princeton, NJ, 1964).

19 Bowman, *Struggle*, pp.119, 172–90; Harry Ammon, *James Monroe: The Quest for National Identity* (New York, 1971), pp.112–22; Elkins and McKitrick, *Age*, pp.498–500.

Jay's Treaty was signed on 19 November 1794. The only major conces- [4 7]
sion that the British made was to agree to withdraw from the Northwest
posts by 1 June 1796. They were to live up to this agreement, but it could be
pointed out that they were supposed to have done this in 1783. Britain also
agreed to pay for spoliations on American shipping that had resulted from
the Orders in Council. The amount was to be fixed by a mixed commission
of representatives from the two countries (two from each country, and one by
lot). The same arrangement was to be used to decide American debts owed
to British merchants from before the Revolution, and to try to settle the true
northeastern boundary between the United States and Canada; the two
countries had failed to agree which river was meant to be the dividing line.

The commercial provisions in the treaty infuriated the American opposition. It was agreed that neither country would impose discriminatory duties
against the other for ten years. Since 1789 Madison had been trying to persuade Congress to discriminate against British commerce, and as Secretary
of State Jefferson had urged the same action. In regard to the British imperial
system, the main concession the British granted was to allow the Americans
a direct trade to the British East Indies; this brought about a modest American trade with India. It was also agreed in regard to trade that fur traders
from both countries could cross the American/Canadian border, and that
the Mississippi River was open to the citizens of both countries. The article
of the treaty regarding American trade with the British West Indies was so
limited that it was eventually eliminated when the treaty was ratified by the
American Senate. Under this article, only American vessels of less than 70
tons could trade there, and the principal West Indian products – molasses,
sugar, coffee, and cotton – could not be exported from the United States.[20]

The obvious omission in the treaty was any recognition by the British of
American neutral rights. Great Britain was going to make its own decisions
about the way that blockades should be carried out, about what goods could
be carried on neutral ships, and about the way in which neutrals would be
stopped and searched. The British had the naval power to fight whatever
type of maritime war they desired against the French, and throughout this
period they never had the slightest intention of modifying this power.

The treaty caused a furore in America. The opposition viewed it as a
capitulation to Great Britain, a confirmation of their warnings about
Hamilton's desire to promote British influence. In reality, the treaty represented the best terms that the United States could obtain. It also represented a

20   Jay's Treaty is printed in Bemis, *Jay's Treaty*, pp.453–88.

[4 8] realignment of the United States in its relationships with Britain and France. Instead of adopting the Jefferson/Madison position of commercial retaliation to punish Great Britain for its policies, and a friendly neutrality towards France, the United States had taken the best British terms that it could get; terms that many considered completely inadequate because they ignored the American position on neutral rights.

American opinion was polarized because much more was involved than the question of what terms could be obtained. Although Britain had traded extensively with the United States in the years since the Revolution, she had also treated her badly. Understandably at the end of a war for independence, Britain had excluded America from her imperial trading system, but she had also refused to sign a commercial agreement that would have acknowledged the extensive trading relationship between the two countries. More than this, Britain had retained American territory in the Northwest, encouraged the Indians to resist the American frontier advance, had refused to send a minister to the United States until 1791, and at the beginning of the European wars had treated American commerce with a ruthlessness that betrayed an indifference about the reaction of the United States.

To Hamilton and his supporters all this was irrelevant. It was clearly in the economic interest of the United States to retain close ties to Great Britain. The solvency of the government depended on the duties on imported British goods, but more than this United States foreign commerce was flourishing. The opportunities presented by the European wars were providing vastly increased profits. An estrangement from Great Britain would end these opportunities. Britain was an overbearing friend, indifferent to American desires or feelings, but from the Hamiltonian point of view she was a very good friend to have. For the time being, the treaty removed any possibility of war, and the Hamiltonians believed that war with Great Britain would be a disaster for the United States.

Jefferson, Madison, and their supporters thought much differently. They objected that the only American response to British aggression was to send a special envoy to England, and they objected even more strongly to a treaty that failed to recognize American neutral rights. But their objection went far beyond that. They realized that in bringing about this treaty Hamilton had, temporarily at least, aligned the United States with Great Britain in the struggle in Europe. It meant deserting the old ally France, and Jefferson and Madison believed that the British influence they so feared would now be paramount in the United States, enhancing the moneyed interests, and presenting a threat to the independent republicanism they desired.

The administration was satisfied that Jay's Treaty had eased tensions with [4 9] Great Britain, and quickly discovered that it had the additional advantage of paving the way for an agreement with Spain. By far the most pressing problem with Spain was the need to secure permission for western settlers to ship their goods freely down the Mississippi River through New Orleans to the sea. The United States also wanted Spain to acknowledge the 31st parallel as a boundary, and to stop backing the Indians.[21]

Since 1789 the United States had achieved no success in persuading the Spanish to make these concessions. With good reason, the Spanish feared the American advance into the Mississippi Valley. But the situation was changing. The presence in the United States of a government far more effective than that of the 1780s, and the growing American population in the Mississippi Valley, led the Spanish government to think that their old hopes of detaching portions of the American trans-Allegheny West were disappearing. This realization was now to combine with a changing European situation to make an agreement possible. Although the French Revolution had led the Spanish to reverse their traditional stand to ally with the British against the French, in 1794 they were considering abandoning the British and signing a separate peace with France. The Anglo-American negotiations that led to Jay's Treaty disturbed the Spanish. An agreement between the United States and Great Britain could pose a threat to Spanish possessions on the Gulf of Mexico.

In the summer of 1794 the Spanish government informed the United States that it was prepared to negotiate, and asked that the two American commissioners in Madrid be replaced by an envoy with more authority. In response the American government sent Thomas Pinckney, the American minister in London, as special envoy to the Spanish court. He did not arrive there until June 1795. The Spanish knew that the Americans had signed a treaty with the British, but they did not know its details. They were ready to make concessions to the United States. Soon after Pinckney's arrival, Spain signed a separate peace treaty with France.

In the negotiations in Spain Pinckney was in a very different position than Jay had been in England. In London, Jay had been the suitor and could only obtain what the British wanted to concede. In Madrid, the Spanish now believed that they needed an agreement because of potential danger to their

---

21 Arthur P. Whitaker, *The Spanish American Frontier, 1783–95: The Westward Movement and the Spanish Retreat in the Mississippi Valley, 1783–1795* (1927; rpr, Gloucester, Mass, 1962), pp.63–122; Thomas P. Abernethy, *The South in the New Nation, 1783–1819* (Baton Rouge, La, 1961), pp.47–73.

[5 0] American possessions. The first proposal of Manuel de Godoy, the Spanish negotiator, was that the United States and Spain should form an alliance to guarantee their territories in the New World, and should include France in the alliance. Pinckney declined. The American government wanted no more European alliances, and they hoped that Spanish territory on the Gulf would ultimately be yielded to the United States.

Godoy realized that if he wanted the agreement he would have to concede what the United States had wanted since the Revolution. Pinckney's Treaty was signed at San Lorenzo on 27 October 1795. Spain's most important concession was that citizens of the United States had the right to navigate the Mississippi through Spanish territory, and the right to deposit their goods duty free at New Orleans for a period of three years. At the end of that period this concession could be renewed either at New Orleans or elsewhere in Spanish territory. The treaty also recognized the 31st parallel as the boundary, provided for a mixed commission to decide the question of spoliation claims against Spain, and contained a provision that each power would act to restrain the Indians. Spain also agreed that the American definition of neutral rights would be incorporated in the treaty. The only major American desire the Godoy would not satisfy was to open the Spanish empire to American trade. Pinckney's Treaty was so obviously favorable to the United States that it was approved unanimously by the Senate.[22]

Ironically, an American administration that was coming under increasingly bitter attack for its Hamilton-inspired emphasis on northeastern moneyed interests had achieved major diplomatic successes in the Mississippi Valley. American trade on the Mississippi River increased dramatically after the signing of Pinckney's Treaty; settlers from as far away as western Pennsylvania benefited from the opportunity to ship their goods freely down the rivers to the Gulf.

In the Northwest, the British had agreed to leave their military posts on American territory and respect the boundary established in 1783. Also, in the summer of Jay's negotiations in England, American troops had finally won a decisive military action against the Indians in that region. At the battle of Fallen Timbers in August 1794 General Anthony Wayne led his troops to a complete victory. A year later, at the treaty of Greenville, the Indians ceded large areas of land northwest of the Ohio River. Defeated, and now lacking

---

22 Samuel F. Bemis, *Pinckney's Treaty: America's Advantage from Europe's Distress, 1783–1800* rev. edn (New Haven, Conn, 1960), pp.245–314; Whitaker, *Spanish American Frontier*, pp.201–22.

British support, the Indians could do nothing to stop American settlers pouring across the Ohio River in the following years.[23]

Jay's Treaty had also persuaded the British that the United States had abandoned the French alliance, and was willing to cooperate. For nearly ten years they were to treat American shipping with consideration. American shipowners and merchants were able to take full advantage of the extensive opportunities created by Europe at war.

Yet, while the diplomacy of 1794–5 had been a success, it was also highly controversial. The American position on neutral rights had been abandoned along with the special relationship with France. The United States had thrown in her lot with Britain, the old revolutionary enemy and the country that Jefferson and Madison thought presented the greatest threat to American republicanism. Many believed that the United States had put profit and convenience before honor and laid herself open to the corruption and insidious influences that brought down republics. The idea of a unified, national government that had been weakening since at least 1791 collapsed in the aftermath of Jay's agreement with Great Britain.

23   Reginald Horsman, *Expansion and American Indian Policy, 1783–1812* (East Lansing, Mich, 1967), pp.99–103.

CHAPTER 4

THE RISE OF POLITICAL PARTIES

The common assumption in 1789 was that 'parties' and 'factions' – and the terms were often linked – were disruptive of national unity and good government. There had been a struggle over the Constitution and its ratification between Federalists and Antifederalists, but it was hoped that once a government under Washington began to function all good men would rally around the president to support republicanism. When new divisions arose in the course of the 1790s there was a tendency for each side in the argument to look upon the other not as a legitimate party, but rather as a disruptive, conspiring faction that endangered the republic. Politicians were apt to see the insidious influence of a corrupt England or the destructive radicalism of a revolutionary France as moving factors in the actions of those they opposed and distrusted. Politicians poured out invective against their opponents, brazenly used the press to further their political ends, and had not the slightest hesitation in attacking the motivations of those with whom they disagreed. Antagonisms were increased because there were basic disagreements in foreign as well as domestic policy. In the course of the 1790s two widely divergent political programs emerged as to how the republic could best be preserved, and how its future power and prosperity could be assured.

The Federalist coalition that had pushed through the Constitution and fought for its ratification began to crumble within a year of the inauguration of the new government. The coalition collapsed in response to Hamilton's financial and economic plans. Hamilton and his supporters wished to use the power of the government to promote the growth of capital and its investment. While Hamilton had no doubt about the importance of agriculture, he thought that future growth depended on diversifying the American economy. He was also convinced that the substantial elements in society – the moneyed classes – should direct the nation's affairs. His supporters admired many aspects of the English monarchical society, and believed that close commercial ties to Great Britain were essential for the achievement of economic growth and independent power.

The opposition party that arose in the course of the 1790s found its [5 3] original unifying force in its opposition to Hamilton's policies. The early opposition was led in Congress by James Madison, Hamilton's old Federalist ally. Madison in 1789–90 sharply disagreed with Hamilton on two policies at the very center of his plans – close ties with Great Britain, and the full funding of government securities to all holders. To reward speculators, Madison believed, was to risk the corruption of the republic. He feared the degree to which the trade of the new nation was tied to Great Britain, and he resented the way in which the British profited from trade with America while refusing to allow the United States entry into the ports of her empire.

The sources of the emerging division between Hamiltonians and Jeffersonians has produced vigorous discussions among historians; discussions connected to the more general argument about the timing of the emergence of a modern, liberal, capitalistic United States. Some have placed great emphasis on the degree to which the Jeffersonians, in their opposition to Hamilton, reflected the values of those who opposed the English establishment in the seventeenth and eighteenth centuries. They have emphasized the degree to which Jeffersonians were imbued with ideas of classical republicanism, and the ways in which they feared a government inspired by Hamilton would bring a return to the vices in the British system that had been resisted in the Revolution. They have stressed Jeffersonian fears that public virtue and independence would be threatened as Hamiltonian financial policies cemented an alliance with moneyed interests, corrupted Congress, and allowed the centralization of power.[1]

Other historians, while acknowledging the importance of classical republican ideas to the revolutionary generation, have emphasized the degree to which the Jeffersonians looked not to the past but to the future in pursuing policies that would allow American farmers the lands and markets that would enable them to pursue their individual advantage. Jeffersonians sought freedom in the economic as well as in the political sphere. In this view, emphasis is placed on the degree to which the Jeffersonians admired not some static agrarian past but rather a nation of yeoman farmers advancing across the

---

1   This position has been argued most vigorously in Lance Banning, *The Jeffersonian Persuasion: Evolution of a Party Ideology* (Ithaca, NY, 1978). He modifies it somewhat in Lance Banning, 'Jeffersonian ideology revisited: liberal and classical ideas in the new American republic,' *WMQ*, 3rd Ser., 43 (1986), pp.3–19. There is an examination of the way in which Republican arguments affected historians in Robert E. Shalhope, 'Republicanism and early American historiography,' *WMQ*, 3rd Ser., 39 (1982), pp.334–56.

[5 4] continent and increasing in prosperity while selling their goods throughout the world.[2]

These different arguments and different emphases reflect the degree to which the United States was in a process of transformation in these post-revolutionary years. Existing values and modes of thought were being challenged across the whole of American society. Traditional values existed side by side with new opportunities and fresh expectations. In the emerging division of Hamiltonians and Jeffersonians there was no simple division between old and new. Hamiltonians looked to the future in stressing the importance of the business community and the necessity for a diversified economy, but were tied to the past in seeking a deference-based political system. Jeffersonians placed a much greater faith in the political role of the common man, were able to envisage a future of individual opportunity and commercial success for farmers, but feared the financial apparatus of a modern state and resisted the development of any large-scale manufacturing.

When Jefferson returned from France in 1790 he responded to Hamilton's policies as Madison had done. Both Madison and Jefferson thought that Hamilton's national bank encouraged the same unhealthy speculation as his funding plans, while demonstrating a willingness to use the Constitution in any way he thought necessary to further his objectives. By 1792 Hamilton's opponents, to emphasize their fears, began to use the name Republican. The Federalists were no longer the old coalition that had successfully won the battle for the Constitution but were those who thought that Hamilton was generally right in the policies he was proposing.

In the course of the 1790s the Hamiltonian approach to government and economic growth proved particularly attractive to Americans who thought of themselves as above the common run of the population. Many of the long-established families, with 'old' money, became Federalists, as did those in the most respectable professions, and those with most education. The Federalists were much stronger in long-established regions than in the newer areas of settlement. They were also much stronger among long-established churches than among the new evangelical groups. Adherents of the new evangelical churches – the rapidly expanding Methodists and Baptists, and other denominations – generally gave strong support to the Republicans. They wished to challenge older patterns of authority in political matters as

---

2   The Republican paradigm for these years has been challenged most strongly in Joyce Appleby, *Capitalism and the New Social Order* (New York, 1984). See also the essays in Joyce Appleby, *Liberalism and Republicanism in the Historical Imagination* (Cambridge, Mass, 1992).

well as in religious life. Ethnic divisions also helped shape political alle-   [5 5]
giance. At first the Germans generally voted Federalist; later in the 1790s
many were to change. The Irish consistently favored the Republicans.[3]

The Jeffersonians increasingly feared a government that was determined
to rest its power on the moneyed interests, and on a tight connection with
Great Britain. They wanted to limit Hamilton's broad construction of the
Constitution because they thought it threatened a republic based on a sharing of state and federal powers. Many rank-and-file Republicans wished to
end the deference that had formed such a large element in pre-revolutionary
society, and believed that the Revolution had granted new political power
to the common people. Ordinary citizens were becoming more willing to
participate in political action, and felt freer to challenge those who viewed
themselves as their betters.[4]

The rapid proliferation of newspapers helped publicize the emerging
divisions over Hamilton's policies throughout the country. John Fenno's
Gazette of the United States ardently defended Hamiltonianism, and Hamilton
made use of the paper to defend his position. The newspapers that supported
the Federalists used the *Gazette* as their major source of information about
the national political struggle. Philip Freneau's *National Gazette* served the
same function for the opposition as Fenno's *Gazette* did for the Hamiltonians. It did not long survive Jefferson's resignation at the end of 1793,
because it lost much of the financial support that Jefferson had provided.
Newspapers throughout the country had no qualms about adopting extremely
partisan positions, and entered vigorously, and at times venomously, into the
political debates. Their number increased from about 90 in 1790 to well
over 200 in 1800.[5]

Although the supporters and opponents of Hamilton clashed fiercely
from 1790 to 1793, parties had not yet taken shape. Personal and sectional
allegiances still often determined the voting patterns of individual members
of Congress. Hamilton gained most of his voting support from the Northeast, Madison from the South. As yet, there were no 'party' organizations,

---

3 David Hackett Fischer, *The Revolution of American Conservatism: The Federalist Party in the Era
   of Jeffersonian Democracy* (New York, 1965), pp.201–26 (Appendix 1); Nathan O. Hatch, *The
   Democratization of American Christianity* (New Haven, Conn, 1989), pp.9–11, 23–34.
4 Ronald P. Formisano, 'Deferential-participant politics: the early republic's political culture, 1789–1840,' *American Political Science Review* 68 (1974), pp.473–87; Simon Newman,
   Parades and Politics of the Street: Festive Culture in the Early Republic (Philadelphia, 1997),
   pp.1–10.
5 Carol S. Humphrey, *The Press of the Young Republic, 1783–1833* (Westport, Conn, 1996), pp.42,
   45–7.

[5 6]   and at the local level individual politicians depended on their personal friends and allegiances for activity on their behalf.[6] The two decisive events in transforming a struggle over Hamilton's policies into more formal, organized political parties were the outbreak of war between England and France in 1793 and the signing of Jay's Treaty in 1794.

The war between Britain and France deeply intensified existing divisions, for it was now no longer a question of the United States leaning too closely towards Great Britain, or being subjected to subtle corrupting influences, but rather of having to make definite choices between the two belligerents. The war in Europe showed that within the United States there was a broad basis of popular support for France; a support that had its roots in the backing France had given America in the Revolution, but which gained great strength from the French Revolution's attack on privilege at home and on Britain abroad. This vein of support for France was to help the opposition gain adherents, and, as the United States government increasingly favored Great Britain, it became easier for many to engage in formal opposition to a government led by Washington.[7]

The most radical manifestation of the pro-French stance of 'ordinary' Americans was provided by the Democratic–Republican societies that sprang up in 1793 to express support for France, opposition to Great Britain, and suspicion of any American policy that appeared to show coolness towards the old revolutionary ally. These societies expressed strong opposition to Hamiltonian elitism, and to any policies that seemed to threaten the popular liberties won in the Revolution. The societies had their origin in the early months of 1793. In April, in a letter to the *National Gazette*, the German Republican Society of Philadelphia argued that societies should be formed throughout the United States to support equality and resist aristocracy. In May, after French envoy Genêt arrived in Philadelphia to an enthusiastic welcome, a more influential Philadelphia society was formed – the Democratic Society of Philadelphia.[8] The use of 'Democratic'

6 John F. Hoadly, 'The emergence of political parties in Congress, 1789–1803,' *American Political Science Review* 74 (1980), pp.757–79; also John F. Hoadly, *Origins of American Political Parties, 1789–1803* (Lexington, Ky, 1986); James R. Sharp, *American Politics in the Early Republic: The New Nation in Crisis* (New Haven, Conn, 1993), pp.10–11, 26–50.

7 Newman, *Parades and Politics*, pp.121–85, discusses popular enthusiasm for France. See also David Waldstreicher, *In the Midst of Perpetual Fetes: The Making of American Nationalism, 1776–1820* (Chapel Hill, NC, 1997), pp.126–37.

8 Philip S. Foner (ed.), *The Democratic–Republican Societies, 1790–1800: A Documentary Sourcebook of Constitutions, Declarations, Addresses, Resolutions, and Toasts* (Westport, Conn, 1976), pp.5–7 (introduction); Sharp, *American Politics*, pp.85–9.

in the name was provocative to the Hamiltonians. In the 1790s all Americans could ardently defend 'republicanism,' but to many Federalists 'democracy' implied excess and the worst features of the French Revolution. The Democratic–Republican societies never had general support, but they publicized and intensified in a popular and more dramatic form arguments that opponents of Hamilton and his policies had long used.

In early July the members of the Democratic Society of Pennsylvania sent a circular letter asking for the formation of other societies and pointing out that European powers were threatening freedom by trying to defeat the 'glorious efforts of France.' They referred to the 'seeds of luxury' that had taken root in American soil. In subsequent meetings the society reiterated its support for France and its hatred of Great Britain. In January 1794 the society attacked the 'cruel and unjust war' being waged against France, and in April protested the 'insults and injuries' Great Britain was inflicting on American trade. The members resolved that 'the progress of British influence in the United States has endangered our happiness and Independence.' There was to be a dinner in honor of the victories of the French Democrats 'over the horde of Royalists and Aristocrats.'[9]

Although the societies generally lasted, at most, for only a few years, they sprang up rapidly in 1793 and 1794, when over 40 were founded. They were usually small, but the biggest – the Democratic Society of Pennsylvania – had over 300 members, and the New York Society over 200. Although some men of wealth and professionals belonged, most of the members were artisans and there were a few laborers. They met regularly, called each other 'citizen,' and publicized their activities by letters to the press, circulars, and memorials. They invoked the spirit of the American Revolution, attacked privilege, defended freedom of speech, and supported education and a number of other social issues, including ending imprisonment for debt. Above all else, they backed France and its revolution in its struggle against Great Britain.[10]

The tone of many of the resolutions and pronouncements of the Democratic Societies shocked Hamilton and his supporters. The preamble of the constitution of the Democratic Society of the City of New York, published in February 1794, began with the assertion that 'all legitimate power resides in *the People*, who have at all times the natural and inherent RIGHT to

9   Foner (ed.), *Democratic–Republican Societies*, pp.66–7, 69, 75, 77, 78.
10   Ibid., pp.6–23 (introduction); Stanley Elkins and Eric McKitrick, *The Age of Federalism* (New York, 1993), pp.451–61.

[5 8] amend, alter, or abolish the form of Government which they have instituted.'
It asserted that the great object of the Society was 'to support and perpetuate
the EQUAL RIGHTS OF MAN.' On 4 July 1794 the Democratic Society of
Wythe County, Virginia, attacked the conduct of the American government.
'Under the corrupt influence of the paper system,' the Society announced,
the government had 'crouched' to Great Britain and neglected France. A year
later on the 4th the Juvenile Republican Society of New York City rose to a
toast which urged 'Less respect to the consuming speculator, who wallows in
luxury, than to the productive mechanic who struggles with indigence.'[11]

The societies gave a new strength to criticisms of Hamiltonian policies
that had developed in the previous years, and helped to radicalize the
opposition press. They also helped to drive the Federalists into the more
extreme elitist position that ultimately helped to undermine them. The event
that most inspired the Federalists to an open denunciation of the societies
was the Whiskey Rebellion in western Pennsylvania.

Since the passage of the excise tax in March 1791, western Pennsylvania
had been a center of opposition. When this opposition climaxed in the
summer of 1794, members of two recently formed Democratic societies
were involved. Some of their opponents argued that they were at the heart of
the resistance that produced fiery public meetings denouncing the law, and
led to attacks on revenue collectors and buildings. Resistance culminated in
a clash in which two of the protestors attacking the house of an Inspector
of Excise were killed. The house was burned down. The 13,000 militia
called out by Washington were not needed to put down resistance that had
already evaporated, but the Federalists tied the societies to the events in
western Pennsylvania. In September, in his proclamation on these events,
Washington referred to 'a treasonable opposition,' and the propagation of
the 'principle of anarchy' in the region.[12]

The adverse publicity helped destroy the societies, but before they disappeared they became involved in the major national debate over the signing
of Jay's Treaty. This debate, more than any other single event, helped shape
parties at both the national and local level. Even the appointment of Jay had
aroused opposition among the societies, and the news of the treaty he had
signed brought a more general uproar among the anti-Hamiltonians. Many
were now convinced that Hamilton had cemented an alliance with Great

---

11 Foner (ed.), *Democratic–Republican Societies*, pp.151, 233 (New York), p.353 (Virginia).

12 Ibid., pp.29–32 (introduction); Elkins and McKitrick, *Age*, pp.461–87; Thomas P.
Slaughter, *The Whiskey Rebellion: Frontier Epilogue to the American Revolution* (New York, 1986),
pp.175–221; *MCP*, 1, pp.161–2 (25 Sept. 1794).

Britain that would be destructive of internal liberties and ruinous to the cause [5 9] of France. The signing of Jay's Treaty capped Hamilton's role as the prime shaper of the policies of the new government. He had achieved a substantial part of the internal financial and economic policies he thought essential for a strong and prosperous nation, and, in spite of the crisis produced by the outbreak of war in Europe, had brought the nation closer to Great Britain than it had been since before the Revolution. He was ready to return to his New York law practice, anxious to recoup his finances, and still ready to serve as an intimate advisor of what had become a Federalist party administration. He left the administration at the end of January 1795, but in the following years was never far removed from the shaping of Federalist policy.

For a man so disliked by the opposition, Hamilton had escaped comparatively unscathed by scandal. Since 1790 his opponents had frequently accused him of devising policies to line the pockets of his friends and supporters, but only once had he been accused of using his office for his own advantage. In November 1792 two businessmen – James Reynolds and Jacob Clingman – who had speculated in government securities were arrested for attempting to defraud the government. In jail, and anxious to get out, Reynolds let it be known that he had injurious information about the head of a government department. A secret Congressional investigation, by James Monroe and two other members of the opposition, examined charges that Hamilton had used his privileged position to make money on government securities.

When Hamilton, in private, was confronted with the charges he had to reveal that this had all arisen because of his affair with James Reynolds' wife, Maria. In the summer of 1791, when Hamilton's wife and children were away, Maria had visited Hamilton, said her husband had deserted her, and asked for money. Later that day he gave her money and went to bed with her. They began an affair that apparently ended within a few months. However, while it was still going on, Maria's husband returned and asked for a job at the Treasury. Hamilton declined to give him one, but gave him money. Hamilton had good reason to believe that Maria had connived at all this, and he explained to the Congressional committee that the money given to Reynolds had not been for private speculation in government securities but rather a pay-off because of the affair with Reynolds' wife. The committee believed him, and kept the matter secret. Inevitably, however, rumors flew about Hamilton's financial dealings.

In January 1793 William Branch Giles of Virginia asked the House to investigate the Treasury, on the grounds that Hamilton was using government

[6 0] power to make money for his friends, the speculators. Hamilton again was quickly able to dispose of the charges against him. When, in February, Giles went ahead and tried to get the House to censure Hamilton, his motions were easily defeated. The affair with Maria Reynolds did not become public until 1797, when muckraking journalist James Calendar wrote of it in two pamphlets, again tying the affair to corruption. Hamilton first answered the corruption charges in the *Gazette of the United States*, and later publicly admitted the adultery.[13]

Hamilton had left the administration before Jay's Treaty reached Philadelphia in March 1795. The way in which the treaty was handled contributed to the eventual uproar. Washington decided that the terms should be kept secret until the Senate acted upon it. By this time the opposition was irate. They knew that a treaty had been signed, and secrecy only helped confirm them in their belief that the United States had sold out to Great Britain. The Senate considered the treaty in a secret special session in June. The Federalists had a two-to-one majority in the Senate, but the treaty needed a two-thirds vote for approval. It received exactly the majority it needed, with all of the Republicans voting against it.[14]

Washington had intended to release the treaty on 1 July, but by that time its terms had been revealed. The French minister, Pierre Adet, had obtained a copy from one of the senators, and gave it to a Republican newspaper editor, Benjamin Bache of the *Aurora*. He published a summary on 29 June. He also printed the whole treaty in pamphlet form. This began a period of intense debate, and it also began a period in which the French representatives in the United States made considerable efforts to influence the course of the American political and diplomatic argument.[15]

In August, despite considerable public opposition, Washington signed the treaty. The divisions extended into Washington's cabinet. From French dispatches intercepted by the British and turned over to the Americans, Washington learned that Secretary of State Randolph had given confidential information to the previous French minister, Joseph Fauchet, and that he thought that Jay's Treaty was a mistake. Although at the time it was

13 Jacob K. Cogan, 'The Reynolds affair and the politics of character,' *JER* 16 (1996), pp.389–417; Elkins and McKitrick, *Age*, pp.293–302.

14 Jerald A. Combs, *The Jay Treaty: Political Battleground of the Founding Fathers* (Berkeley, Cal, 1970), pp.159–61.

15 Albert H. Bowman, *The Struggle for Neutrality: Franco-American Diplomacy during the Federalist Era* (Knoxville, Tenn, 1974), pp.203–4; Alexander DeConde, *Entangling Alliance: Politics and Diplomacy under George Washington* (Durham, NC, 1958), pp.424–8; James Tagg, *Benjamin Franklin Bache and the Philadelphia Aurora* (Philadelphia, 1991), pp.244–7.

suspected that Randolph might have been corrupt, it appears that he [6 1] was simply very indiscreet in informing the French minister of the deep American divisions on policy. Randolph was obliged to resign, and there was now a very clear demarcation between a Federalist administration led by Washington and inspired by Hamilton, and a Republican opposition led by Jefferson and Madison.[16]

The ratification of Jay's Treaty did not end the vocal opposition that had continued throughout the summer. Some of the Democratic–Republican societies, along with other die-hard opponents of the treaty, urged the Republicans to make last-ditch efforts in the House to impede the treaty by opposing the appropriations needed to carry it into effect.[17] As the Senate not the House had constitutional authority in the matter of treaties, this raised questions beyond specific objections to the agreement that had been signed.

When Congress assembled in December 1795 the Republicans in the House were ready to launch a major assault on Jay's Treaty, and while they waited for Washington to submit the treaty for the necessary appropriations their determination increased. By March, when the treaty was sent, many in the House were prepared both to oppose the treaty and to fight for their right to have a say in what constitutionally was the prerogative of the president and the Senate. The tone of Republicans in the House was revealed in a circular letter from Virginia representative Samuel J. Cabell to his constituents. He objected bitterly to Jay's Treaty and the supposed way that the rights of the House were being ignored, and stated that 'it is very doubtful whether our dear and magnanimous allies the French can be reconciled to our Conduct respecting the British Treaty.'[18]

The Republican members of the House, who were in the majority in this 4th Congress, tried to convince their colleagues that the House needed to assert its separate rights in regard to treaties. In March the House voted 62 to 37 to ask the president to submit to them all the papers regarding the Jay negotiations that would not violate the secrecy of any ongoing negotiations. Washington turned down this request, pointing out that the Constitution had given the Senate and the president power over treaties, and that the members of the Constitutional Convention had specifically defeated an

16 Bowman, *Struggle*, pp.207–18; Elkins and McKitrick, *Age*, pp.425–31; DeConde, *Entangling Alliance*, pp.119–25, 406–16.
17 Foner (ed.), *Democratic–Republican Societies*, p.38.
18 Noble E. Cunningham (ed.), *Circular Letters of Congressmen to their Constituents, 1789–1829* 3 vols (Chapel Hill, NC, 1978), 1, p.39.

[6 2]   effort to grant the House a role in this process. For a time an impasse developed. In the House Madison defended a different interpretation of what had happened at the Constitutional Convention, and tried to persuade even those who considered themselves Federalists that the prerogatives of the House of Representatives were at stake. Resolutions were introduced that claimed for the House the right of deliberating on treaties when a Congressional law was necessary to carry a treaty into effect. They passed by a vote of 57 to 35, and the treaty was still in limbo. At the end of April the House was evenly split on the question of voting the appropriations needed to put Jay's Treaty into effect. In the Committee of the Whole the vote was 49–49. The chairman, a Republican, gave a casting vote in favor of advancing the treaty to the open floor of the House. It now passed by a vote of 51–48. Jay's Treaty went into effect, but the Republicans continued to attack the pro-British Federalist policies that it represented.[19] In the aftermath, when the full effect of Jay's Treaty became known, the Republicans were able to claim that they had fought to the end to oppose policies that had brought about the collapse of relations with France.

In the spring of 1796 the problems that the treaty was to create in relations with France were not yet fully apparent, while its advantages were becoming more evident. An important factor was that in February news had arrived of the signing of Pinckney's Treaty, which had achieved what the United States had long sought in the Southwest. With trade down the Mississippi now freely opened to the western Americans, the British withdrawing from the Northwest posts, and the Indians in the Northwest defeated, the Federalists had achieved the major American diplomatic objectives in the Mississippi Valley. To match the achievements in the West, the Federalists could point out that their policy of friendship with Britain was enabling American shippers to take full advantage of the extensive opportunities opened up by the revolutionary wars of Europe. If one looked at concrete profit rather than abstract honor, and many did, Federalist policies were paying dividends. The advantage for the Federalists in the mid-1790s was that, for all the objections to the tendencies of Hamiltonian policies, most Americans did not want to return to the ineptness and impotence of the 1780s. Jefferson and the Congressional Republicans were pointing out the ultimate threats to republicanism that were present in the internal financial policies and the pro-British foreign policy of the Hamiltonian system, but in

---

19   *AC*, 4th Cong., 1st Sess., pp.759–83, 1289–91; Elkins and McKitrick, *Age*, pp.444–9; John C. Miller, *The Federalist Era, 1789–1801* (New York, 1960), pp.172–4.

practical terms these were proving remarkably beneficial. For many, the insults [6 3] to American shipping brought about by the outbreak of European wars were more than offset by the vastly enhanced commercial opportunities.

The presidential and Congressional elections of the fall of 1796 were the first elections to be fought on party lines. As yet, political organization was rudimentary, and some politicians tried to maintain an independent stance, but the debates surrounding Jay's Treaty had for the most part forced members of Congress to commit themselves either to the Federalist policies or to the active opposition of the Republicans. As in 1792 Washington had made no prior announcement of his intentions. It was assumed that as he had been reluctant to continue as president in 1792 he would in all probability step down in 1796. By May his close associates were convinced that this time he would not allow himself to be drafted, but his public announcement of retirement did not come until September.

As vice-president for two terms, John Adams assumed that he was the natural successor to Washington. This conviction was increased by the fact that the election of president and vice-president was still on one ticket. Adams had twice been runner-up in the election for president. He had a long and distinguished record of public service. The difficulty for Adams was that Hamilton, who was still at the heart of the Federalist party, did not really support him. For all his qualities, Adams was not an easy man to like. He had none of the relaxed easy personal charm of a Jefferson. He was extremely suspicious of those around him, and had a cool manner that made it difficult for him to win friends. Another difficulty he faced in his desire to become president was that he could not actively offer himself for office. The political and personal culture of the 1790s was such that it was considered demeaning actively to seek an office that held such prestige. The ideal model was Washington; wanted by all but reluctant to accept. Yet, though there were problems, it was clear that Adams would have to be one of the men for whom the Federalists voted.

The other Federalist candidate was less obvious, but Hamilton and his friends saw the desirability of having a southerner to give Adams strength in a region in which he was not particularly popular. They settled on Thomas Pinckney of South Carolina, not one of the major figures of the era, but he was from a prominent political family in a state in which the Federalists had strength. The South in general was also delighted with the treaty he had just signed with Spain.

Although James Madison had served with distinction in the Constitutional Convention and in Congress, there was no doubt that his friend

[6 4]   Thomas Jefferson was the first and natural choice for the Republicans. Jefferson had the ability to elicit personal admiration and liking that Madison lacked. He was no orator, but around a dinner table or in personal conversation he often won over those who heard him. He also had the remarkable ability of distilling in lucid and memorable language the thoughts and feelings of many people. He had achieved this in the Declaration of Independence, and he often did it in private letters; ultimately he was also to do it as president. But Jefferson, like Washington, had to be sought. Not only in his public posture, but also in his private communications with friends, he talked and wrote as though he did not want the presidency.

By the summer of 1796 it was clear that the Republicans were united behind Jefferson as their leading candidate, although they were unsure who to back for vice-president. The untypical figure who emerged as the leading contender to be elected with Jefferson was Aaron Burr of New York. He was untypical in that he did what he could to promote his own candidacy. Born in New Jersey, Burr had impressive family credentials. After serving in the Revolution he had settled in New York. In a state that developed local political organizations more quickly than most, Burr proved himself a master at organizing a vote for those men and principles he wanted to support. As a leading Republican he became a major rival of Hamilton, who came to dislike and distrust him. For most of the 1790s New York was a Federalist state. The Republicans, however, were developing strength there in the turmoil produced by the Federalist friendship for Great Britain and Jay's Treaty. New York provided some artisan backing for the Republicans as well as the more extreme support represented by the Democratic societies.[20] In 1796 Burr faced the problem that the Republicans were weak in the Northeast, and nationally he did not find Republicans who were prepared to make any great exertion for him. Republican leaders in the various states concentrated their efforts on backing Jefferson.

As Washington's vice-president, Adams should have been the logical choice in 1796, but he was hurt by the surge in support for the Republican party that had arisen in the direct aftermath of Jay's Treaty. If the election had been in the fall of 1795 he could have been in even more trouble, but by the fall of 1796 the good effects in the Mississippi Valley of the treaties with Britain and Spain, and the burgeoning foreign trade, had dulled the edge of opposition. The nation was now much stronger both politically and economically than it had been in 1789.

---

20   Alfred F. Young, *The Democratic–Republicans of New York: The Origins, 1763–1797* (Chapel Hill, NC, 1967), pp.568, 575–6.

Adams and Jefferson made no public appeal in the months before the [6 5] election, and state organizations were still primitive. In the seaboard cities various clubs and fraternal organizations tried to get out the vote for their candidates, and newspapers were often partisan. The Democratic societies were no longer flourishing as they had done in 1793 and 1794, but those that survived made every effort to support Republican candidates. A more surprising feature of the election was that the French minister, Pierre Adet, threw his support behind the election of Jefferson and openly attacked Federalist foreign policy.[21]

Popular participation was still limited in electing the president. There were only six states in which the presidential electors were directly chosen by the people. In the other states the state legislatures either chose them or at least played a role in the selection. It was in the states with popular choice that most electioneering occurred, particularly in Pennsylvania. Another difficulty in choosing the president was that it was not yet an unwritten custom that presidential electors would automatically vote for a particular candidate. This meant that campaigning by letters and personal meetings went on even after the electors had been chosen. Until the electors actually cast their votes, which was weeks after they had been elected or chosen, it was not certain who would win.

Hamilton never came out openly against Adams, but he worked in private to secure as many votes for Pinckney as possible. If Adams showed a weakness in the southern states then it seemed possible that Pinckney might get more electoral votes. New England electors thwarted any hopes that Hamilton might have had of this happening by casting their second vote not for Pinckney but for someone with no chance of winning. On the Republican side, Jefferson had solid support from Republican electors, but there was little effort to secure similar support for Burr. The result was a victory for Adams, but not the victory by the acclamation that Adams had hoped for. He obtained 73 electoral votes, Jefferson had 68, Pinckney 59, and Burr 30.[22] The presidential electoral system created by the Constitution was now shown to have a major weakness: because there was no separate ticket for vice-president, the leader of the opposition would serve as vice-president. Those who had written the Constitution had not allowed for a party system. The electoral situation was to worsen to produce a crisis in 1800.

---

21 Bowman, *Struggle*, pp.264–70; DeConde, *Entangling Alliance*, pp.471–7.
22 Richard P. McCormick, *The Presidential Game: The Origins of American Presidential Politics* (New York, 1982), pp.51–8; Page Smith, 'Election of 1796,' in S&I, 1, pp.59–80.

The heated debate over Jay's Treaty had not caused the electorate to desert the Federalist cause, and the Federalists won a majority in both Houses of Congress. Yet, Adams had to contend with being the immediate successor to Washington. In his last year as president even Washington had not been immune from the attacks of the opposition, but those who might have had qualms in challenging Washington had no problem in launching an attack on Adams. He also had to assume the presidency with a vice-president from the opposition and only lukewarm support from those close to Hamilton.

Washington had made the public announcement of his retirement on 19 September in his Farewell Address. The address had originated in 1792, at a time Washington was thinking of retiring, and had asked Madison to give him suggestions for a statement. In 1796 Washington asked Hamilton to help him with Madison's draft, and what emerged was, originally, much less a document for the ages than it was a statement of the Federalist position on domestic opposition and foreign policy in the aftermath of the controversies of the first half of the 1790s.

Although the permanent importance of the address has rested primarily in its statements on foreign policy, Washington devoted much of his discussion to the domestic situation. He asked for a unified America, free of foreign influences, and not beset by sectional and party divisions. In discussing foreign policy, Washington warned against foreign entanglements. 'The Great rule of conduct for us, in regard to foreign Nations,' Washington stated, 'is in extending our commercial relations to have with them as little *political* connection as possible.' As Europe had a set of primary interests, with which the United States had little relation, Washington argued, ''Tis our true policy to steer clear of permanent Alliances, with any portion of the foreign world.' He advocated only 'temporary alliances for extraordinary emergencies.'[23] The argument that the United States had a distinct set of interests from those of Europe has been cited as a forerunner of the principles contained in the Monroe Doctrine, but at the time it would seem that Washington was far more concerned with enunciating the Federalist position on the problems of the French alliance. Rather than shunning foreign connections, Hamilton had made one with Great Britain a corner-stone of Federalist domestic and foreign policy, and though Jay's Treaty was not an alliance it represented an acknowledgment of close ties to Great Britain.

---

23 John C. Fitzpatrick (ed.), *The Writings of George Washington* 39 vols (Washington, DC, 1931–41), 35, pp.214–38, 233–5 (quotations).

By the time Washington retired the closeness to Great Britain encouraged
by Hamiltonian policies was in the course of precipitating a crisis in relations
with France; a crisis that was to dominate Adams' presidency, and make a
major contribution to the downfall of the Federalists. Franco-American relations began to decline sharply after the signing of Jay's Treaty, although the
full impact was delayed because James Monroe, the American minister in
Paris, tried to convince the French that the treaty would never be approved
in the United States. France believed the treaty, not Monroe, and informed
him that France would treat American commerce in the same manner as the
British had been treating it. When news of the ratification of Jay's Treaty
arrived Monroe was also told that, as the United States had obviously unilat-
erally abrogated the 1778 treaties, diplomatic relations would be broken off.
In November 1796 Adet informed the American government that this action
had been taken. The United States was discovering that Washington's dream
of taking full advantage of commercial ties to Europe while avoiding the
diplomatic entanglements was impossible.

CHAPTER 5

THE ADAMS ADMINISTRATION

John Adams, like Washington, heartily disliked political parties. As president, he had to deal with the problem that few Federalists outside New England felt any strong allegiance to him. He was a conservative who had devoted himself to the cause of independence, working tirelessly on a host of details. Serving in the Continental Congress in the early years of the Revolution, he had worked on numerous committees. Like Jefferson he was widely read, but he lacked Jefferson's ability to turn his reading into lucid statements of principle. In years in which party allegiance and party friends were becoming increasingly important, Adams had difficulty making close friends and in inspiring loyalty. As a diplomat in Europe he had felt alienated from his colleagues, and had exhibited a profound suspicion of Benjamin Franklin. Although his instincts drew him closer to Britain than to France, he had none of the passionate one-sided commitment that Hamilton and Jefferson exhibited in their relations with those two countries. Adams would have followed Washington's advice of impartiality in dealing with the European powers, and sought only the interests of the United States, but he discovered that in trading across the Atlantic in time of war the United States could never avoid offending one side or the other. To reap the benefits of neutrality meant to endure the dangers of potential war.

Both because he was succeeding Washington as president, and because of his own inclinations, Adams did not change the cabinet. This was unfortunate for he inherited a cabinet with allegiance to Hamilton, and Hamilton became one of Adams' severest critics. Secretary of State Timothy Pickering, Secretary of the Treasury Oliver Wolcott, and Secretary of War James McHenry were all Hamilton men. They did not have the distinction of the men who had served Washington in his early years.

Along with his Hamiltonian cabinet, Adams inherited a major crisis with France. Hamilton and his friends did not fear total estrangement from that country, but Adams wanted the United States to avoid war and to maintain an independent stance. His possible actions were limited both by the problems he faced within his own party and by France's anger at the United States [6 9] for ignoring its French treaties to pursue friendship with the British. When Adams assumed office in March 1797 he had to deal immediately with the problem that the French were seizing American merchant ships and that they had refused to receive Charles Cotesworth Pinckney, who had been sent to replace James Monroe as minister.

Adams hoped to end the French crisis by negotiation, but he also wanted military preparations to convince the French that the United States was capable of defending itself. In a message calling for a special session of Congress to meet on 15 May 1797, Adams asked for a strengthening of the navy by completion of the three frigates that were already being built, protection for commerce, defense of the seacoast, and a reorganization of the militia, but he left the question of an increase in the army to Congress. The Republicans opposed all military preparations on the grounds that the Federalists were preparing for war against France.[1]

To fulfill his desire of conducting the presidency without the obvious bias of party, Adams wanted to involve the opposition in negotiations. He hoped that Madison could be persuaded to go to France as part of a three-man commission.[2] This betrayed a political naivety on Adams' part. The Republicans did not want to be involved in the actions of a Federalist administration because this would mean taking part of the blame if failure occurred, and Adams's own Federalist cabinet was strongly opposed to bringing in the opposition. Adams had to abandon any plans of a bipartisan approach to foreign policy. Ultimately, after one nominee declined, the special mission came to consist of Charles Cotesworth Pinckney, John Marshall, and Elbridge Gerry. Pinckney and Marshall were Federalists, but though Gerry later was a Republican governor of Massachusetts he was not as easy to characterize, having supported various Federalist programs. Adams had more faith in him than his cabinet had.[3]

Although Adams had great hopes of achieving a settlement, French policy since Jay's Treaty had been ratified gave little indication that they were prepared to treat. In the previous winter American ships bound to and from British ports had been seized, and on 2 March 1797 the French announced

1   *M&P*, 1, pp.232–9 (25 Mar., 16 May 1798); Ralph A. Brown, *The Presidency of John Adams* Lawrence, Kans, 1975), pp.39–43.
2   Stanley Elkins and Eric McKitrick, *The Age of Federalism* (New York, 1993), pp.542–7.
3   Alexander DeConde, *The Quasi-War: The Politics and Diplomacy of the Undeclared War with France, 1797–1801* (New York, 1966), pp.18–35; Albert H. Bowman, *The Struggle for Neutrality: Franco–American Diplomacy during the Federalist Era* (Knoxville, Tenn, 1974), pp.283–5.

that they would seize any enemy goods on American ships, and the ships carrying them, if they were evading French regulations.[4] In these years of the 1790s, and later under Napoleon, French policy towards the United States was erratic. It could be argued that even after the signing of Jay's Treaty it was in the interest of France to maintain friendship with the United States. Given British naval power, American neutral shipping had the capacity to be of great help to the French, and, in spite of Federalist leanings towards Great Britain, American shipowners would trade wherever they could make a profit.

The main object of the American commission was to stop the drift towards war. If possible, the envoys were to secure from France what Jay had secured from Britain – agreement to discuss compensation for spoliations on American commerce. The United States would also have liked the French to agree to a change in the 1778 Treaty of Alliance to remove the American commitment to defend the French West Indies. From the point of view of Adams, the most important task of the commission was to convince the French that Jay's Treaty did not mean that the United States was now siding with Great Britain in the European war.

The negotiations began in Paris in October 1797. Like the British, but with less reason, the French did not think they needed to treat the United States with respect and consideration. They had difficulty realizing that American commercial strength was more important than American military weakness. The French minister of foreign affairs, Talleyrand, believed that the United States needed to compensate France for signing Jay's Treaty. Also, the fires of the French Revolution had cooled, and in the period of the Directory French leaders were turning to more traditional eighteenth-century habits. Corruption was rife, and Talleyrand thought this was an opportunity for lining his own and a few other pockets.

The American commissioners had to deal with a succession of intermediaries. In the documents relating to the mission, three of the agents who had contacted the envoys were identified simply as X, Y, and Z. It was made clear by these underlings that if the Americans wanted an agreement they would have to pay. This would involve a 'loan' to the French government, and private payments to Talleyrand and other French leaders. The American commissioners were less concerned at the prospect of the private money to French leaders than they were at the prospect of a loan to the French government. If the United States made a loan to France, this would be a clear violation of its neutral status. The strained negotiations went on throughout the

4   Bowman, *Struggle*, pp.275–7.

winter of 1797–8. At one point Pinckney fended off the French with a testy [7 1]
'It is, no, no, not a sixpence.'[5] In the aftermath of this débâcle the American
press were to transform this into a triumphant cry of 'Millions for defense,
but not one cent for Tribute.'

By March 1798 it was clear that neither side was willing to move from its
position. Pinckney and Marshall left Paris. Gerry unwisely stayed on, for
there was nothing he could accomplish. The envoys had begun to report to
the United States in the course of the winter, and by the time Marshall and
Pinckney left Paris the American government knew that the negotiations
were failing. As the dispatches revealed the full extent of France's disdain for
the United States a wave of anti-French feeling swept the country. The
Republicans still wanted above all else to avoid a conflict with France, but
the Federalists now talked of war.

Adams was offended by the way his overtures had been rejected, but
he was not as bellicose as some in his party and in his cabinet. In messages
to Congress he asked for comprehensive military preparations, and made
it clear that he would not send another minister to France unless he was
assured that the French would receive him 'as the representative of a great,
free, powerful, and independent nation.' In April Congress asked for all the
papers relating to the mission. These were made public, and the nation read
of the arrogance with which its representatives had been treated. Politically,
the Federalists were given a considerable boost, and in Congress it now
became relatively easy for Adams to obtain the military preparations he
needed. France had badly hurt the pride of a nation sensitive of its newly
independent status.[6]

Relations with France were severed, and in the late spring and early summer of 1798 Congress placed the country on a war footing. All trade with
France and her colonies was prohibited, and the treaties with France were
abrogated. Public armed ships were given the authority to capture French
public armed ships, and merchant ships were given the power to defend
themselves. If they were able, they were also empowered to make prizes of
the French armed ships that attacked them. A Navy Department was created,
separate from the War Department, and Benjamin Stoddert of Maryland
appointed to run it.[7]

5   DeConde, *Quasi-War*, pp.43–59; William C. Stinchcombe, *The XYZ Affair* (Westport, Conn,
    1980).
6   *M&P*, 1, pp.264–5 (19 Mar. 1798), p.266 (21 June 1798); Elkins and McKitrick, *Age*,
    pp.582–8.
7   Brown, *Presidency of Adams*, pp.51–8.

[7 2]   The Federalists now pressed for a sizeable increase in the American regular army, a particularly sore point with many of the Republicans. Jefferson, Madison, and their supporters resented the increased taxation made necessary for military increases and, steeped in classical history, they had a fundamental fear of the dangers of large regular military forces to a republic. Although military forces were very small through most of the 1790s, they accounted for a large percentage of federal expenditure. By 1794 military costs were already nearly 40 per cent of all spending, and these costs increased greatly during the period of the quasi-war with France from 1798 to 1800. The trade expansion of the 1790s had increased tariff income, but the crises generated by the war in Europe brought new taxes. In June 1794 Congress imposed a tax on refined sugar, carriages, snuff, and other items, including sales at auction; in July 1796 a stamp tax on legal documents; and in July 1798 a tax on houses, land, and slaves. Tariffs still raised most of the money – over $10,750,000 of the nearly $13,000,000 raised in 1801, but Republicans objected to the principle of increased federal taxation.[8]

Even as a private citizen Hamilton took an active role in urging increases in the military. In March he wrote to Secretary of State Timothy Pickering suggesting that the army should be increased to 20,000, with a provisional army of 30,000, and that not only should the frigates be completed but that if war came ten ships of the line should be built. When in May 1798 Congress authorized 10,000 more troops there were shudders among the more ardent Republicans.[9]

In this time of crisis the nation again turned to Washington. Adams had general support for bringing him out of retirement, but difficulty was caused by the Federalist maneuvering to make Hamilton his second-in-command. Hamilton himself, and some of the cabinet, wanted this, but Adams was reluctant. Against his wishes, Adams was obliged to yield to Washington and appoint Hamilton as Inspector-General of the army. This increased Republican fears.[10]

When no French invasion materialized Hamilton raised the possibility of attacking Louisiana and Florida – the possessions of France's ally, Spain –

---

8   Curtis B. Nettels, *The Emergence of a National Economy, 1775–1815* (New York, 1962), p.317; J. C. A. Stagg, *Mr Madison's War: Politics, Diplomacy, and Warfare in the Early American Republic, 1783–1830* (Chapel Hill, NC, 1983), p.127. For the Republican distrust of regular forces, see Lawrence D. Cress, *Citizens in Arms: The Army and the Militia in American Society to the War of 1812* (Chapel Hill, NC, 1982), pp.127–34.

9   Brown, *Presidency of Adams*, p.53.

10   Richard H. Kohn, *Eagle and Sword: The Federalists and the Creation of the Military Establishment in America, 1783–1802* (New York, 1975), pp.219–38; Elkins and McKitrick, *Age*, pp.600–6; Brown, *Presidency of Adams*, pp.63–71.

and combining with the British in Joint operations against Latin America. For Hamilton, this would have the advantage of shaping an alliance with the British as well as opening Spanish possessions to American trade.[11] Ultimately, all the squabbles over the army and its possible use came to nothing. The French never invaded, the United States did not attack Spanish possessions, and recruitment never brought the army anywhere near the numbers that had been authorized. The quasi-war with France was fought only at sea.

The undeclared naval war helped American seamen enhance the reputation they had built during the Revolution. The three frigates – *Constitution, United States,* and *Constellation* – completed in 1798 were superior to practically all French or even British vessels of that class, and Congress authorized the building and purchase of other ships. In the course of the hostilities the new navy put some 45 ships to sea, and American forces were augmented by hundreds of privateers. While the French were causing great problems for American merchant vessels, the United States fought only a defensive war. American ships were authorized only to take French armed vessels.

Much of the war was fought in the West Indies. In 1797 and 1798, after the breakdown of Franco-American relations, the French seized hundreds of American ships. By 1799 the United States had several naval squadrons operating in the West Indies, and was able to reduce these losses. American ships were also able to take the war to the French armed vessels. In the course of the conflict they captured some 80 French ships, and proved capable of causing the French severe problems. Captain Thomas Truxton, who had won a major reputation during the Revolution, achieved new fame early in 1799 when his frigate the *Constellation* took the French frigate *L'Insurgenté*. The United States was in her element at sea, and American warships, augmented by numerous privateers, effectively harassed a powerful enemy.[12]

While Republicans feared Federalist elitism, Federalists feared Republican extremism. With war with France appearing likely, a particular source of concern for the Federalists was the support that the Republicans had gained from a core of immigrants who had fled from Europe because of their sympathy for revolutionary change. In these years the United States had already become a refuge for the persecuted of Europe, and many Republicans

---

11 John C. Miller, *Alexander Hamilton: Portrait in Paradox* (New York, 1959), pp.495–9.
12 Howard P. Nash, *The Forgotten Wars: The Role of the US Navy in the Quasi-War with France and the Barbary Wars, 1798–1805* (South Brunswick, NJ, 1968), pp.61–170; Michael A. Palmer, *Stoddert's War: Naval Operations during the Quasi-War with France, 1798–1801* (Columbia, SC, 1987).

[7 4] welcomed this. In November 1794 the New York Tammany Society had passed the resolution 'The United States of America; May they prove an asylum to the prosecuted [sic] throughout the globe.'[13]

The Federalists were concerned at the activities and potential activities of the friends of the French Revolution who had fled from Great Britain, as well as those of the Irish patriots who had found refuge in the United States. These *emigrés* had often been inspired both by the radical ideas of Thomas Paine and by the French Revolution itself. They were not numerous – perhaps less than 100 – but they were extremely vocal. From their activities in Great Britain they were used to organizing and to writing, and they often used extreme language. The English and Scots *emigrés* had usually wanted parliamentary reform and much greater participation of the general population in government; the Irish had wanted to throw the English out of Ireland. In the 1790s the radicals had suffered repression throughout the British Isles, and they sought a refuge across the Atlantic.

In the United States the *emigrés* were immediately attracted to the emerging Republican party, and many of them turned to journalism. They thought they saw in Hamilton and his friends the same tendencies they had resisted in Europe, and they lambasted Federalist policies. Some of their newspapers became very influential. The *Aurora* in Philadelphia flourished under the editorship of William Duane, and James Callender worked for that paper before going on to other newspapers and to scurrilous pamphleteering. It was Callender who brought Hamilton's affair with Mrs Reynolds before the American public. Joseph Gales fled from Yorkshire to edit the North Carolina *Raleigh Register*. The radical *emigrés* were feared and hated by the extreme Federalists, and in the heat of the crisis with France they helped inspire the Federalist desire to curb those they viewed as dangerous critics.[14]

In June and July 1798 the Federalists accompanied their military measures against France with four internal measures. Three were designed to make it more difficult for immigrants to settle in America and easier for them to be deported, and one was designed to stifle newspaper criticism.

---

13 Philip S. Foner (ed.), *The Democratic–Republican Societies, 1790–1800: A Documentary Sourcebook of Constitutions, Declarations, Addresses, Resolutions, and Toasts* (Westport, Conn, 1976), p.204 (26 Nov. 1974).

14 Michael Durey, 'Thomas Paine's apostles: radical emigrés and the triumph of Jeffersonian Republicanism,' *WMQ* 3rd Ser., 44 (1987), pp.661–88; Richard J. Twomey, 'Jacobins and Jeffersonians: Anglo-American radical ideology, 1790–1810,' in Margaret Jacob and James Jacob (eds), *The Origins of Anglo-American Radicalism* (London, 1984), pp.284–99. There is a full discussion of the *emigrés* in Michael Durey, *Transatlantic Radicals and the Early American Republic* (Lawrence, Kans, 1997).

The measures emanated from Federalists in Congress. Adams gave them his approval, but he was not their ardent advocate. In enacting these measures the Federalists were playing into the hands of their Republican critics, who had long argued that the Federalists were determined to overturn the republican gains of the Revolution. [75]

The Naturalization Act changed the period of residence required before an alien could become a citizen. An act of 1795 had said citizenship could be obtained after a five-year residence. The 1798 act increased this period to 14 years, and the intention to apply for citizenship had to be indicated five years in advance. The act did not apply to those already resident in the country. Some Federalists had favored a more extreme law that would have stopped the foreign born from voting, but this more extreme measure was defeated.

The Alien Act gave the president the power to expel aliens he thought dangerous, even in time of peace. The president did not have to give reasons or grant a hearing. The Alien Enemies Act gave the president the same powers in time of war. These measures were never used by President Adams. Their impact was political. By granting arbitrary powers to the president the Federalists had, in the eyes of many, confirmed the Republican accusation that the Federalists had no respect for individual liberties.

All of the measures were opposed by the Republicans, and some of the Federalists doubted their wisdom, but by far the most controversial measure was the Sedition Act, which passed the House of Representatives by a vote of only 44 to 41. The measure provided for fines and imprisonment for anyone convicted of writing, publishing, or speaking 'false, scandalous and malicious writing' against the government or its officers. Federalists argued that the Sedition Act was less extreme than English common law because it allowed the use of truth as a defense, and put the power of decision in the hands of a jury rather than a judge. These arguments carried little weight with Republicans, who realized that the Federalists were determined to curb the more extreme newspaper critics of Federalist policies.[15]

In enacting this sedition measure the Federalist Congressmen were supporting attempts at stifling the press that had already begun at the local level. Local indictments were brought against Benjamin Franklin Bache of the Philadelphia *Aurora* and John Daly Burk of the New York *Time Piece*.

---

15   See James Morton Smith, *Freedom's Fetters: The Alien and Sedition Laws and American Civil Liberties* (Ithaca, NY, 1956), pp.22–155, 435–42; Henry S. Commager, *Documents of American History* 7th edn, 1 (New York, 1963), pp.175–8.

[7 6] Bache, the grandson of Benjamin Franklin, had used the *Aurora* to attack the Federalists, and had taken an extreme pro-Republican position. Burk had fled from Ireland to America in 1796. Neither was tried. Bache died, and Burk's newspaper ceased publication.

Fifteen indictments were brought under the federal Sedition Act, and there were ten convictions. Secretary of State Timothy Pickering took the lead in trying to stifle the leading Republican newspapers. Bache's death did not stop the efforts to gag the Philadelphia *Aurora*, and the paper was continued under William Duane, who had served as assistant editor. In early 1799 he was twice indicted, although not convicted. Later, after the United States Senate took action against him, he had to flee to avoid arrest. He was charged again in the fall of 1800, but the Federalist loss of power brought his troubles to an end. At the Boston *Independent Chronicle*, editor Thomas Adams was charged under both the federal Sedition Act and by the Massachusetts authorities, under the common law. Adams was too ill to be tried, but his brother was jailed. Samuel Holt of the New London *Bee* was given a three-month jail sentence and a $200 fine.[16]

The political *emigrés* came under particular attack. Thomas Cooper, the chemist and free-thinker, had fled from England after his conspicuously pro-French activities had made him unwelcome there. In England, he had defended the right of revolution, equality, and freedom of expression; settling in Pennsylvania, he responded to the Sedition Act by attacking the Federalists in the *Sunbury and Northumberland Gazette*. His trial for seditious libel before the notoriously biased federal judge Samuel Chase resulted in a six-month jail sentence and a $400 fine. Cooper, who was much admired by Thomas Jefferson, was to prosper after the defeat of the Federalists.[17]

Another British dissident who particularly raised Federalist ire was the notorious James Callender, who made his living by writing. He had defended the Democratic societies, bitterly opposed Jay's Treaty, and attacked Washington and Hamilton. In the late 1790s Jefferson corresponded with him, and he moved to Richmond, Virginia. Indicted in 1800 for one of his pamphlets, he was tried before Justice Chase and given nine months in jail and a $200 fine. Unlike Thomas Cooper, Callender later

16   The enforcement of the Alien and Sedition acts is discussed in ibid., pp.159–433; see also Carol S. Humphrey, *The Press of the Young Republic, 1783–1833* (Westport, Conn, 1996), pp.47–8, 59–61, 63–7; Kim T. Phillips, *William Duane: Radical Journalist in the Age of Jefferson* (New York, 1989), pp.77–91, 118–30; James Tagg, *Benjamin Franklin Bache and the Philadelphia Aurora* (Philadelphia, 1991), pp.366–90.

17   Dumas Malone, *The Public Life of Thomas Cooper, 1783–1839* (1926; rpr, Columbia, SC, 1961), pp.91–130.

broke with Jefferson, and was to publish the rumors that Jefferson had a [77] slave mistress.[18]

The prosecution under the Sedition Act that received the most publicity was that of Matthew Lyon of Vermont, an Irish immigrant who had married the daughter of a Vermont governor. In 1797, as a Congressman, Lyon had literally fought with Connecticut Congressman Roger Griswold on the floor of the House. After suffering a verbal attack, Lyon had spit on Griswold. Griswold had subsequently attacked him with a cane. The Federalists tried to expel Lyon from the House, but failed.

In the summer of 1798 Lyon was indicted for attacking President Adams in letters published in the *Vermont Journal*. This was just a few days after Lyon had established his own newspaper, *The Scourge of Aristocracy*. Found guilty, Lyon received a sentence of four months in jail and a huge $1,000 fine. In December 1798, while still in jail, Lyon was re-elected to Congress. For the Republicans, Lyon became the prime example of the degree to which the Federalists were determined to crush the opposition by any means.[19]

The initial popular reaction to the news of France's cavalier treatment of American commissioners had been to rally round the government in a display of patriotic indignation, but in the second half of 1798 and 1799 the Federalists began to lose the advantage they had gained after their 1796 election victory. The quasi-war with France was harming American commerce. Foreign trade had flourished in the aftermath of Jay's Treaty as the British acted leniently towards American shipping, but French hostility brought losses and disruption. Commercial areas, at first delighted that relations with Great Britain had improved, were now anxious that French relations be stabilized to bring an end to the open hostility at sea.

The Federalist military preparations also became a rallying cry for the Republicans. Federalist determination to enlarge an army for which there did not seem to be any particular military need convinced many in the opposition that the Federalists were now beginning to present an active threat to internal liberties. The passage of the Alien and Sedition acts, and their enforcement, gave the Republicans the evidence they needed. Politically the Alien and Sedition acts were a disastrous Federalist mistake.

18   See Michael Durey, *With the Hammer of Truth: James Thompson Callender and America's Early National Heroes* (Charlottesville, Va, 1990); Humphrey, *Press*, pp.65–6.

19   Aleine Austin, *Matthew Lyon: 'New Man' of the Democratic Revolution, 1749–1822* (University Park, Pa, 1981), pp.108–25; John C. Miller, *The Federalist Era, 1789–1801* (New York, 1960), pp.208–9, 235–6.

[7 8]   The response of Jefferson and Madison was to draft anonymous responses – the Kentucky and Virginia resolutions – in an attempt to rally state resistance to the measures. The strongest of the two statements was written by Jefferson and passed by the Kentucky legislature in November 1798. Jefferson asserted that the Constitution was a compact of the states in which only specifically defined powers were given to the federal government; all the rest were reserved to the states. Jefferson maintained that broad construction of the Constitution was unconstitutional, and that the Alien and Sedition Acts were 'void, and of no force.' He argued that when the national government used powers that had not been given to it, each individual state had the right '*to judge for itself, as well as of infractions as of the mode and measure of redress.*' The resolutions written by Madison were adopted by the Virginia legislature in December. Although shorter, and somewhat more moderate than Jefferson's, Madison's resolutions asserted that when the federal government exercised unconstitutional powers the states had the right and duty 'to interpose for arresting the progress of the evil.'

The Virginia and Kentucky resolutions were more effective as a rallying cry to the Republican faithful than as a means of enlisting the states in opposition to the federal government. Most of the states, including all north of the Potomac, rejected them; the rest simply did not reply. Although Virginia and Kentucky did nothing to stop the operation of the acts, Kentucky, in its response to the replies it had received to its original resolutions, said in regard to the Constitution: '*That a nullification of those sovereignties, of all unauthorized acts done under the color of that instrument is the rightful remedy.*' In 1798 the Republicans were more interested in convincing the country that the Federalists were misusing the Constitution than in nullifying acts of the federal government. For a later generation of southerners, nullification itself was the major issue.[20]

While some Federalists were pleased at the collapse of relations with France, and were happy to prepare for what they believed would become a real rather than a quasi-war, President Adams was far more cautious. He had been angered by the way in which his original overtures for a settlement had been scorned, but he did not want war. His original view that it was in the interest of the United States to seek agreement with the French was unchanged.

---

20   Dumas Malone, *Jefferson and the Ordeal of Liberty* (Boston, Mass, 1962), pp.395–424; Irving Brant, *James Madison: Father of the Constitution, 1787–1800* (Indianapolis, Ind, 1950), pp.457–71; Commager, *Documents*, 1, pp.178–85.

French leaders were having second thoughts about the rupture of [79] relations with the United States. France and her colonies needed American trade, and the extreme reaction to Jay's Treaty was being modified. Through William Vans Murray, the American minister in The Netherlands, the French unofficially let Adams know that they were ready to treat. The same message was brought back to the United States by a Pennsylvania Quaker, Dr George Logan, who had gone on his own mission to Paris to seek peace. Angry at Logan's private endeavors, the Federalists in Congress in 1799 pushed through the Logan Act, making it illegal for a private citizen to discuss the United States and its policies with foreign governments.[21]

Adams, who wanted a reason to deal with the French, welcomed the limited signs that the French were changing their American policy, and favored sending a new envoy to France. His cabinet thought that it was up to France to send a negotiator. Secretary of State Timothy Pickering was far more uncompromising in his federalism than Adams. He was a strong supporter of the military preparations, and continued to give his allegiance to Hamilton. The president displeased the more ardent Federalists with his moderation, and in February they attacked his nomination of William Vans Murray as minister to France.

In sending this nomination to the Senate, Adams followed his conviction of what was right rather than the requirements of party unity, and his action pleased the Republicans more than the Federalists. Federalist resistance was so strong that it was clear that Murray could not be confirmed. Adams had to nominate an enlarged mission. He did it by adding two Federalists – Chief Justice Oliver Ellsworth and, ultimately, after Patrick Henry declined, the North Carolinian William R. Davie. These were confirmed by the Senate, but delay ensued as Adams waited to make sure that France would actually receive his commission. He could not afford a repetition of the débâcle that had resulted from the XYZ affair. When in October 1798 he finally ordered the commission to go, he had opposition both within and outside the cabinet. Both Secretary of State Pickering and Hamilton disagreed with Adams' policy.

Speedy diplomacy was impossible in the early republic. Adams had originally nominated an envoy to France in February 1799. By the time he had received assurances that the French would receive his commissioners, and they had sailed across the Atlantic, it was March 1800. The negotiations took half a year before the Convention of Mortefontaine was agreed to on

21   Bowman, *Struggle*, pp.362–5.

[8 0] 30 September 1800. From the American point of view the most important aspect of this agreement was the ending of the quasi-war at sea. Commercial relations were renewed, and the principle that 'free ships make free goods' was included in the agreement. France was still hoping that American ships could substitute for her own in carrying French goods. The United States negotiators could not get a provision providing for French compensation for spoliations against American shipping. This, along with the American desire to end existing treaties, was deferred for future consideration.

By the time the treaty arrived in the United States for ratification Adams was a lame-duck president, and the Federalists who controlled the Senate knew that their control would end in the next session of Congress. Many of the Federalists were disgusted at what they thought was a yielding to France. At first the agreement could not get the two-thirds majority it needed. It finally passed after the article deferring discussion of the questions of spoliations and the existing treaties was struck out. The United States was no longer linked to France by treaty.[22]

The ending of the quasi-war with France was very much the result of the personal efforts of President Adams. In responding to tentative French overtures he had incurred the wrath of his own party, and had ensured that many of its leaders would give him only lukewarm support in the election of 1800. Yet, when he extricated the United States from its clash with France he sealed a decade of what had been successful Federalist diplomacy. The United States had come close to formal conflict with both Britain and France, and had fought a limited naval war with the French, but ultimately had managed to maintain its neutrality in the European conflict. Out of this neutrality had come rich commercial gains. In the West, the border problems in the North and South had been solved, British and Spanish backing for Indian resistance had ended, the Mississippi River had been opened to American commerce, and settlers were now advancing in great numbers across the Alleghenies. The contrast to the relative impotence of the 1780s was striking.

But, while shaping a successful diplomacy, the Federalists had also done much to enable the Republicans to unseat them. Although Adams had achieved an agreement with France in 1800, Federalist policy of the 1790s had shifted American foreign policy from friendship with France and distrust of Great Britain to the ending of the French alliance, a coolness with the French, and comparatively good relations with the British. This won support for the Federalists among many commercial leaders, and in much of

22   Ibid., pp.386–435; Elkins and McKitrick, *Age*, pp.606–41, 662–90.

New England, but it was not popular with many Americans. The distrust [8 1] of Great Britain that Jefferson preached was not simply a personal attitude. In that, as in so many other of his stands, Jefferson well represented a more general American position. Britain was the old revolutionary foe, France the country that had helped in the Revolution, and many thought had emulated the United States in shaping her own Revolution. The bloodshed and extremism that had emerged in France had alienated some but certainly not all. It was to take Napoleon to make most Americans cast a jaundiced eye on France, and to become even more convinced that the future of republican liberties lay in the New World.

Hamilton had succeeded brilliantly in establishing government credit, and making sure that capital became available for America's entrepreneurs, but in doing so he had not disguised his belief that political power should lay more in the hands of this commercial elite than in the hands of ordinary men. Many of the common run of Americans believed that the American Revolution had given a fatal blow to the deference that had characterized pre-revolutionary politics. They were no longer prepared to accept direction from any narrow elite. Farmers and artisans had joined merchants in voting Federalist when federalism meant supporting a government that gave the stability lacking in the period of the Confederation, and when they believed that they were backing the national government of George Washington. A majority had continued to support the Federalists and Adams when Washington stepped down because, once the initial shock of Jay's Treaty had worn off, the positive advantages of Jay's and Pinckney's treaties had become apparent, and it seems possible that the fiery rhetoric of some of the more radical Republicans had convinced many that to change parties might mean a return to the instability of the late 1780s.

But the events of the Adams administration gave a majority of Americans reason to believe that the long-uttered warnings of the opposition were coming to pass. There was a shooting war with France, a country admired by ordinary Americans, and trade was disrupted. Above all, the Federalists, in passing the Alien and Sedition acts, and enforcing the new laws against seditious libel, appeared to be sliding from elitism into autocracy. To prosecute and imprison Republican newspaper editors, however virulent or irresponsible their attacks on governmental officers, was an act of political idiocy. In the mid-1790s 'extremism' had emanated from radical Republicans, particularly those in the Democratic societies; in 1798 and 1799 'extremism' was coming from the arch-Federalists who were eroding their base of support by betraying a lack of trust in basic freedoms achieved by the Revolution.

[8 2]   To add to the attack on republican liberty, many of the Federalists displayed a great eagerness to use the crisis with France to create a stronger military establishment; a military establishment that the Republicans had long warned could be a way of crushing republican liberties. The crisis and the increased military also brought the need for increased taxes. The federal tax of 1798 on land, houses, and slaves caused considerable resentment. As in the case of the Alien and Sedition acts, many thought this an unwarranted use of federal power, and, like the earlier excise tax, it was a type of levy that caused maximum irritation.

The way in which the Federalists lost the majority support they had enjoyed in the mid-1790s can be illustrated by patterns of voting in both New York and southeastern Pennsylvania. When the Republican party began its development in New York in the 1790s its support was mostly agrarian, among yeoman farmers. It also had some support among the artisans in New York City. Most of the mercantile interest were Federalists, but the Republicans had the support of some merchants and professionals. As the decade advanced the urban wing of the Republicans grew in strength.[23]

In Washington's first term the Federalists were in the majority in New York, but after 1793 the Republicans gained a larger following as a result of the pro-British Federalist foreign policy. In New York City their basis of artisan support expanded with the growth of the Democratic societies, and as it became clear that the Republican leadership supported the idea of a broadly based republican government that had arisen in the Revolution. The artisans reacted adversely to the elitism of the Federalists, and to the suspicion of immigrants that became an element in Federalist philosophy as the decade advanced. The Republican press gave wide dissemination to anti-Federalist ideas. The Federalists, however, were able to stress the extremism of the Democratic societies, and the stability their government had achieved, to win both the presidential and the Congressional elections in the state in 1796. In the years from 1797 to 1800, as the mantle of extremism passed from the Democratic–Republican societies to the arch-Federalists, as France became the overt Federalist enemy, and as Federalist elitism and fear of disruptive immigrants flowered in the Alien and Sedition acts, the Federalist majority began to erode.[24]

A similar erosion of backing for the Federalist government occurred in southeastern Pennsylvania, a region that had supported the Federalists. In

23 Alfred F. Young, *The Democratic–Republicans of New York: The Origins, 1763–1797* (Chapel Hill, NC, 1967), pp.566–82.
24 Ibid., pp.401–2; *NYCA*, pp.71–7.

this strongly German area there was great resentment against the federal [8 3] tax on houses and land imposed in 1798, and considerable evasion. When arrests were made, a mob led by John Fries broke them out of prison. Adams responded as Washington had responded to the whisky rebellion, sending regular troops and militia to put down the 'rebellion.' There was no resistance, but there were many arrests, and imprisonments. Three of the men, including John Fries, were tried for treason and sentenced to be hanged.

When Fries appealed and was granted a new trial he had the misfortune to have Samuel Chase as his presiding judge. Chase had become notorious for his impassioned anti-Republican charges to juries. The verdict and the sentence were confirmed. In April 1800 Adams pardoned Fries and others who had been convicted as a result of the events in southeastern Pennsylvania. This decision by Adams alienated him still further from the arch-Federalists. Secretary of State Pickering thought the pardoning a great mistake, and Hamilton condemned Adams' action. This reaction of Federalist leaders is a measure of the extent to which they were becoming out of touch with the mass of the American population. To hang a man for resistance to an unpopular tax was hardly in the revolutionary tradition. The series of events since the passage of the 1798 tax had converted the German areas of southeastern Pennsylvania from Federalist to Republican.[25]

For all the Federalist political mistakes the election of 1800 was to be a difficult one for the Republicans to win, particularly at the presidential level where popular will was deflected by the diverse ways of naming the presidential electors. As late as the elections of 1798 the Federalists still had good reason to be confident. Victories in the elections of that year left them with a majority in Congress. Adams seemed more in tune with the general popular will than many of the Federalists on whom he had to depend for support, and clearly many in the electorate were reluctant to dispense with the party that had achieved the stability and prosperity of the 1790s.

The presidential election of 1800 was complicated by Adams' unpopularity with leaders within his own party. In the spring of 1800 Adams reorganized his cabinet. Secretary of War James McHenry was forced to resign, and Secretary of State Timothy Pickering was dismissed. Throughout the Adams presidency these men had showed far more loyalty to Hamilton than to Adams. Secretary of the Treasury Oliver Wolcott, another Hamiltonian, survived. Adams appointed Samuel Dexter of Virginia as Secretary of War, and John Marshall of the same state as Secretary of State. This move gave Adams

[8 4]   a little more peace among his immediate advisors, but it did even more to convince Hamilton that it was necessary to maneuver to replace Adams as president without throwing the election to the Republicans.[26]

In 1800, as in the earlier presidential elections, the process of deciding which men would be backed by each party was a limited affair. Each party in Congress caucused to decide who would be supported, and then depended on the partisan press and the usual process of private contacts with the key leaders in the various states to publicize the choices. There was still no separation of presidential and vice-presidential candidates, and no campaigning by the men who expected to be chosen. As in 1796, Jefferson and Burr had the support of the Republicans, but the party was now more solidly behind Burr than it had been in the previous election. President Adams and Charles Cotesworth Pinckney were the choices of the Federalists, but the caution with which Hamilton had worked against Adams in 1796 had been replaced by a simple directness. In the early fall of 1800 Hamilton wrote an anti-Adams letter in the form of a pamphlet entitled 'Letter from Alexander Hamilton, Concerning the Public Conduct and Character of John Adams, Esq. President of the United States' to circulate among the Federalist leaders. It was published in late October.[27]

The election for president was long drawn-out because voting took place not on one day, but at different times from October to December. A further complication was added because in more than half of the states the state legislature still named the presidential electors. This meant decisive votes were taking place well before the fall elections. In New York the key vote was in the spring, and here the artisan vote in New York City proved to be vital. By electing their assembly candidates in New York the Republicans won a majority in the state legislature, and a vital state for the Federalists in the presidential race of 1796 now swung to the Republicans.[28]

The election was a deadlock at the presidential level. Both Jefferson and Burr received 73 votes, Adams had 65, Pinckney 64. Hamilton's plan of persuading some of the electors to throw away their vote on Adams to give the victory to Pinckney had misfired. There was a strong sectional cast to the voting; 53 of the 73 Republican electoral votes came from the South, 12 were from New York, and 8 from Pennsylvania. Of the Adams votes, 53 came from the North, 3 from Delaware, and 9 from the South.

26   Brown, *Presidency of Adams*, pp.168–71.
27   *PAH*, 25, pp.169–234.
28   *NYCA*, pp.79–80.

Those who drafted the Constitution had not expected party voting, but [8 5] they had allowed for a good deal of the scattering of votes in the election for president. The Constitution provided that if there was a tie then the choice would be given to the House of Representatives, but in the House the vote would be by states, not by individuals. A state delegation would first have to agree among themselves how to cast the state vote.

The Congressional elections of 1800 had produced a more decisive result than the voting for president. Because of direct voting, a popular shift in opinion registered more easily at the Congressional level. The Republicans would now have large majorities in both Houses of Congress. This Republican victory, however, did not help the tangled situation in the voting for president. The new Congress elected in the fall of 1800 did not take office until the fall of 1801. The House of Representatives, which would have to decide between Jefferson and Burr for president, would still have a Federalist majority. Had Burr been a different man, he could have made it quite clear that, like the rest of the party, his choice for president was Jefferson; but Burr had character flaws that eventually were to ruin him. He made no effort to withdraw from the presidential contest, knowing full-well that Federalists bent on embarrassing the Republicans were likely to vote for him.

In February 1801, when voting began in the House, it appeared that the Republicans could count on 8 of the 16 states casting their vote for Jefferson. One more state was needed, and this presented a serious problem as the Federalists, against the advice of Hamilton, determined to support Burr. The first vote was eight for Jefferson, six for Burr, and two divided. For 36 ballots the Federalists held firm, and blocked Jefferson. Even at the end, it was very close. The Federalist Congressman from Delaware, James A. Bayard, who was the only representative from his state, decided to abstain, and he used his influence with the Federalist representatives from Maryland and Vermont to have them do the same. This meant that Maryland and Vermont went from Burr to Jefferson. A major crisis was solved, and Jefferson would become president, with Burr as his vice-president.[29]

When the Federalists left office in 1801 there seemed no reason to believe that they would not be back. They had left a record of solid accomplishment. What ultimately was to ruin them was their lack of faith in the general population, and an inability to accept the changes in personal and political

29   Noble E. Cunningham, Jr, 'Election of 1800,' in S&I, 1, pp.101–34; Richard P. McCormick, *The Presidential Game: The Origin of American Presidential Politics* (New York, 1982), pp.66–70.

[8 6]   relationships that had been produced by the Revolution. If the Republicans could now prove that they were capable of managing the federal government, the Federalists would have great difficulty in regaining office. Only if the Republicans showed a tendency to return to the confusion produced by individual state power in the 1780s would the Federalists be able to claim that popular government did not work. It was soon revealed that while Jefferson and his party had objected bitterly to the ways in which the Federalists had expanded federal powers under the Constitution, they were quite willing to use those powers themselves, even if for different purposes.

CHAPTER 6

THE ECONOMY

When the American colonies declared their independence from Great Britain they had no doubts about their ability to continue the economic growth that had characterized their colonial years. This was no group of rebels desperate for freedom, but a group of leaders confident in their broadly-based prosperity. The British-American colonies had succeeded in attracting immigrants in far greater numbers than the colonial areas of other European powers. By the middle of the eighteenth century, when French Canada had attained a non-Indian population of only some 70,000, the British colonies were approaching a population of 1,500,000.[1] This number increased with great rapidity in the next 50 years. Agriculture was at the heart of colonial economic success, but this had been accompanied by remarkable commercial expansion. American shipping had flourished within the British imperial system; so much so that by the time of independence the American merchant fleet was ready to become the major rival of the old colonial ruler. The new United States had broken away from Europe politically but was entwined with Europe economically.

The United States experienced difficulty in reaching its economic potential in the years immediately following the Revolution. Although there has been debate as to the extent of economic depression in these years, there is no doubt that disruptions in America caused by the war, the necessity for the realignment of trade made necessary by leaving the British imperial system, and the lack of any federal role in economic development, slowed progress. Before the war American shippers had traded extensively within the British system, particularly to and from the West Indies. After the war they were officially shut out of that trade, although unofficially some of it continued. The commercial treaty with France allowed limited access to the French

---

1   *A Century of Population Growth: From the First Census of the United States to the Twelfth, 1790–1900* (Washington, DC, 1909), p.9; J. M. Bumsted, *The Peoples of Canada: A Pre-Confederation History* (Toronto, 1992), p.92.

[8 8]   West Indies, but Spain excluded American shipping from her colonies. The main American export – tobacco – had a reduced volume in the years following the war. Imports of British manufactured goods continued at a high level, and the resulting trade imbalance brought severe problems.

The adoption of the Constitution and the beginning of the new American government in 1789 brought immediate benefits to the American economy, and the outbreak of general European war in 1793 gave extensive new opportunities for foreign trade. The new government was of key importance. Hamilton's financial program gave a great boost to the American economy, and federal control of commerce made possible a national commercial policy. The funding of the national debt and the creation of the First Bank of the United States achieved Hamilton's object of putting usable capital into the hands of American entrepreneurs.[2]

When Hamilton organized the First Bank of the United States there were only three banks in the country, but there was an explosion of banking in the following decades. There were 29 by 1800, 90 by 1811, and nearly 250 by 1816. They provided abundant capital that had not been available before the Revolution, and they also issued the notes that provided the United States with a currency. Hamilton had established a United States mint, which began its operations in Philadelphia in 1794, but the gold and silver coins it produced provided only a small proportion of the circulating medium.[3]

Banks were only one type of the corporations that began to flourish in the early years of the republic. Corporations had been chartered by governmental authorities since colonial times, but only after 1789 did corporations flourish in large numbers. There was particular interest in investing in internal communications. A large proportion of the charters issued were for turnpike and bridge companies. Banks and insurance companies were the next most important. Between 1775 and 1801 states chartered over 320 corporations, and from 1801 to 1817 they issued some 1,800 more charters. After 1806 charters to manufacturing companies, which had been very few in

2 Curtis B. Nettels, *The Emergence of a National Economy, 1775–1815* (New York, 1962), pp.47–63; Douglass C. North, *The Economic Growth of the United States, 1790–1860* (Englewood Cliffs, NY, 1961), pp.18–20; Claude D. Goldin and Frank D. Lewis, 'The role of exports in American economic growth during the Napoleonic wars, 1793 to 1807,' *Explorations in Economic History*, 17 (1980), pp.7, 11–12; Gary M. Walton and James F. Shepherd, *The Economic Rise of Early America* (Cambridge, 1979), pp.182–9.

3 Bray Hammond, *Banks and Politics in America: From the Revolution to the Civil War* (Princeton, NJ, 1957), pp.40–76, 144–8, 227; Edwin J. Perkins, *American Public Finance and Financial Services, 1700–1815* (Columbus, Ohio, 1994), pp.266–81; Nettels, *Emergence*, pp.120, 295–300; Thomas Cochrane, *Frontiers of Change: Early Industrialism in America* (New York, 1981), pp.32, 36.

the 1790s, increased rapidly. New York alone chartered 161 manufacturing companies in the years from 1809 to 1815.[4]

The Federalist administration of the 1790s, inspired by Hamilton, did all it could to encourage this emerging world of investment and commerce, but tensions accompanied the transformation. While the southern Republican leaders were committed to the importance of foreign commerce to American agriculture, they were deeply distrustful of the creative use of capital. In their minds, and in those of many of their followers, debt and speculation were linked to the presence of an English-loving, moneyed elite. The Federalist desire to pass a bankruptcy law, based on that of Great Britain, was a deeply controversial issue. Federalists argued that the United States was reaching a stage of society where such a law had become necessary, but their Republican opponents stressed the agricultural nature of the United States. When the measure was finally enacted in 1800, it passed the House by one vote. When the Republicans came into power, it was soon repealed.[5] The Republicans always had the vain hope that the extensive foreign sale of their agricultural products would enable the United States to remain primarily an agricultural country. They wanted to participate in the market, but they also wanted to confine its scope.

Historians have argued about the extent of capitalist development in the early years of the American republic. The slow growth of factory-based industry and the persistence of household manufacture has helped to convince some that pre-revolutionary patterns persisted into the nineteenth century. Yet, whatever the doubt about the rate of transformation in the work-place, there is little question of the growth of commercialization. Republicans in the early national period often attacked the activities of the new moneyed interests, but an interest in selling, in reaching new markets both at home and abroad, pervaded the whole period.[6]

In defending the agricultural nature of the United States the Republicans were stressing an activity that occupied well over 90 per cent of the American people. But while the vast majority of Americans lived on farms, there were great differences in the types of farming they were engaged in. The Middle and Northern states, the Upper and Lower South, and the frontier regions farmed and sold in different ways.

4 Nettels, *Emergence*, pp.289–95.
5 Drew McCoy, *The Elusive Republic: Political Economy in Jeffersonian America* (Chapel Hill, NC, 1980), pp.178–84.
6 See Michael Merrill, 'Putting "Capitalism" in its place: a review of recent literature,' *WMQ* 3rd Ser., 52 (1995), pp.315–26; Paul A. Gilje, 'The rise of capitalism in the early republic,' *JER* 16 (1996), pp.159–81; Gordon Wood, *The Radicalism of the American Revolution* (New York, 1992), pp.313–18.

[9 0] New England and the Middle states generally were engaged in provision farming. The average farm was not more than 100 or 200 acres, and the production of grain was important. Corn, wheat, and rye were all grown, and in the Middle states the production of flour from wheat resulted in a lucrative cash crop. With the outbreak of European wars an important market developed in Europe, and necessity often obliged foreign colonies in the West Indies to admit American ships. There was also extensive keeping of livestock in the North, but difficulties of preservation limited large-scale, distant sales. In general, farmers on the rich soils of central Pennsylvania and the Hudson Valley in New York were in a far better position to produce for distant markets than those who had to endure the rocky soils and shorter growing seasons of large parts of New England. There were good reasons for the New Englanders to look to the sea for their wealth.[7]

New Englanders found that the sea was a greater source of profit than the land. The New England cod fishery had been devastated in the Revolution, when the fishermen could not reach their fishing grounds on the Grand Banks off Newfoundland and near the Gulf of St Lawrence. It improved in the 1780s, but only came into its own after 1790. Massachusetts and Maine provided most of the vessels and the men. The fishermen found an excellent market for their dried and pickled fish in the West Indies, and they also sent it to southern Europe. Only the embargo and the War of 1812 interrupted their growth in prosperity in the early nineteenth century.

The second arm of the prosperous New England fishing industry was whaling. The industry centered in Nantucket and New Bedford. The whalers roamed great distances after the sperm and baleen whales, which provided oil for candle making and lamps and stays for corsets. In the course of these years they extended their whaling grounds from the far North Atlantic to the waters off South America and round Cape Horn into vast reaches of the Pacific.[8]

The South was the home of large-scale commercial agriculture. Tobacco produced in the Chesapeake states of Virginia and Maryland had been the great American export crop of the colonial years. It remained the most important American export until 1820, but in these years the Upper South was undergoing sharp changes. In her writings Joyce Appleby has emphasized

7   Percy W. Bidwell and John I. Falconer, *History of Agriculture in the Northern United States, 1620–1860* (Washington, DC, 1925), pp.84–144; Wayne A. Rasmussen, '*History of Agriculture in the Northern United States, 1620–1860* revisited,' *Agricultural History* 46 (1972), pp.9–17.

8   Nettels, *Emergence*, pp.216–19; Harold A. Innis, *The Cod Fisheries: The History of an International Economy* rev. edn (Toronto, 1954), pp.219–26.

how Republican thought was influenced by the degree to which the planters [9 1] in the Chesapeake were beginning to move their production from tobacco to wheat in response to the growing European market for grain. Virginia and Maryland shared in the prosperity that wheat growers experienced from the Chesapeake through the Middle states up into the Connecticut River Valley. Much of the land in the Chesapeake was suffering from soil exhaustion brought on by many years of continuous tobacco production. Wheat brought new opportunities for the planters of the Upper South to participate in a prosperous overseas market.

In the years before the War of 1812, however, tobacco remained the most important southern crop. In these years some interest began to develop in practising less wasteful farming, and finding ways to improve depleted soil, but most of the new opportunities came from moving on to new land. The piedmont of Virginia and North Carolina succeeded the Chesapeake as the most important tobacco region. Tobacco also followed the Virginia frontier into Kentucky and into central Tennessee. The production of tobacco was at its greatest in the early 1790s; it began to decline after 1793, and suffered greatly in the period of economic restrictions and war from 1807 to 1815.[9]

The Lower South was undergoing an extensive transformation in its agriculture in the 30 years after independence. Rice continued to be important in low country South Carolina, but indigo, which had been supported by British bounties, was no longer profitable to grow. The Lower South's great opportunity came with the development in cotton cultivation. In 1790 cotton was of practically no importance. Its expansion had been limited by the difficulty of removing seeds from the short staple (or green seeded) cotton. They were easier to remove from the long staple, but this could not be grown inland. The general introduction of the short staple cotton became possible in 1793 when New Englander Eli Whitney, while staying at a plantation in Georgia, invented the cotton gin. This made possible a much more rapid, mechanical separation of the seeds. There was no problem in finding a market. The English Industrial Revolution had brought new technology to the spinning and weaving of cotton. Lancashire cotton factories were ready to supply the world, but they needed a good and convenient supply of cotton, and were having difficulty securing it from their existing sources in the West

9   Joyce Appleby, *Liberalism and Republicanism in the Historical Imagination* (Cambridge, Mass, 1992), pp.257–75; Lewis C. Gray, *History of Agriculture in the Southern United States to 1860*, 2 vols (Washington, DC, 1933), 2, pp.595–609, 752–62, 799–810; Nettels, *Emergence*, pp.193–5, 243–50.

Indies, Brazil, India, and the eastern Mediterranean. The American South was to provide what they needed. Before the War of 1812, England was obtaining over half its cotton from the United States, and that supply was to increase dramatically in the years after the war.[10]

The changes in the Lower South were striking. American production rose from under 3 million pounds in 1793 to 80 million pounds by 1811; by 1820 it was the main export. Farming in South Carolina was transformed, and cotton cultivation spread rapidly into the upcountry. In the years before the War of 1812 the change to cotton helped expand Georgia settlement into the interior of the state. Cotton cultivation also began to reach the eastern half of the Mississippi Valley; developing in central Tennessee, in the areas of Natchez and Baton Rouge along the Mississippi River, and in the region that later become Alabama.[11]

A decisive factor in the trade opportunities of the early national period was the outbreak of general European war in 1793. The great expansion that was to result was to last until the period of economic coercion and war from 1807 to 1815. With Europe at war, the European countries needed supplies and provisions of all types. The war also opened up great opportunities in the West Indies. As France had difficulty in maintaining connection to her West Indian colonies, she was willing to throw all of them open to American shipping. Even the British West Indies were frequently accessible to American ships as governors invoked emergency powers to admit American supplies that they so desperately needed. American ships were welcome in ports all over Europe and the West Indies. The cost of this expansion came in a variety of diplomatic incidents, quasi-war, and, ultimately, war itself, as the American government attempted to maintain its self-asserted neutral right to trade freely in time of general war. The shipowners and the seamen were far less perturbed by the blockades, the harassment, and the seizures than the general American population and the government, for there were great profits to be made. These profits were so great that shipowners could afford to lose ships in pursuing them.

Both farmers and shippers profited from the expanded markets, but the shipping industry profited more than American agriculture because the opportunities went far beyond carrying American produce. American ships

---

10 Constance M. Green, *Eli Whitney and the Birth of American Technology* (Boston, Mass, 1956), pp.12–94; Gray, *Agriculture*, 2, pp.610–11, 673–81, 721–31.

11 Gray, *Agriculture*, 2, pp.681–90; Joyce E. Chaplin, *An Anxious Pursuit: Agricultural Innovation and Modernity in the Lower South, 1730–1815* (Chapel Hill, NC, 1993), pp.277–329; Nettels, *Emergence*, pp.183–8, 192.

now began to replace European ships on a variety of ocean routes. The American re-export trade became more important than the trade in domestic products. Money generated from the great increase in foreign trading helped fuel the domestic economy. The Northeast was the greatest beneficiary of the expanded foreign trade, not only through shipbuilding, but a variety of support industries served the burgeoning shippers – warehouses, docks, agents, banks, and insurance companies expanded to boost the prosperity of northeastern ports.[12]

Export and re-export figures showed dramatic increases. The increase of domestic exports was less striking than that of re-exports, but the value of domestic exports more than doubled between 1790 and 1807, from about $20,000,000 in 1790 to nearly $50,000,000 in 1807. The most important growth was in export of cotton, but the European demand for wheat and flour also substantially increased. In 1790, the value of re-exports had amounted only to some $500,000, by 1807 it was nearly $60,000,000. The main items involved in this re-export trade were coffee, sugar, pepper, and cocoa brought from European colonies. American ships also often supplied these colonies with manufactured goods from Europe. Imports increased from a value of about $30,000,000 a year in the early 1790s to $138,500,000 in 1807. Most American imports from Europe came from Great Britain, and the United States consistently had an adverse balance of trade with the British. As prosperity increased in the years before 1807 there was an increased demand for British-manufactured goods.[13]

American ships did not confine themselves to Europe. The United States opened a trade to China in 1784 when the *Empress of China* left New York for Asia, and the trade to China developed steadily in the 1790s. American ships went round Cape Horn, traded for furs on the far northwest coast in what became known as the Oregon Country, and sailed across the Pacific to China to trade furs for Chinese products. In 1810 John Jacob Astor, who had earlier organized the American Fur Company, formed the Pacific Fur Company, and attempted to establish a fur trading post at the mouth of the Columbia on the Pacific.[14]

---

12 North, *Economic Growth*, pp.36–8, 46–54; Walton and Shepherd, *Economic Rise*, pp.1–4; but also see the discussion in Goldin and Lewis, 'Exports,' pp.6–25.

13 Emory R. Johnson, *et al.* (eds), *History of Domestic and Foreign Commerce of the United States* 2 vols (1915; rpr, New York, 1967), 2, p.20; North, *Economic Growth*, pp.24–5, 28–9, 38–41; Nettels, *Emergence*, pp.231–2, 235–6.

14 Johnson, *et al.* (eds), *Domestic and Foreign Commerce*, 2, pp.25–6; Samuel E. Morison, *The Maritime History of Massachusetts, 1783–1860* (Boston, 1941), pp.44–78; John D. Haeger, *John Jacob Astor: Business and Finance in the Early Republic* (Detroit, Mich, 1991), pp.115–37.

[94]   The disruption to European shipping brought about by the European wars meant that the proportion of America's foreign trade carried in American ships increased strikingly in these years; from less than 60 per cent in 1790 to over 90 per cent in 1807. In the 1790s alone the American share of shipping in the Anglo-American trade increased from under 50 per cent to some 95 per cent. The Northeast experienced the greatest benefit from this increase. Boston, other New England ports, New York, and Philadelphia were at the center of the re-export trade. Further south, Baltimore also shared in the new opportunities. In 1806 over 80 per cent of re-exports passed through Massachusetts, New York, Pennsylvania, and Maryland. Domestic exports were less highly concentrated because of the considerable exports of tobacco and cotton from the South; Charleston and Savannah were the most important ports for the export of cotton, although New Orleans was also beginning to expand its activities.[15]

The new opportunities meant that shipbuilding expanded dramatically in the years to 1807. The tonnage of American shipping engaged in foreign trade increased from some 355,000 in 1790 to over 1,000,000 in 1807. Although there was some shipbuilding in the main southern ports, the center of the industry was in the Northeast – in New York, Philadelphia, and the ports of New England. Demand was so great in the early years of the nineteenth century that the industry even expanded into the region beyond the Alleghenies. Marietta, on the Ohio River, which was settled by New Englanders, for a time became a minor center of shipbuilding, sending ocean-going vessels down the Ohio and Mississippi Rivers to the Gulf.[16]

A variety of subsidiary manufactures, ranging from sails to anchors, grew up to support shipbuilding, and the demand for rope gave a great boost not only to the establishment of ropewalks but also to American hemp growing. The 1810 census listed over 170 ropewalks in the United States. All the seaports had ropewalks, and, in the interior, Kentucky had 15. From an early date the growing of hemp became of great importance in that state, and it was also grown in Virginia, Massachusetts, and New York.[17]

The greatly increased use of American shipping meant that a great deal more capital became available, particularly in the Northeast. Before 1807

15   North, *Economic Growth*, pp.41–5; Nettels, *Emergence*, p.223–4, 234; Johnson, *et al.* (eds), *Domestic and Foreign Commerce*, 2, p.28.

16   John G. B. Hutchins, *The American Maritime Industries and Public Policy, 1789–1914* (Cambridge, Mass, 1941), pp.170–95; Leland D. Baldwin, *The Keelboat Age on Western Waters* (Pittsburgh, Pa, 1941), pp.161–74; Johnson *et al.* (eds), *Domestic and Foreign Commerce*, 2, p.28.

17   Nettels, *Emergence*, pp.197–8, 284; *ASP, F*, 2, p.428; James F. Hopkins, *A History of the Hemp Industry in Kentucky* (Lexington, Ky, 1951).

much of this capital that was not reinvested in shipping was invested in land [9 5] and in construction. After that date, when economic restrictions and then war slashed the import of manufactured goods from Great Britain, much of the capital was diverted into manufacturing.[18]

American banks and insurance companies also benefited greatly from the expansion in shipping. Banks in those areas devoted to foreign trade gained much of their business by advancing money to pay for foreign goods, and to enable importers to advance credit to buyers away from the coast. Before 1789 American shipowners usually obtained their insurance in Great Britain, but the securities created by Hamilton's funding program and the creation of the Bank of the United States became the basis for the organization in Philadelphia of the Insurance Company of North America. Its 1794 state charter specified that its $600,000 capital was to be in United States securities, stocks of the Bank of the United States, or stocks of companies incorporated in Pennsylvania. By 1800 there were over 30 operating companies, two-thirds of them in the Northeast and Pennsylvania. Their expansion and success came to an abrupt end after 1807, when the restrictions and extensive seizures made their financial position increasingly precarious.[19]

American ships and American trade went abroad to penetrate the oceans of the world, but the expansion of internal trade encountered great difficulties in these years. In 1789 there were no real roads, merely wider or narrower tracks, beaten down by the passage of traffic, and with the larger holes filled by pouring in rubble or small stones. In spring and fall, when there were heavy rains, they were often virtually impassable. They could be used by individuals on horseback, or by high-wheeled coaches or wagons, but it was impractical to try to move bulk produce or goods by land over anything but the shortest distances. The difficulty and the cost were prohibitive.

The only marked improvement in movement by road in these years came with the development of turnpikes. Turnpikes were private commercial ventures. Companies were organized to build a turnpike between specific locations, stock was sold, and the investors hoped to profit from tolls levied on traffic on the turnpike. The first turnpike was built between Philadelphia and Lancaster, Pennsylvania, from 1792 to 1794. Use was made of the crushed stone surface Macadam system developed in England. This first effort was a great success, and it inaugurated a craze for turnpikes in the years before the War of 1812. Hundreds of turnpike companies were chartered by the states.

18 Cochrane, *Frontiers of Change*, pp.51, 57–8.
19 Nettels, *Emergence*, pp.301–2, 314; Johnson, *et al.* (eds), *Domestic and Foreign Commerce*, 2, pp.132–3.

[9 6] Many companies never built the roads they proposed, but by 1812 most of the major cities were connected and there were many subordinate connections. The turnpikes made it much easier for individual travelers or coaches to move more swiftly from area to area, but did not solve the problem of moving bulk produce. Freight rates were high, and it was impractical to pay the tolls and make a profit.

Water was the only feasible way of transporting produce or goods in bulk, but here producers were restricted by accessibility, by the terrain, and by the flow of rivers. For those near the coast, the ocean was the best means of moving goods north and south. In the southern states there was a clear demarcation between the tidewater and the piedmont. Those in the tidewater region could ship their goods down the rivers to the sea, but for those who had moved above the fall line, where the rivers became unnavigable, produce had to be dragged around the falls. In all regions, settlement had clung to the navigable rivers. Although Britain was in the process of partially solving her communication problems by the construction of canals, the difficulties of terrain and distance in the United States made this solution slow to arrive. There were only about 100 miles of canals in the United States by the end of the War of 1812.[20]

New, and more formidable, problems were created in these years by the advance of settlement across the Allegheny barrier into the eastern half of the Mississippi Valley. The shipment of any large quantity of goods across the mountains was impractical. Manufactured goods from Great Britain were sent into the interior, but it was totally uneconomical to send farm produce eastwards over the mountains; only livestock, which could be driven on the hoof, brought any large trade opportunities in populated areas to the east. Originally the pack-horse had been the primary means of sending goods westward over the mountains, but by 1789 this was being superseded by the use of Conestoga wagons. In the first decades of the nineteenth century, freight rates for shipping goods from Philadelphia to Pittsburgh by wagon varied between $6 and $10 per hundredweight, at a time when a laborer was earning $1 a day.[21]

Although westerners were becoming interested in the possibility of the federal government using its resources for internal improvement such as roads, the constitutional objections to this were still viewed as insuperable.

20 Balthasar H. Meyer and Caroline E. Mitchell, *et al.*, *History of Transportation in the United States before 1860* (Washington, DC, 1917), pp.3–279; Nettles, *Emergence*, p.261.
21 Charles H. Ambler, *A History of Transportation in the Ohio Valley* (Glendale, Cal, 1932), pp.36–7; Baldwin, *Keelboat Age*, p.184.

To meet some of the pressure for links with the West, without opening up [9 7] the whole question, Congress in 1803, at the time Ohio was admitted to the Union, agreed that 5 per cent of the proceeds from the sale of public lands in the state would be used to make roads. Three-fifths of the money would be used for roads within Ohio, and the rest would go towards the cost of a road to connect the state to the East. From this arrangement a plan for the Cumberland, or National, Road emerged. By 1806 it was agreed that a road should be cut across the mountains from Cumberland, Maryland, to Wheeling, on the Ohio River. After years of political maneuvering over the question of the exact route that the road should take, construction began in 1812. The road ultimately stretched all the way to Illinois, but it took until 1818 to reach the Ohio River.[22]

Those who advanced across the mountains settled when possible on navigable rivers connected to the Ohio–Mississippi system, and sent their produce by water to New Orleans. Even for the settlers in western Pennsylvania, it was easier and cheaper to send produce to New Orleans by way of the Ohio and Mississippi Rivers than eastward by land over the mountains. Yet, for those east of Louisville even this water route presented problems, as there were falls at Louisville that were dangerous when the water was low. As early as 1804 a company was incorporated with the object of cutting a canal at that spot, but it was 1826 before construction began.[23]

After the negotiation of Pinckney's Treaty with Spain in 1795 the shipping of goods down the Mississippi increased rapidly. By 1799 the value of goods sent through New Orleans was over $1,000,000. The Louisiana Purchase in 1803 ended any possible doubt about the future of this trade, and by 1807 the worth of goods received in New Orleans had increased to over $5,300,000.[24]

In this period before 1815, when rafts, flatboats and barges were used to send produce by water, the water trade in the Mississippi Valley and elsewhere was complicated by the lack of any efficient means of moving against the flow of the rivers. Most of the rafts and flatboats that were used to send goods south on the Mississippi were simply broken up when they reached their destination. There was little trade up-river. The problem of movement against the stream was ultimately to be solved by the development of the steamboat, but in the years before 1815 the steamboat was just passing out

22 Karl Raitz (ed.), *The National Road* (Baltimore, Md, 1996), pp.93–197.
23 Baldwin, *Keelboat Age*, pp.68–70.
24 Johnson, *et al.* (eds), *Domestic and Foreign Commerce*, 1, pp.206–10.

[9 8] of its experimental stage. Robert Fulton's *Clermont* steamed on the Hudson in 1807, and in 1811 the *New Orleans*, which had been built at Pittsburgh, traveled to New Orleans. It then opened a steamboat connection between New Orleans and Natchez. But it was not until after the War of 1812 that regular steamboat navigation both up and down the Mississippi was to begin.[25]

The need for linking the various sections of the United States by an efficient communication system was realized in these years, but as yet the combined financial and constitutional problems thwarted all plans. In 1808 Thomas Jefferson's Secretary of the Treasury, Albert Gallatin, presented a plan that suggested the main elements of what was needed. Gallatin laid out a scheme for linking the different sections of the nation by roads and canals. He estimated that the cost of $20,000,000 could be paid in ten years.[26] This was an unusual dream for the usually financially cautious Gallatin, and it came to nothing. The financial status of the United States became precarious in the years from 1808 to 1815, and there was strong resistance to a broad interpretation of the Constitution that would have been necessary for any large-scale federal commitment to internal improvements.

Lacking an efficient communication system, the difficulties in creating any large-scale internal market for American manufactures were insuperable, but in these early years of the republic the market revolution was beginning to gain speed. Although there was some development of factory production, particularly in the years of economic coercion and war from 1807 to 1815, more important were the gradual changes that were taking place in the traditional production and sale of goods. Increasingly households and shops, both in rural areas and in the towns, were expanding the area of their sales. Women in households more often were spinning or weaving specifically for sale as well as for household consumption. In the artisan shops, masters now more frequently turned to additional apprentices or to wage labor to achieve greater production, rather than working in the traditional manner with a few journeymen. In these years the move towards capitalism was far more to be seen in the emergence of a market economy than it was in the growth of a factory system.[27]

25 Richard C. Wade, *The Urban Frontier: The Rise of Western Cities, 1790–1830* (Cambridge, Mass, 1959), pp.39–42; Baldwin, *Keelboat Age*, pp.47–9, 66, 124–5; Nettels, *Emergence*, p.260.
26 *ASP, MI*, 1, pp.724–41 (4 Apr. 1808).
27 Bruce Laurie, *Artisans into Workers: Labor in Nineteenth-Century America* (New York, 1989), pp.15–16, 49–50; Paul A. Gilje and Howard B. Rock (eds), *Keepers of the Revolution: New Yorkers at Work in the Early Republic* (Ithaca, NY, 1992), pp.1–11; Nettels, *Emergence*, pp.265–6; Cochrane, *Frontiers of Change*, pp.55–7.

Even without an industrial revolution, Gallatin could report in 1810 that [99] the United States was able to supply all of its needs in wooden articles, leather, soap, candles, flaxseed oil, refined sugar, and coarse earthenware. In addition, a considerable part of the country's needs were being provided by the producers of iron, cotton, wool, hats, paper, liquor, hemp, gunpowder, window glass, jewelry, clocks, and lead.[28]

The gradual emergence of a market economy began to put a strain on relationships within the traditional artisan shops, particularly in the towns. Seeking greater profits, masters began to bring greater 'efficiency' into the traditional relationships between master and journeymen in trades such as shoemaking, cabinetmaking, and tailoring. Tensions increased as masters expanded the number of workers in their enlarged shops by going beyond the traditional journeymen to hire additional apprentices or even semi-skilled labor that began to form a wage-labor force. The successful masters, as they expanded their operations, also employed a putting-out system, having shoes or other articles made in the homes of their workers. The various ways of increasing production and cutting costs had an adverse effect on the journeymen. In Boston between 1790 and 1825 the number of journeymen carpenters who advanced to the status of master dropped from 45 per cent to 11 per cent.[29]

In response to their weakening position, journeymen in New York and Philadelphia tried to organize both to provide help to individuals and families in trouble, and to resist the move of the masters away from the traditional master–journeyman relationship. Shoemaking was one of the first trades to undergo sizeable changes, and, both in Philadelphia and New York, societies of cordwainers were established by journeymen to try to maintain or improve their position.

In Philadelphia, the journeymen cordwainers attempted to act as a union to resist the coming of market values to shoemaking. They tried to enforce a 'closed shop,' and in 1805 they went on strike, clashing with the workers who were being hired to take their place. The masters struck back by bringing charges of criminal conspiracy against the strikers under English common law. Declaring for the masters, the court decided that organizing to raise wages was illegal, and fined the journeymen. In 1809 the New York

28 *ASP, F,* 2, pp.425–6.
29 Richard Stott, 'Artisans and capitalist development,' *JER,* 16 (1996), p.268; Nettels, *Emergence,* p.282; Gary J. Kornblith, 'The artisanal response to capitalist transformation,' *JER* 10 (1990), pp.315–21; Sean Wilentz, *Chants Democratic: New York City and the Rise of the American Working Class, 1788–1850* (New York, 1984), pp.23–60; *NYCA,* pp.179–80.

[1 0 0] masters also took the journeymen shoemakers to court for conspiracy, and won a conviction. There were a number of other journeymen strikes in these years, and other instances of masters bringing charges against them. In New York, striking journeymen house carpenters attacked the buildings and newspaper offices of those who opposed them.[30]

The masters also organized to try to protect their position as they met increasing competition from even larger producers. In Philadelphia a major reason for the masters in shoemaking resisting journeymen demands was that the wages they were paying journeymen in the years from 1806 to 1815 were twice as much as shoemakers were receiving in Massachusetts. In New York, the Mechanics Society, formed in 1785, became a prominent organization of many of the most important masters. New York masters also attempted to make better arrangements to secure the capital they needed to expand their businesses. Finding that the established banks favored investment in large merchant operations, they helped organize the Manhattan Bank. When that failed to serve their needs, they backed the Mechanics Bank which was chartered in 1810.[31] In these years a gulf was beginning to appear between master and journeymen in those trades that were responding most strongly to market forces.

The enlargement of manufacturing beyond the household and the existing shops of the artisans into large-scale manufacturing in factories with power-driven machinery, and a large wage-labor force, was limited in these years by a number of factors. An overriding problem was the domination of Great Britain in supplying the United States with a whole variety of manufactured goods. Already in the throes of a large-scale industrial revolution, Great Britain could supply large quantities of quality goods at a cheaper price than the Americans could make them.

The United States had a widely dispersed population that was often engaged in the rapid transformation of new areas. Most of the immigrants from Europe had come with the reasonable hope, in a land-rich nation, of acquiring land and becoming farmers. There was no large, surplus population to serve as a wage-labor force. The population was overwhelmingly rural, and there were no large cities. The distances were great, and the communications were primitive. Internally, a great proportion of national energy was devoted to clearing and building. As capital was created in the boom

30 Richard J. Twomey, 'Jacobins and Jeffersonians: Anglo-American radical ideology, 1790–1810,' in Margaret Jacob and James Jacob (eds), *The Origins of Anglo-American Radicalism* (London, 1984), pp.289–91; Nettels, *Emergence*, pp.265–6; *NYCA*, pp.199–242.
31 *NYCA*, pp.21–2, 137–9, 243–54; Nettels, *Emergence*, p.297.

years before 1807 it was poured back into shipping or into land and construction. There was simply no need to use it in investing in risky infant
manufacturing operations that would have to cope with extensive British
competition.

Hamilton realized the need for the United States ultimately to achieve a
balanced economy, and to free itself from economic dependence on British
manufactures. In December 1791 he sent Congress his Report on Manufactures. In it he advanced reasons for the United States to industrialize. He
acknowledged the problems of lack of capital and the shortage of labor, but
he wanted to encourage investment in manufacturing by a system of pro-
tective tariffs on imported manufactured goods, duty-free importation of
necessary foreign raw materials, and governmental bounties. This proposal
for federal government-backed development of manufacturing encountered
the strong resistance of those who saw it as another instance of Hamilton's
desire to expand the power of the federal government while helping a
moneyed elite, and it was not carried into effect. In the conditions of the first
years of the republic it seems unlikely, in any case, that it could have succeeded in its intentions.[32]

Thwarted in any more general plan, Hamilton gave his encouragement
to the incorporation of the Society for Establishing Useful Manufactures,
which in 1791 was given a charter in New Jersey. It was capitalized at
$1,000,000. This capital was mostly in the securities of the funded federal
debt and the First Bank of the United States. The Society attempted to create
a whole manufacturing community at Paterson, New Jersey, but failed by the
mid-1790s.[33]

While most production in the United States in these years still took place
in the household or in small shops, there had long been some manufacturing
activities that required a larger level of operation with more expensive equip-
ment, and some power-driven machinery. In the years after the Revolution,
as markets expanded, these operations often increased in level of investment
and in size.

Even in colonial America, metal industries had benefited from larger
investment and a larger scale of operation. An America dominated by farming provided an extensive market for a variety of iron products, used both
in building and in the daily life of the farm. The raw material was produced
in the many furnaces and forges of the Northeast. These were usually

---

32   *PAH*, 10, pp.230–340 (5 Dec. 1791).
33   McCoy, *Elusive Republic*, pp.159–65.

[1 0 2] established in rural areas in close proximity to iron ore and to water power. There was abundant timber for fuel. Before 1815 American forges were providing much of the crude iron needed in the United States, and the foundries were supplying all the cast-iron cooking utensils needed in the home, as well as the iron needed for the constant construction. In 1810, Gallatin estimated that four-fifths of the bar-iron used was produced in the United States. The rest – some 9,000 tons – was imported from Russia, England, and Sweden. The finer metal products were still imported from England.[34]

One major advance in these years was the uniformity system of Eli Whitney. Muskets had previously been made individually by hand. By 1801 Whitney was producing muskets with some interchangeable parts, after making the machinery necessary to turn out the lock mechanism with sufficient accuracy. In these years of crisis, the federal government encouraged the manufacture of arms because it wanted to end its earlier dependence on those of foreign manufacture. National armories in Springfield, Massachusetts, and at Harper's Ferry could not produce enough, and the government turned to private contracting with private manufacturers such as Whitney, who by 1808 employed some 50 workmen in his operation near New Haven.[35]

Much of the larger-scale American production in these years was still intimately connected with the land, with mills and tanneries numerous throughout the country. Sawmills were constantly expanding in number as the frontier advanced into the Mississippi Valley, and as construction boomed. The sawmills had long depended on water power, but by 1800 steam had been introduced, and the number of steam mills increased rapidly after that date. Steam engines were being built in Philadelphia by 1810. Water power still dominated in the numerous flour mills, but after 1810 efforts to use steam increased.[36]

While a variety of other long-established industries, such as papermaking and glassmaking, continued to expand in these years, the greatest innovations came in the production of textiles, for it was here that an infant factory system began to emerge. Progress was slow before 1810 – in that year 90 per cent of American textiles were of household production – but the sharp reduction of British imports after 1807 encouraged the use of capital to establish larger manufacturing operations.

34 *ASP, F,* 2, pp.428–9; Nettels, *Emergence,* pp.270–4; Paul F. Paskoff, *Industrial Evolution: Organization, Structure, and Growth of the Pennsylvania Iron Industry, 1750–1860* (Baltimore, Md, 1983).

35 Green, *Whitney,* pp.119–50.

36 Nettels, *Emergence,* pp.278–82; *ASP, F,* 2, 429; Cochrane, *Frontiers of Change,* p.58.

The large-scale production of cotton thread began to appear in America [1 0 3] at about the same time as the inauguration of the new government. There had been experiments with the spinning jenny before that, but in 1790 Samuel Slater, an immigrant Englishman, began to operate a mill in Pawtucket, Rhode Island, which made use of Richard Arkwright's more efficient frame. The building of new cotton mills was slow before 1807, but from 1807 to 1815 economic coercion and war led to numerous new cotton factories in the United States. The efforts of the British government to prevent knowledge reaching America, by blocking the emigration of skilled workmen, failed. In 1811 Augustus Foster, the British minister in the United States, reported that American manufacturing, particularly in coarse cloth and cotton, was progressing in every quarter, and that there were frequent arrivals of workmen from England.[37] Most of this expansion was in spinning not weaving. By 1815 there were over 200 mills operating in the United States, most of them in New England.

Woolen manufacture grew much more slowly than cotton. American farmers contending with recently cleared land much preferred hogs to sheep, although after 1807 there was a flourishing importation of Merino sheep specifically to provide wool for the new industry. The great mass of woolen goods continued to be items of household manufacture in this period, but there were many fulling mills, which cleaned and prepared the cloth woven in the home, and an increasing number of carding mills for combing the wool before it was spun. Only during the War of 1812 was there any significant advance in weaving on power looms.[38]

As the new spinning mills developed, they began to depend on the labor of women and children. In 1810 Gallatin estimated that of the 4,000 workers employed by cotton mills, 3500 were women and children. The growth in the number of employees was rapid in the War of 1812, but women and children continued to provide most of the labor force. Women and children were often adept in handling the delicate threads, and they had the advantage for employers that they were paid less than men.[39]

Because of the wide availability of land and the shortage of labor, wages both for laborers and skilled workmen were higher in the United States than in Great Britain. Gaps in income were widening. More opportunities were

---

37 Cochrane, *Frontiers of Change*, pp.62–3; Nettles, *Emergence*, pp.203–4, 274–5; *IBM*, pp.347–8 n.11; Barbara M. Tucker, *Samuel Slater and the Origins of the American Textile Industry, 1790–1860* (Ithaca, NY, 1984).

38 Nettles, *Emergence*, pp.276–7; Cochrane, *Frontiers of Change*, p.64.

39 *ASP, F*, 2, p.427; Nettels, *Emergence*, p.269.

[104] arising for some to develop wealth, but the market was operating to make it more difficult for others to maintain their standard of living. Fortunately, for most white Americans, the opportunity both to avoid sinking into poverty, and even to prosper, was still much higher than in Europe. Early nineteenth-century America by no means guaranteed success, but for the ordinary people of European extraction it provided both better living conditions, greater freedom, and a much better chance of social and economic mobility than Europe. While some were employed in the new factories, or sought to earn a living in the slowly expanding towns, the great majority wanted to make their living from the land, and as the population grew their desire fueled a constant movement into new areas. The opportunity to own farms was made possible by the constant expansion of the areas under cultivation as the advancing frontiersmen wrested land from the American Indians.

CHAPTER 7

THE ADVANCE OF SETTLEMENT

The desire for expansion into new areas had survived even the most dangerous years of the Revolution. American settlers were advancing into western Pennsylvania, Kentucky, and Tennessee as the Revolution began, and, in spite of combined British–Indian attacks, settlement continued. While some easterners, particularly from New England, feared that the unrestrained emigration of pioneers might weaken social cohesion, and even the bonds of nationhood, most Americans of the revolutionary generation looked confidently to a rapid advance into the Mississippi Valley.

For the American Indians the advance of non-Indian settlement was a devastating experience. A combination of disease and warfare had wiped out most of the Indians east of the Alleghenies by the time of the American Revolution. Some survivors had moved west, but only in areas where European settlement was lacking did Indians survive in the East in any large numbers. Most of Georgia was still occupied by Creeks and Cherokees, the Cherokees still hung on in western North Carolina, and the Iroquois occupied western New York. The Iroquois had been badly weakened by the Revolution, and they were vulnerable in the early national period.

Indian tribes were numerous from the Great Lakes to the Gulf, practising a mixed economy of farming and hunting. In the summer, Indian women farmed often-extensive fields; in winter the men traveled to hunting grounds to supply meat and skins. In some regions, particularly in the Great Lakes area, tribal members also gathered wild rice or tapped maple trees as an essential part of their economy. In the Old Northwest, Indian villages were thickly scattered from western Pennsylvania to the Mississippi, and northwards to the Canadian border. In the Southwest, the state of Georgia, and the region that would become the states of Tennessee, Alabama, and Mississippi had large Indian populations. Kentucky had few Indian settlements as it was a major hunting ground for tribes both north and south of the Ohio River.

To the first settlers who began to move across the mountains the whole region appeared to be in a pristine, untouched state. To them it was a Beulah

[1 0 6] land, given by their God to those who would till it and make it fruitful. To the Indians it was their homeland, given to them by their God in the distant past. For a time, in the decade after the Revolution, the Indians of the eastern half of the Mississippi Valley believed that they would be able to retain their lands and expel the interlopers. The comparatively small number of settlers, isolated from the East by the mountains, appeared to be a manageable foe.

At root, a desire for land lay at the heart of all nineteenth-century American Indian policy. The settlers who came from Europe were mostly landless at home, but they came from societies in which land was all important. Most Europeans who emigrated to America, and their descendants, regarded land as their route to wealth and social mobility. Their European cultures also gave them a specific view of how land should be used. It should be farmed and fenced by men. Their wives would take care of the house and children, spin and weave, and engage in numerous other tasks necessary for daily living. They believed that those who labored in the soil were especially blessed because they were obeying biblical commands to make the land fruitful. To these men, the Indians were savages, part of the natural environment that had to be overcome.

The leaders who shaped American Indian policy in the early republic desired land, but they combined this desire with a hope that the Indians could be transformed; a transformation that they believed would benefit the Indians as well as the United States. They were imbued with the Enlightenment view that human beings were improvable, that environment not innate nature had shaped human differences, and that American Indians were in a state of savagery that the Europeans had passed through long before. Pioneers often thought of the Indians as bloodthirsty savages to be destroyed or removed, but to men of the Enlightenment they represented man at an earlier stage of his existence.[1]

Before 1789 the Confederation government and the states squabbled about jurisdiction over the Indians while attempting to use force to compel tribes to yield lands in the Mississippi Valley. The policy produced chronic warfare, and while settlers continued to advance into Kentucky and Tennessee, settlement north of the Ohio River was slowed to a trickle. By 1789 Secretary of War Henry Knox, who had served in the same position in the Confederation government, had begun to devise what he believed would be a more effective Indian policy. He was convinced that force was

---

1 Reginald Horsman, *Race and Manifest Destiny: The Origins of American Racial Anglo-Saxonism* (Cambridge, Mass, 1981), pp.104–8.

not enough. He wanted to provide for the advance of settlement across the [1 0 7] Mississippi Valley with a minimum of warfare and a minimum of cost, and with an untarnished reputation for the new republic.[2]

Knox's first objective was to have hostile tribes on the frontiers of the United States deal only with the federal government, not with individual states. In this hope, which he had striven for in vain before 1789, he was greatly helped by the United States Constitution. Although European powers divided the Americas without regard for the territory claimed by individual Indian tribes, and though the Indians east of the Mississippi were encompassed within the national bounds of the United States, the Constitution dealt with the Indians as foreign powers. From 1789 treaties with Indian tribes were negotiated under the authority of the president, and were ratified by a two-thirds vote of the Senate. American leaders might think of these treaties as quite different from those with France or England, but legally they were exactly the same, and such treaties became part of the supreme law of the land.[3]

In having the federal government take control of Indian policy, Knox hoped to bring order to the advance of settlement. He wanted to purchase Indian land in formal treaties. He was willing to acknowledge that the Indians had a 'right of soil' that had to be paid for. This right of soil stemmed from the actual Indian residence on the land. It did not affect the territorial sovereignty of the American government. The payment would be much less than land prices in deals between non-Indians, because it was considered that Indians made only limited use of the land.

Knox was willing to acknowledge Indian ownership of unceded land, with the understanding that if the land was sold in the future it would be sold only to the United States government. Knox, and other American leaders, were not worried by the possibility of the Indians adamantly refusing to sell, because past experience had shown them that as non-Indian settlers advanced, game disappeared, the Indians lessened in numbers, the survivors became demoralized, and they were unable to resist pressure for further land sales. Knox wrote in 1789 that a policy of peace and conciliation would not prevent expansion. 'As the settlements of the whites shall approach near to the Indian boundaries established by treaties,' Knox wrote, 'the game will be diminished, and the lands being valuable to the Indians

---

2 Reginald Horsman, *Expansion and American Indian Policy, 1783–1812* (East Lansing, Mich, 1967), pp.3–52.
3 See Dorothy Jones, *License for Empire: Colonialism by Treaty in Early America* (Chicago, 1982).

[108] only as hunting grounds, they will be willing to sell further tracts for small considerations.'[4] Knox, like Jefferson, persisted in regarding the mixed-economy eastern Indians as nomadic hunters.

Under Knox's policies, Indian land cessions were followed by an attempt to provide strict protection of the new boundaries against white encroachment until such time as the government desired further cessions. Violations of Indian areas by non-Indians were resisted, and laws were passed to license traders and to provide for the punishment of crimes within Indian country. These measures were put into effect both by the treaties themselves and in a series of Trade and Intercourse acts. The first was passed in July 1790, and the measures were much strengthened by subsequent acts in 1793, 1796, and 1802. To enhance its influence among the tribes, and in an attempt to keep out unlicensed American traders and traders from Canada, the government in 1796 established the Indian 'factory system'; government trading posts were established in Indian country both to centralize the control of trade and to provide a means of influencing the Indians.[5]

The 1793 Trade and Intercourse Act included another essential ingredient in the Indian policy that was shaped in the 1790s. The act empowered the president to appoint temporary agents to promote 'civilization.' From the beginning of the new government in the spring and summer of 1789 Knox had emphasized that both self-interest and national honor required that negotiation, payment for land, and the strict enforcement of boundaries should be accompanied by civilization policies. Knox argued that the only way to avoid staining the national character by destroying the Indians was to 'civilize' them. He dismissed the arguments of those who argued that the Indians were incapable of civilization. 'To deny that, under a course of favorable circumstances, it could not be accomplished,' he wrote, 'is to suppose the human character . . . as to be incapable of melioration or change – a supposition entirely contradicted by the progress of society, from the barbarous ages to its present degree of perfection.' How much better it would be, he argued, if 'instead of exterminating a part of the human race,' the United States had 'imparted our knowledge of cultivation and the arts to the aboriginals of the country, by which the source of future life and happiness had been preserved and extended.'[6]

---

4   *ASP, IA*, I (Washington, 1832), pp.13–14 (15 June); Horsman, *Expansion*, pp.35–6, 38–41, 44–5, 54–9.
5   See Francis P. Prucha, *American Indian Policy in the Formative Years: The Indian Trade and Intercourse Acts, 1790–1834* (Cambridge, Mass, 1962), pp.41–50, 86–8.
6   Ibid., *ASP, IA*, I, pp.12–14 (15 June), 52–4 (7 July, quotations).

From 1790 the United States pursued a policy of Indian land cessions, [109] strict boundaries, and the furtherance of Indian 'civilization.' Agricultural implements were provided in the hope that the men would stop hunting and start farming. Spinning wheels and looms were given to Indian women to persuade them to leave the fields and turn to spinning and weaving. Missionaries urged the Indians to become Christians. The government wanted to encourage the end of tribalism and the adoption of private property. Thinking in optimistic eighteenth-century terms of the ease by which such a transformation could be achieved, American leaders saw the 'civilization' policy as the answer to how the United States could obtain the lands of the American continent while living up to its revolutionary and republican ideals of benefiting mankind in general. In this rosy view of the future, both the United States and the Indians would be satisfied; the United States by obtaining the land it needed for its expanding population, the Indians by receiving the inestimable blessings of an advanced civilization. The idea that the Indians wanted to preserve their way of life with the same tenacity as American leaders wanted to change it was not within the patterns of thought that the revolutionary generation had inherited.

The Indian policy of the early republic did not achieve the results hoped for by Knox. Westward expansion was not peaceful, most of the Indians did not readily accept American civilization, and greed for land overcame any dream of policies that would satisfy both sides. A basic problem was that the federal government wanted land for its pioneers more than it wanted the civilization of the Indians. Pressure for land was relentless, money and effort spent on 'civilization' was meagre, and little time was given to what was an extremely complicated and difficult process. Time could not be given because pioneers advanced constantly in great numbers, and most of the pioneers did not want the Indians civilized; they wanted them removed or killed. To move westwards meant clashing with the Indians, who wished to keep their lands and their way of life. The deaths and suffering that resulted bred hatreds, and westerners constantly pressed the federal government for action not talk. Ultimately, the federal government yielded to its own pioneers and their political representatives.

The Indians for the most part wanted to retain their own way of life. Some adopted the ways of the dominant society that was overwhelming them, but most resisted, either actively or passively. In the early 1790s, after comparative success in retaining their lands in the 1780s, the Indians north of the Ohio felt confident and were not prepared to accept the American policies; they were willing to fight to stop the advance from the East. As a

[1 1 0] result, the government could not put its new policies into effect until it had waged war beyond the Ohio River. Failures by Josiah Harmar and Arthur St Clair early in the 1790s were followed by a decisive victory by the troops of Anthony Wayne in August 1794 at the battle of Fallen Timbers. In the following year the Treaty of Greenville established a boundary that allowed the pioneers to advance into what was to become eastern and southern Ohio.[7] South of the Ohio, the growth of new settlements in Kentucky and Tennessee had become so extensive by the mid-1790s that they were no longer in any real danger from Indian attack.

The treaties of the 1790s – with the Creeks and Cherokees in the South and with a dozen tribes in the North – tried to put into effect the policies that had been outlined by Knox. Thomas Jefferson ardently endorsed them when he became president in 1801. Writing of the Indians in his second inaugural in March 1805, he said that 'humanity enjoins us to teach them agriculture and the domestic arts . . . to prepare them in time for that state of society which to bodily comforts adds the improvement of the mind and morals.' In 1809, shortly before he left office, when Knox's policies were already in ruins, he told a visiting delegation of Indians that 'we wish you to live in peace, to increase in numbers, to learn to labor as we do. . . . We wish to see you possessed of property and protecting it by regular laws.'[8]

Jefferson, however, also deeply believed that it was in the interest of the United States and the world for the United States to advance across the American continent. Throughout his administration he urged his agents to press for more land. Jefferson believed that the success of republicanism depended on providing land for the settlers advancing across the Mississippi Valley. Indian tribes were constantly harassed into making cessions. Land, not the civilization policy, dominated discussions between government agents and Indians.

Both north and south of the Ohio River Indian tribes attempted to resist the treaties that were taking their lands. From 1805 Tenskwatawa (the Shawnee Prophet) and his brother Tecumseh attempted to unite the Indian tribes to resist the two main thrusts of federal policy. Gathering supporters first in Ohio, and then on the Tippecanoe River in Indiana, they attempted to preserve the Indian way of life and Indian lands. Tenskwatawa urged Indians to throw off the ways of the newcomers, while Tecumseh argued

---

7 Horsman, *Expansion*, pp.84–103.
8 *M&P*, 1, p.380; War Department, Secretary's Office, Letters Sent, Indian Affairs, B: pp.412–13, National Archives, Washington, DC.

that no tribe should cede lands because the Indians owned the lands in common.[9] [1 1 1]

In the South the tribes of the region, after constantly yielding lands to government pressure, from 1806 dug in their heels and tried to say 'no more.' The fighting in the War of 1812, when some of the tribes again tried to ally with the British in an effort to resist the American advance, was effectively to end Indian hopes of resistance east of the Mississippi River, and after 1815 the government was gradually to move to a policy of removal, by which even the minority of the Indians who had accepted the civilization policy were to lose their lands. The dream of expansion with a good conscience evaporated in an overwhelming desire for land, in a failure to understand the reluctance with which any people would give up their way of life, and in a frontier unwillingness to accept Indians as fellow citizens.

The basis for the relentless advance westwards in these years came not from immigration, but from a natural increase. The population of the United States grew from under 4,000,000 in 1790 to over 7,200,000 in 1810, and to over 9,600,000 in 1820. Yet many eastern counties of the older states hardly increased in population as their inhabitants left to find better lands and greater opportunity in new areas. In a nation in which well over 90 per cent of the population was engaged in farming, the rapid population growth presented major challenges in older areas. There was not enough good land for the sons and daughters of the older inhabitants. There were also reasons to leave for some who already owned farms. Areas that had long been planted with the same crops were suffering from soil exhaustion. This was a particular problem in the tobacco lands of the Chesapeake. Also, the Revolution had brought social unrest. The talk was of freedom and of new opportunities. There was a greater unwillingness to accept the patterns of social deference that had been an integral part of colonial life. In New England, establishment ministers no longer had the influence they enjoyed in earlier years. Emigrants sought good land, prosperity, social mobility, and more of the opportunity and freedom that had been promised in revolutionary rhetoric.[10]

While the most striking advance of these years was into the lands beyond the Alleghenies, emigrants also moved into the undeveloped lands in the

9 R. David Edmunds, *Tecumseh and the Quest for Indian Leadership* (Boston, Mass, 1984), and *The Shawnee Prophet* (Lincoln, Neb, 1983); John Sugden, *Tecumseh: A Life* (New York, 1998).
10 *A Century of Population Growth: From the First Census of the United States to the Twelfth, 1790–1900* (Washington, DC, 1909), p.57; Avery O. Craven, *Soil Exhaustion as a Factor in the Agricultural History of Virginia and Maryland, 1606–1860* (Urbana, Ill, 1925), pp.72–84, 118–20; Reginald Horsman, *The Frontier in the Formative Years, 1783–1815* (New York, 1970), p.21.

East. From Maine to Georgia the areas under cultivation increased dramatically. Colonial territorial growth was to be dwarfed by the expansion in the first half-century of the new republic.

In northern New England Vermont had been of interest to settlers since the middle of the eighteenth century. For emigrants from southern New England, it had the advantage of comparative accessibility and safety. Settlers did not encounter the Indian resistance present beyond the Alleghenies, for New England Indian resistance had been crushed at an earlier date. Vermont's advantages were offset by a harsh climate, a short growing season, and a limited availability of good land, but it had a population of some 30,000 by 1780. This population nearly tripled in the next ten years, and by 1810 it had reached almost 218,000. The region had established its own government in the revolutionary years, and had long wanted to join the Union. It entered in 1791 as the first addition to the original 13 states.

Between 1783 and 1810 Vermont passed from being a frequent destination for pioneers to being a source of emigrants to western New York and the Ohio Valley. Settlers had discovered that much of the land away from the rivers was not particularly fertile, and the population growth meant that little desirable land was now available. The region also suffered greatly in the years of economic restriction after 1807. Difficulties in communications meant that Vermont's economic ties were northwards to Canada via Lake Champlain, not southwards into the United States. The cutting of economic ties to Great Britain and her possessions was a disaster for the residents of Vermont.[11]

While the settlement of Vermont represented the hopes of the small farmers of New England, movement into Maine very much involved another aspect of expansion in these years – the part played by the land speculator. After the Revolution Massachusetts made determined efforts to promote Maine's growth, both by giving land to actual settlers and by the sale of large tracts to speculators. For those with money to invest, and with political influence, large-scale speculation in land was one of the hoped-for routes to great wealth. Both in the older states with undeveloped areas, and in the Ohio Valley, speculators acquired huge tracts in the hopes of reselling the land at a profit. Both the states and the federal government were often ready to make quick, large sales at a discount in order to raise money immediately, rather than waiting for the slower returns of sales to actual pioneers. Like Vermont, Maine showed steady growth in these years. Its population had

11   Horsman, *Frontier*, pp.22–3.

been about 40,000–50,000 in the Revolution; it had reached over 151,000 [1 1 3] by 1810. Most of its best land was taken up before 1815, and, like Vermont, it suffered greatly from the economic restrictions and war against Great Britain.[12]

Once the power of the Iroquois had been broken the rich lands of western New York were much more desirable to emigrants than northern New England. In the aftermath of the Revolution some of the Iroquois were dispersed from their homeland. Some who had fought with the British fled to Canada, others tried to join with Indians beyond the Ohio to resist the American advance. Those who stayed, including some who had fought with the Americans, quickly lost most of their lands in treaties dictated by the state of New York. Massachusetts also had land claims in the region, and in 1786 had agreed that New York could have sovereignty while the land would be divided between the two states.

Western New York was largely disposed of through land speculators, although the state of New York also laid out a tract of 1,500,000 acres for its revolutionary veterans. Speculators made ambitious efforts to promote the rich lands east of the Genesee River. They issued pamphlets extolling the wonders of the Genesee country, and engaged in the more practical work of building roads, erecting mills, and laying out small towns. Over 200,000 pioneers entered the region in the years before the War of 1812, most of them from eastern New York and New England. Even the more desolate northern areas on the eastern shore of Lake Ontario and along the St Lawrence River became the scene of large-scale speculation. The population growth was less dramatic than in the western parts of the state, but settlers pushed up to the Canadian border.[13]

In the South Atlantic states, except for Georgia, much of the good land had already been taken up by 1789. Population growth and soil exhaustion in the Chesapeake provided a major impetus for the first large trans-Allegheny settlements in Kentucky and Tennessee. Virginia still included what was later to be the state of West Virginia, and that region began to be settled in these years. Wheeling became of great importance as a jumping-off point for emigrants down the Ohio. It was often used instead of Pittsburgh, because in low water the river from Pittsburgh to Wheeling was difficult to navigate. The pioneers who moved along the western Virginia

12 Ibid., pp.23–4.
13 Neil A. McNall, *An Agricultural History of the Genesee Valley, 1790–1860* (Philadelphia, 1952), pp.1–77; Horsman, *Frontier*, pp.24–8; Shaw Livermore, *Early American Land Companies: Their Influence on Corporate Development* (New York, 1939), pp.197–214.

[1 1 4] side of the Ohio and into the valleys of the Great and Little Kanawha were often poor, and followed an Indian pattern of living by hunting as well as farming. Slavery was much less important in west Virginia than in the eastern part of the state.[14]

Of the original states the least transformed by Europeans in 1789 was Georgia. At the end of the Revolution, its non-Indian population was less than 50,000. The Creek Indians occupied much of the state, and were in possession of large villages and extensive fields. Although they also hunted as an integral part of their mixed economy, they made nonsense of the constant governmental rhetoric about nomadic Indians making their living by the chase. Georgia put relentless pressure on its Indians throughout these years, and settlers gradually advanced across the eastern part of the state, particularly with the expansion of cotton growing in the late 1790s and after 1800. This was a slave frontier. Much of the arduous work of settlement – chopping and girdling trees, clearing underbrush, and breaking the new land – was carried out by slaves. By 1800 the population was over 162,000, including almost 60,000 slaves.[15]

Georgia was the last of the states to cede western land claims, and until 1802 owned what was to become Alabama and Mississippi. With this vast acreage, and wanting to attract settlers, the state had very generous land policies, at times giving land away by lottery. There were also huge grants to land companies, and widespread corruption. In 1789 and 1794 speculators acquired the extensive Yazoo land grants in the Alabama–Mississippi region of the state. The 1794 grants involved the bribery of most of the Georgia legislature, and a new legislature canceled them. This produced endless litigation, for innocent purchasers of land company lands tried to maintain their rights to what they had bought in good faith. Ultimately, the Supreme Court under John Marshall was to overturn the state's reversal of its original decision, and used the case to enforce the sanctity of contract.[16]

The political and legal basis for expansion into the Mississippi Valley had been provided in the era of the Confederation. One of the major accomplishments of the Confederation government had been establishing policies to provide for land sales and government in the region beyond the

---

14   Horsman, *Frontier*, pp.4, 50–1.

15   E. Merton Coulter, *Georgia: A Short History* rev. edn (Chapel Hill, NC, 1960), pp.196–7, 219–20; James C. Bonner, *A History of Georgia Agriculture, 1732–1860* (Athens, Ga, 1964), pp.38–9; Horsman, *Frontier*, pp.54–5.

16   C. Peter Magrath, *Yazoo: Law and Politics in the New Republic: The Case of Fletcher v. Peck* (Providence, RI, 1966).

mountains. The states had been persuaded that they should yield their own [1 1 5] land claims to the region to create a public domain. Some delayed in making the cession, but by the time the new national government took office in 1789 the federal government owned a huge domain north of the Ohio River. A general system for the survey and sale of the public land had been established in the Ordinance of 1785. The principle of prior, rectangular survey and sale had been established, but at first it was difficult for settlers to buy land. It was priced at only $1 an acre, but the least amount that could be bought was 640 acres, and there was no credit system. At a time when laborers earned $1 a day, and skilled workers often not more than $1.50 or $2.00, $640 was a huge amount. Many of the more substantial citizens of New England resisted providing easy access to the public lands because they feared that unrestrained westward expansion would weaken the fabric of society, lower land prices in the East, and perhaps lead to western areas breaking away from the Union.[17]

In the late 1780s the government had begun to survey lands to the west of Pennsylvania for direct sale to pioneers, but sales were slow, and, like the states, the Confederation government turned to speculators for the rapid disposal of land. Large tracts of land along the north bank of the Ohio were sold at a discount to speculative companies. The Ohio Company received 1,500,000 acres, its subsidiary the Scioto Company a massive 5,000,000 acres. Judge John Cleves Symmes obtained 1,000,000 acres.[18]

The governmental system that was established by the Northwest Ordinance of 1787 embodied the idea of republican not traditional empire. It was agreed that settlers beyond the mountains could ultimately form new states and gain admission to the Union on an equal basis with the original 13. Temporarily, one great governmental unit was created for the whole area between the Ohio and the Mississippi Rivers – the Northwest Territory. Settlers would have to pass through two earlier political stages before achieving statehood. It was stated that in the future there would be between three and five states there. One momentous decision in the Northwest Ordinance was that slavery was banned in the whole region between the Ohio and the Mississippi Rivers. This decision was momentous not only

---

17 Clarence E. Carter (ed.), *The Territorial Papers of the United States* (Washington, DC, 1934–), 2, pp.12–18; William D. Pattison, *Beginnings of the American Rectangular Land Survey System, 1784–1800* (Chicago, 1957).

18 Livermore, *Early American*, pp.134–46; Malcolm J. Rohrbough, *The Land Office Business: The Settlement and Administration of American Public Lands, 1789–1837* (New York, 1968), pp.9–11; Horsman, *Frontier*, pp.36–7.

[1 1 6] because it banned slavery in that region but also because it tacitly allowed it south of the river. The original ordinance for the future government of the trans-Allegheny West, drafted by Jefferson in 1784, had proposed ending slavery in the whole western region. That part of Jefferson's plan had been rejected by the Confederation Congress. Some slaves were taken north of the Ohio by southerners, but they did not succeed in altering the general ban.[19]

Before 1795 the difficulties of advancing into the region north of the Ohio were very great. To the problems of distance, difficulties of communication, and the heavy forest cover was added widespread Indian resistance. The tribes in the path of the pioneer advance – the Shawnee, the Wyandot, the Delaware – and many others scattered west and north along the Wabash and through the Great Lakes region were determined to retain their lands. Not until Wayne's victory at the battle of Fallen Timbers in 1794 was it reasonably safe to settle in what was to become the state of Ohio.

The only practical route of entry for most settlers was down the Ohio River by flatboat or raft. In the early 1790s, they clustered close to the north bank of the Ohio, at the mouths of the various tributaries, but after Fallen Timbers they advanced further north into the interior of the state. Settlement also began in the northeast corner of the state in a region reserved by Connecticut as its own Western Reserve.

In these years, the Old Northwest was primarily a region of small farms. At first, corn was the basic crop, and hogs the main livestock. Wheat developed as an important cash crop, and cattle were soon kept along with the ubiquitous hogs. Marketing was a great problem. It was impractical to send bulk produce eastwards by wagon over the mountains, and the main route to market was to the south – down the Ohio and Mississippi to New Orleans and the sea. The only practical way of farmers making a profit to the east was by driving cattle, hogs, and horses up to and over the mountains, selling along the way.[20]

As settlement and farm production grew, small western towns became of increasing importance as marketing and trading centers. Pittsburgh, which was the main point of entry for pioneers preparing for the journey down the Ohio, flourished by selling supplies. It soon developed infant industries – nail factories, breweries, glassworks, an iron furnace, a cotton factory, and a host of smaller establishments, and found a ready market for its products in

---

19 Carter (ed.), *Territorial Papers*, 2, pp.39–50; *Journals of the Continental Congress*, 34 vols (Washington, DC, 1904–37), 26, pp.118–20, 246–52, 255–60, 274–9.
20 Horsman, *Frontier*, pp.4–5, 148–56.

the settlements down the Ohio River. The town had been a frontier outpost [117] in 1789, but by 1815 a visitor commented that it 'promises to be one of the greatest *manufacturing* towns in America.'[21]

Cincinnati became the most important town of what was to become the state of Ohio. Founded in the winter of 1789–90, it endured its dangerous early years as a base from which military expeditions were launched against the northwestern Indians. After 1795 it benefited from the rapid rural population growth, and became the marketing center for the southwestern Ohio region. Companies arranged the export of farm produce to New Orleans, and distributed manufactured goods from upriver. Like other western towns it became a center for new banks, and by 1815, when its population had reached some 5,000, it was beginning industrial development.[22]

In 1800 it was at last made reasonably simple for settlers to buy land directly from the central government. Settlers could now buy their land over time. The price of land had been raised to $2 in 1796, but from 1800 only a quarter of the purchase price had to be paid within 40 days; the other three-quarters were not due until the end of the second, third, and fourth years. Also, land west of the Muskingum River could be sold in half-sections of 320 acres. 750,000 acres were now sold by the government in less than two years, and in 1804 purchase was made still easier when the minimum purchase was reduced to 160 acres. In 1785 a purchaser had needed an immediate $640 to buy land from the government. From 1800, $160 was enough, and from 1804, $80.[23]

The population of Ohio increased from 45,000 in 1800 to over 230,000 in 1810. It became a state in 1803, although its northwestern corner was Indian country until after the War of 1812. Both in territorial Ohio and in the new state, the citizens of Ohio engaged in vigorous political debate. The division between Federalists and Jeffersonian Republicans at first was as bitter beyond the mountains as it was in the East. After 1800, however, the Jeffersonians began to dominate throughout the eastern half of the Mississippi Valley. Although some who wanted an older elite-dominated, deferential society emigrated to the West, it proved far more attractive to those who had interpreted the Revolution as a victory for popular sovereignty. Many ordinary citizens wanted to rid politics of an old elite, and

21 Lorenzo Dow, *History of Cosmopolite* (Wheeling, Va, 1848), p.339; Richard C. Wade, *The Urban Frontier: The Rise of Western Cities, 1790–1830* (Cambridge, Mass, 1959), pp.7–13, 41–9.

22 Wade, *Urban Frontier*, pp.22–7, 53–9.

23 Rohrbough, *Land Office*, pp.18–50; Horsman, *Frontier*, pp.72–3.

[1 1 8] were hoping to create a society in which free men would be able to engage in the vigorous pursuit of individual prosperity. Andrew Cayton has shown that in Ohio the elite had to reach a compromise with those who were demanding a more egalitarian society. Western state constitutions generally recognized the popular demand that free white males should participate extensively in government.[24]

Even before Ohio became a state adventurous settlers had begun to press on down the Ohio River. Indiana Territory was created in 1800, when what was to become the state of Ohio was broken off from the rest of the Northwest Territory. Shortly after it was created, the eastern portion of Indiana Territory (modern Indiana) had a population of some 2,500, of whom nearly half were under 16 and less than 200 45 or older. Cayton has characterized the frontier population of Indiana as highly mobile, rural, youthful, and high in fertility. Labor was in short supply, and large families supplied it. By 1810, the area that was to become the states of Indiana and Illinois had a population of nearly 37,000. Although Michigan Territory was created in 1805, and Illinois Territory in 1809, much of the upper lake country was Indian controlled until after the War of 1812. Only isolated French–Canadian settlements at Detroit, Mackinac, Green Bay, and Prairie du Chien broke the pattern of Indian occupancy. The fur trade was still dominated by traders from Canada.[25]

In the early years of settlement the different regions of the trans-Allegheny West had numerous qualities in common, but one vital difference was that south of the Ohio River slavery was an integral part of the frontier advance. The backbreaking work of clearing land, which was carried out in the North by free white farmers hoping to create a better life for themselves and their families, was carried out in the South by slaves. When pioneers, most of them poor, began to move into Kentucky and Tennessee directly before and during the American Revolution, their slaves were comparatively few, but as settlement increased slavery became of much greater importance.

In 1790 Kentucky had a population of over 73,000, including 12,000 slaves, and in the following years the state rapidly became as much southern as western. In the early days, many pioneers had taken the hard route through the mountains by way of the Cumberland Gap, but the most popular route in the 1790s was down the Ohio River. When the new federal

---

24 Horsman, *Frontier*, pp.5–9, 51–3, 86–7, 161–3; See Andrew R. L. Cayton, *The Frontier Republic: Ideology and Politics in the Ohio Country, 1780–1825* (Kent, Ohio, 1986).

25 Andrew R. L. Cayton, *Frontier Indiana* (Bloomington, Ind, 1996), pp.178–9; Horsman, *Frontier*, pp.73–83.

government began its operations, Kentucky was already pressing for state- [1 1 9]
hood. Virginia's 1784 cession of her western land claims had not included
Kentucky, and the region was not a part of the federal territorial system. In
the 1780s Kentucky was a Virginia county, but its settlers had discussed the
possibility of separate statehood since soon after the Revolution. The state
entered the Union in 1792.

In Kentucky, as in Ohio, there were tensions among the free white population between those who wished to retain the influence of an elite – in this
case the large planters – and those who desired a greater degree of popular
sovereignty. The Kentucky Constitution represented a moderate victory
for those who desired change in that members of the lower House were
to be elected by free male suffrage. Those who feared unlimited popular
sovereignty succeeded in providing that the governor and the senate would
be elected by an electoral college.

After statehood was accomplished there was rapid economic growth.
Tobacco plantations spread from Virginia, and the cultivation of hemp also
became of great importance. Lexington became the main center of trade, and
shortly after 1800 became the location of Kentucky's first bank. Even before
the War of 1812 the region around Lexington reminded visitors of Virginia.
By 1820 the state's population was over 464,000, and among these were
over 126,000 slaves.[26]

Tennessee followed the same pattern as Kentucky, but was a little slower
to develop. The first settlers had followed valleys southwest from Virginia to
settle in the eastern part of the state, centering on Knoxville, but ultimately a
more prosperous development occurred in the central Nashville region,
where cotton became an important crop in the years before the War of 1812.
The two population centers were separated by large areas of Cherokee country. Like Kentucky, slavery quickly became an integral part of the area.
Tennessee entered the Union in 1796. The state went further than Kentucky
in the drive towards popular sovereignty by letting adult males elect both
houses and the governor. There was also a bill of rights incorporated in the
constitution. In newly created southern states, the contradictions of slavery
in a nation inspired by republican ideals became particularly apparent.[27]

---

26 Horsman, *Frontier*, pp.5–9, 51–3, 86–7, 161–3; John D. Barnhart, *Valley of Democracy: The
    Frontier versus the Plantation in the Ohio Valley, 1775–1818* (Bloomington, Ind, 1953),
    pp.80–105.
27 Horsman, *Frontier*, pp.5–13, 51–4, 95–6, 149–52, 161–3; Barnhart, *Valley*, pp.111–19;
    Thomas P. Abernethy, *From Frontier to Plantation in Tennessee: A Study in Frontier Democracy*
    (Chapel Hill, NC, 1932), pp.135–7.

Throughout the 1790s settlement in the Lower South was far less than that in Kentucky and Tennessee. The great problem for white southerners who hoped to move west in this region was that most of Georgia, and the area that was to become Alabama and Mississippi, was occupied by powerful, well-established Indian tribes. Creeks, Cherokees, Chickasaws, and Choctaws had large villages and towns and abundant fields. When Mississippi Territory was created in 1798 the main white settlement in the region was around Natchez, where cotton cultivation began to assume importance in the late 1790s and developed rapidly after 1800. The population of the modern state of Alabama was slower to grow, although there was some settlement on the rivers north of Mobile. Development was badly hampered by the lack of an open access to the Gulf. Spain remained in control of Mobile until the War of 1812. After 1806 cotton planters began to move into what was to become the extreme northern part of the state. They were able to use the Tennessee River for navigation. By 1810 the non-Indian population of Mississippi Territory had increased to over 40,000, of whom some 17,000 were slaves.[28]

The most dramatic American expansion in the Southwest came in 1803 with the Louisiana Purchase. This brought the Spanish and French populated area of what was to become the state of Louisiana under American rule, as well as the Indian-occupied regions northwards to Canada and westwards to the Rockies. The Louisiana region had a non-Indian population of some 40,000 in 1803, with many slaves. New Orleans was the biggest city in the Mississippi Valley, with a population of some 10,000. It was the great center for American trade from as far away as western Pennsylvania. The area that was to become the state of Louisiana became the Territory of Orleans in 1804. It was admitted to the Union as Louisiana in 1812. In the years between 1803 and 1812 Louisiana attracted many from the East. The new American settlers engaged in extensive cattle ranching, as well as the cultivation of cotton and sugar. The region, however, retained its own distinct style, which had developed in the period of French and Spanish dominance. Roman rather than common law played an important part in its courts, a parish rather than a county system prevailed, and the Catholic Church retained great influence, a situation unknown in most of the new areas of the West, where the evangelical religions, particularly the Methodists and the Baptists, had great success in winning converts.[29]

---

28 Horsman, *Frontier*, pp.58–9, 97–9, 152; Thomas Perkins Abernethy, *The South in the New Nation, 1789–1819* (Baton Rouge, La, 1961), pp.446–57.

29 Horsman, *Frontier*, pp.59–62, 100–1.

With the purchase of Louisiana the American vision increasingly went
beyond the Mississippi River to the apparently endless western regions.
Even before Louisiana was obtained Jefferson had sent Meriwether Lewis
and William Clark to explore across the continent. Leaving from St Louis
in 1803, they traveled up the Missouri, across the Rockies, and reached
the Pacific at the mouth of the Columbia. They returned with news of endless horizons, abundant game, and a towering mountain range. As recently
as 1789 Jedidiah Morse had written in his *American Geography* of the
Alleghenies as the most formidable American mountains.[30] While some
Americans still thought of the sea as America's province, and links with
Europe as the key to the future, many looked west, and began to dream of a
nation fronting on two oceans. In the years before the War of 1812, when
the United States appeared to be inextricably entangled in the problems of
Europe, expansion into the Mississippi Valley was laying the basis of a con-
tinental empire.

---

30   Jedidiah Morse, *The American Geography* (1789; rpr, New York, 1970), p.17. For Lewis and
     Clark, see Stephen Ambrose, *Undaunted Courage: Meriwether Lewis, Thomas Jefferson, and the
     Opening of the American West* (New York, 1996).

CHAPTER 8

JEFFERSON IN POWER

Jefferson was the first president to begin his term in the new national capital of Washington, DC. Although the agreement to have a national capital on the Potomac had been made in the early 1790s, Congress had not voted the money to make it possible. President Washington had chosen a location near to Alexandria, Virginia, and appointed commissioners to oversee the preparation of the site and buildings, but at first they had to depend on money provided by Virginia and Maryland. As Secretary of State, Jefferson made suggestions and showed a keen interest in the shaping of plans for the new capital. The ambitious formal lay-out was designed by French Major Pierre Charles L'Enfant. For a time his plans seemed well beyond the capacity of the resources available, but more financial assistance came from the purchase of lots by speculators, particularly the group of Robert Morris, James Greenleaf, and John Nicholson, who invested heavily in the project. Ultimately, they went bankrupt.[1]

L'Enfant's plan for the city had to be modified, but construction slowly progressed. In the summer of 1800 the government departments had moved there from Philadelphia, and in November John Adams had taken up a brief residence in the unfinished presidential mansion. Jefferson had spent the winter in a boarding house. On 4 March he walked from his lodgings to the Capitol, of which only one wing was finished, took the oath of office, and delivered his inaugural address. Ex-President Adams had already left. If Jefferson wanted to emphasize the republican simplicity that he said should succeed the élitism of his opponents he could have had no better setting.

When Jefferson took office Washington, DC had a population of little more than 3,000. A visitor who had no knowledge of its history might well have thought that it was some fantastically planned frontier town, which for some reason had large, unfinished classical buildings spaced apart on the

---

1 Wilhelmus B. Bryan, *A History of the National Capital* 2 vols (New York, 1914), 1, pp.105–298; Dumas Malone, *Thomas Jefferson and the Rights of Man* (Boston, Mass, 1951), pp.371–87; Saul K. Padover, *Thomas Jefferson and the National Capital, 1783–1818* (Washington, DC, 1946).

partially cleared land. The President's house still lacked some of its plastering and its main staircase. Plagues of mosquitoes made fever endemic in the late summer, a season in which the heat and humidity made the town practically unliveable. The planners had hoped that commercial ventures would be attracted but they were slow in coming. Housing was scarce, and foreign diplomats arriving from London, Paris, or Madrid had difficulty believing that this was where they were expected to live and conduct international diplomacy. When possible, they fled to Philadelphia, which may have been small by European standards, but they felt that it had some of the amenities of civilized living that were lacking in Washington.[2]

Although Jefferson could charm a gathering around a dinner table, he was no public speaker. His inaugural was delivered in his usual quite conversational style. In it, he tried to throw out an olive branch to the moderate Federalists with his famous statement that 'We are all Republicans, we are all Federalists,' but in large part his inaugural was a lucid expression of the Republican principles that he hoped to maintain. The will of the majority, he stated, must prevail, but with a respect for the equal rights of the minority. What was needed was 'a wise and frugal Government.' Men should be restrained from injuring each other, but otherwise they should be left free to their own 'industry and improvement.' His list of the essential principles of the American government emphasized the degree to which he hoped that the Hamiltonian tendencies towards centralization, government involvement in the economy, and élitism would be reversed in his new administration. He spoke of 'equal and exact justice to all men;' commerce and friendship with all nations but no entangling alliances; the support of state governments as 'the surest bulwarks' against anti-republican tendencies; support of the general government 'in all its constitutional vigor,' as the defender of peace at home and safety abroad; care of the right of election; 'a well-disciplined militia'; supremacy of the civil over the military; economy in government; payment of debts; encouragement of agriculture, 'and of commerce as its handmaid;' freedom of religion, the press, and the person; and trial by jury.[3] Jefferson hoped for strict economy, and opposed the creative use of the debt to promote capital investment. The farmer not the speculator would be the object of the government's concern, states would be protected against unconstitutional abuses of federal power, and regular military forces would

---

2   Merrill D. Peterson, *Thomas Jefferson and the New Nation: A Biography* (New York, 1970), pp.653–4; James S. Young, *The Washington Community, 1800–1828* (New York, 1966), pp.22–8.

3   *MC&P*, 1, pp.321–4 (4 Mar. 1801).

[1 2 4] be called on only when the resources of the militia had been exhausted. Jefferson was to find, however, that to achieve some of his objectives he would have to use the Constitution and federal power as broadly as any Hamiltonian.

Although Jefferson spent much of his life in public service, often in executive positions, he usually impressed others by the breadth of his knowledge and the lucidity of his prose more than by any ability as a dynamic leader. But his ability to win political friends and admirers served him well in dealing with Congress and his cabinet; a personal letter from Jefferson or a conversation at dinner would often result in a Republican Congressman eager to carry out his wishes. James Madison never inspired the same personal allegiance. To his Federalist opponents, Jefferson's manner, strong opinions, and ability to take actions that seemingly violated oft-stated principles, smacked of hypocrisy. His Federalist opponent Robert Goodloe Harper of South Carolina, in a letter to his constituents in 1797, said of Jefferson that 'I might think him fit to be a professor in a College, President of a Philosophical Society, or even Secretary of State, but certainly not the first magistrate of a great nation.' He believed him to be too wavering and indecisive.[4] Jefferson's opponents were to discover, however, that he would make use of executive power to pursue what he thought essential for the nation.

Jefferson had written in his *Notes on Virginia* that 'cultivators of the earth are the most virtuous and independant [sic] citizens.'[5] but his view of American society was not of a republic fixed in some static agrarian past. He eagerly sought expansion across the Mississippi Valley. If the nation was to be guided by yeoman farmers with roots in the land rather than by a moneyed élite with roots in the towns, it was essential that a rapidly growing population should have access to new areas on the American continent. Only this would provide the necessary land to avoid landless, urban mobs.

Commercial expansion and the freedom of the seas were also at the heart of Jeffersonianism. Jefferson speculated that wars would be avoided and the United States happier if the nation shunned the seas and simply concentrated on cultivating its own lands, but he also wrote that the nation's inhabitants were wedded to commerce. American farmers needed markets, and in a country that was still largely agricultural they had to sell abroad. Jefferson

---

4 Noble E. Cunningham, Jr (ed.), *Circular Letters of Congressmen to their Constituents, 1789–1829* 3 vols (Chapel Hill, NC, 1978), 1, p.63 (5 Jan. 1797).
5 Thomas Jefferson, *Notes on the State of Virginia* (ed.), William Peden (Chapel Hill, NC, 1955), p.175.

did not want national policies to be shaped by those who financed foreign [1 2 5] commerce or invested in it, but he believed that access to foreign markets was essential. Jefferson and Madison hoped to further the prosperity of American farmers by diverting American exports away from Great Britain into other markets. While bitterly opposing federally stimulated capitalism on the Hamiltonian model, Jefferson encouraged policies that would enable the mass of American farmers to pursue their own individual wealth.[6]

Yet, while Jefferson and the Republicans were convinced of the importance of exports for the American farmer, they were impractical in estimating the ability of the United States to impose its will on the major European powers, particularly on Great Britain. Throughout the 1790s both Jefferson and Madison had argued that the United States needed to gain more favorable trade arrangements with Great Britain, and that these could be achieved by pursuing policies of commercial discrimination. They resented England's unwillingness to give concessions to the United States, but had a more general belief that Great Britain presented a threat to American republicanism.

The danger of Jefferson's opinion that the United States had the power to change British policies by economic means did not become explicit in the first years of his presidency. He had the good fortune of coming into office at a time when Europe was temporarily at peace. This peace, however, was only to last from the spring of 1801 to the spring of 1803. When Europe once again erupted into war, a war which England and France were increasingly to fight with blockades, the dangers of the Republican belief that the United States had the right to trade freely in a time of all-out war became fully apparent. Great Britain wanted trade with the United States. She wanted American raw materials, and the United States was of great importance as a market for her manufactured goods, but for British leaders the maintenance of British maritime supremacy and the defeat of France were more important than retaining American trade. Jefferson and Madison were never prepared to accept this. They wanted an agricultural nation, but they wanted an agricultural nation that could export freely to Europe in war or peace.

While Hamilton believed that ultimately large-scale manufacturing was essential for the American economy, Jefferson and his supporters wanted a nation in which household manufacturing was encouraged to eliminate the dependence on foreign, particularly English, manufactured goods. This would have the dual function of emphasizing necessities rather than the

---

6   Jefferson, *Notes*, p.174; Jefferson to John Jay, 23 Aug. 1785, to G. K. van Hogendorp, 13 Oct. 1785, *PTJ*, 8, pp.426–8, 631–4; Peterson, *Jefferson*, p.459; Drew McCoy, *The Elusive Republic: Political Economy in Jeffersonian America* (New York, 1980), p.237.

[1 2 6] luxuries that sapped the vitals of a nation, and reducing the dreaded British influence. Jefferson may have loved his own imported foreign luxuries, but, like Madison, he believed that a republican nation was best served by widely dispersed, prospering farmers making their own household necessities or buying from local shops. Large factories in large towns would produce unstable populations willing to listen to political demagogues.[7]

The Republican party that took over Congress in 1801 was not a tightly knit group. A variety of different viewpoints had gained some cohesion by opposition to Federalist policies in the 1790s. Some Republicans took the states' rights arguments that Jefferson and Madison had used in the Kentucky and Virginia resolutions more literally than the men who had written them. These Old Republicans were ardent supporters of the states' rights position, and were highly suspicious of any powers exercised by the federal government, for whatever purposes. In time, they were to become disillusioned with their own party for its use of federal power. Another distinct group that had joined the opposition to the Federalists in the 1790s was the small, but vocal, corps of radical *emigrés* from Great Britain. These men had played an influential part in the newspaper opposition to the Federalists. Their tendency was to be suspicious of all governments, and though Jefferson had made use of them in the late 1790s he tried to distance himself from them once he became president.[8]

In his relations with one of the radicals Jefferson discovered that the use of scurrilous writing as a means of attacking political enemies could not easily be controlled. In the late 1790s, Jefferson had given financial support to British immigrant James Callender's unrestrained attacks on leading Federalists. Callender had exposed Hamilton's relationship with Mrs Reynolds, claiming that it involved corruption as well as sex, and had launched wild accusations against Presidents Washington and Adams. Callender had been convicted under the Sedition Act, imprisoned, and fined. When Jefferson became president he pardoned Callender and ordered the fine to be returned.

Relations between the two men quickly soured when there was a delay in refunding the money. Callender blamed Jefferson for the delay, and refused to be placated even when a group of Republicans, including Jefferson, arranged to provide the money. Callender demanded an appointment as postmaster in Richmond, Virginia, threatening that if he was not appointed

---

7   McCoy, *Elusive Republic*, pp.14, 223–31.
8   Richard E. Ellis, *The Jeffersonian Crisis: Courts and Politics in the Young Republic* (New York, 1971), pp.19–35, 267–83.

he would turn his written attacks against the president. Jefferson refused [1 2 7] to appoint him, and Callender, now working for the Federalist *Richmond Recorder*, used that paper to launch his attack. In September 1802 he charged that Jefferson was keeping a slave mistress, Sally Hemings, at Monticello, and had fathered children by her. The accusation, which was ignored by Jefferson, was seized upon eagerly by some of the more extreme Federalists, who were very happy to have another chance to attack a man they viewed as an atheistic hypocrite. The relationship Callender asserted was possible – slave mistresses were not uncommon – but no proofs were advanced. In the twentieth century, Callender's charge has produced extensive writing, which at times has revealed more about the writers themselves than about Jefferson and Sally Hemings. After nearly 200 years of debate, new DNA research has established that almost certainly Jefferson was the father of at least one of Sally Hemings's children.[9]

Jefferson's pardoning of Callender had been part of a general Republican desire to undo Federalist policies they thought harmful to the republic. They were particularly keen to remove the policies that had emerged as a result of the crisis with France in 1798. Along with Callender, the others convicted under the Sedition acts were pardoned, and their fines returned. Yet, while Jefferson wanted a free press, and certainly did not want the federal government intervening to curb all criticism, he did not believe that the press could act without any limits. In the years after 1803 he encouraged actions for seditious libel against those he viewed as totally irresponsible Federalist editors.[10]

The changeover in 1801 was more than simply a switch of parties. The victory of the Republicans encouraged the tendencies towards a more democratic political practice and weakened the older elitism and deferential politics practiced by the Federalists. In the years after 1804 there was much greater voter participation than there had been in the first years under the Constitution. Part of this stemmed from the popular base of support for the

9   Michael Durey, *'With the Hammer of Truth': James Thomson Callender and America's Early National Heroes* (Charlottesville, Va, 1990), pp.111–13, 139–63. There is a good brief account of Jefferson, Callender, and Sally Hemings in John C. Miller, *The Wolf by the Ears: Thomas Jefferson and Slavery* (New York, 1977), pp.148–76, and a comprehensive account of historians and Sally Hemings in Annette Gordon-Reed, *Thomas Jefferson and Sally Hemings: An American Controversy* (Charlottesville, Va, 1997). Paul Finkelman, *Slavery and the Founders: Race and Liberty in the Age of Jefferson* (Armonk, AY, 1996), pp.105–67, is highly critical of Jefferson.

10 Miller, *Wolf*, pp.197–201; Leonard W. Levy, *Jefferson and Civil Liberties: The Darker Side* (Cambridge, Mass, 1963), pp.58–67.

[1 2 8]   Jeffersonian movement, but David Hackett Fischer has stressed the extent to which even the opposition Federalists now found themselves in the position of having to cultivate the electorate. They did not regain national power, but they stirred a vigorous party rivalry.[11]

For the attack on Hamiltonian fiscal policies Jefferson leaned heavily on his Secretary of the Treasury Albert Gallatin. The Republicans wished to adopt policies that would eventually eliminate the national debt, to move away from any need for internal taxes, and to slash military expenditures. This last would have the double advantage of reducing taxes while at the same time ending the dangers they perceived were presented by regular military forces. Both Jefferson and Gallatin wanted a lean government. They thought that the national government should be managed like a well-run household, with economy, strict payment of debt, and no waste. Jefferson intensely disliked the Bank of the United States, but Gallatin had the financial acumen to see the essential function it was serving. He defended the bank against the president, and after the United States obtained Louisiana used his influence to have a branch established in New Orleans.[12]

Gallatin, who had been born in Geneva, had emigrated to the United States in 1780. In the 1790s he had achieved a leading position among the Republicans in Congress, and had shown a deep interest in national finances. He had endeared himself to Jefferson with his attacks on Federalist policies, and with two pamphlets that had accused the Federalists of wasting money on the armed forces.[13] In their desire to reduce the debt and taxes, Jefferson and Gallatin at first were considerably helped by the diplomatic and commercial situation they inherited. The Federalists had established excellent relations with Great Britain, Adams had succeeded in bringing the quasi-war with France to an end, and in the spring of 1801 the European wars temporarily ended. The United States lost the special advantages that came from its position as the main neutral in the middle of a European conflict, but the harassment of American commerce ceased. For all the Republican rhetoric about the ill effects of close commercial ties with Great Britain, it was to be the tariffs on the abundant British imports that would enable them to remove internal taxes and to set about eliminating the national debt. When, in 1803,

11   Gordon Wood, *The Radicalism of the American Revolution* (New York, 1992), p.364; David H. Fischer, *The Revolution of American Conservatism: The Federalist Party in the Era of Jeffersonian Democracy* (New York, 1965).

12   Bray Hammond, *Banks and Politics in America: From the Revolution to the Civil War* (Princeton, NJ, 1957), pp.205–7.

13   J. C. A. Stagg, *Mr Madison's War: Politics, Diplomacy, and Warfare in the Early Republic* (Princeton, NJ, 1983), pp.127–30.

the European wars were renewed American ships again had to run the gaunt-
let of extensive blockades, but there were more opportunities.

In spite of the elimination of most internal taxes, the government's
annual revenues increased sharply. When Gallatin came into office, he
estimated existing national revenues at under $11,000,000 a year. Most of
this – $9,500,000 – was from tariffs, $650,000 was from excise duties, and
$450,000 from land sales and the postal service. Without excise duties,
which he planned to eliminate, the annual revenue of the nation would
be about $10,000,000. He wanted to use nearly three-quarters of this each
year to begin the process of eliminating a national debt that was over
$80,000,000. By that process the debt could be eliminated by 1817.[14]

Gallatin's policies depended both on a flourishing foreign trade and on
very small military forces, and until the time of the 1807 embargo he was
to have striking success in achieving his objectives. He was greatly helped
by the growing governmental revenue coming from the expansion of trade.
His estimated $10,000,000 income had become $13,560,000 by 1805 and
$17,000,000 by 1808. In April 1802 he removed the excise duties, includ-
ing the most important – that on distilled liquor. In 1807 he was able to
remove the tax on imported salt. The national debt was steadily reduced,
even though Gallatin had to find money for some unexpected expenditures.
A naval war with Tripoli was paid for by a special extra tax on imports, the
$15,000,000 for buying Louisiana was obtained by a $2,000,000 down
payment from the surplus and the issuing of stock paying 6 per cent interest.
The Jeffersonian objection to the evil impact of the British financial system
on the United States did not prevent Baring Brothers of London being used
to market bonds used for the purchase, and to provide some of the money
for the initial payment to the French government. Because of the rise of
revenues, Gallatin was able to include money for repayment of the Louisiana
stock in the money he set aside each year for the repayment of the debt.[15]

Although the financial situation of the United States was such that
Gallatin was able to encompass the costs of an unexpected naval war with
Tripoli within his financial system, this war illustrated the dangers of sharply

14   Raymond Walters, Jr, *Albert Gallatin: Jeffersonian Financier and Diplomat* (New York, 1957),
pp.145–7; Alexander Balinky, *Albert Gallatin: Fiscal Theories and Policies* (New Brunswick, NJ,
1958), pp.29–85.

15   Balinky, *Gallatin*, pp.89–127; Walters, *Gallatin*, pp.151–4; Curtis B. Nettels, *The Emergence
of a National Economy, 1775–1815* (New York, 1962), pp.318–19; Davis R. Dewey, *Financial
History of the United States* 9th edn (New York, 1924), pp.119–24; Ralph W. Hidy, *The House
of Baring in American Trade and Finance: English Merchant Bankers at Work, 1763–1861*
(Cambridge, Mass, 1949), pp.33–4.

reducing the military while actively seeking the markets of Europe and the world for American produce. The creation of a small American fighting navy had not ended the dangers to American shipping from the Barbary pirates in the Mediterranean. From 1795 to 1797, when the first frigates were being built, the Federalists had found it necessary to sign treaties with Algiers, Tripoli, and Tunis. Like the European powers, the Federalists had decided it was easier to pay what amounted to protection money than lose ships and seamen. The three treaties cost more than $1,000,000, paid out in annual sums; an amount which was nearly 10 per cent of the federal income that Gallatin expected to collect at the start of the Republican administration.

In spite of the treaties, the situation was again reaching a crisis point when Jefferson became president. The United States was late in her payments, and in 1800 the Dey of Algiers commandeered an American frigate that arrived with tribute money to take his ambassador to Constantinople. In 1801 the new administration sent a small force of four ships to take the next tribute to the Mediterranean, in the hope that this would create an impression of American power. Before they arrived, the problem had escalated. In May the Pasha of Tripoli declared war on the United States by chopping down the flagpole at the American consulate.

This was an embarrassing situation for Jefferson. He wanted to cut the navy, not increase it, but he thought it was beneath the dignity of the republic to pay tribute to Barbary pirates. It was a very quick lesson that foreign policy often depended on the policies, or even the whims, of foreign powers, not simply on a set of principles enunciated by the American government. It was a lesson that Jefferson was slow to learn.

For the next four years the United States fought a war in the Mediterranean. The American navy attempted, without complete success, to blockade Tripoli. In 1803 Commodore Edward Preble was sent to the Mediterranean with reinforcements that included the frigates *Constitution* and *Philadelphia*. At first there was disaster. The *Philadelphia* ran aground off Tripoli. The ship and its crew of over 300 were captured by the Tripolitans. In February 1804, in a daring act that could hardly be claimed as a great victory, Lieutenant Stephen Decatur led a force into the harbor of Tripoli, and burnt the American ship. More American reinforcements arrived, and the campaign took on a novelistic air when William Eaton, the American consul at Tunis, independently led a land force from Tunis with the avowed object of replacing the Pasha of Tripoli with his exiled brother. His force of Mediterranean mercenaries included a handful of American marines. He captured one town, but by that time the Pasha of Tripoli had decided that the blockade and the war was costing him money and had decided to make peace.

The treaty that was signed in 1805 did not include any formal tribute money, but it contained a payment of $60,000 for the restoration of the prisoners from the *Philadelphia*. When the American naval force was withdrawn from the Mediterranean in 1807 the Dey of Algiers again sent his corsairs to capture American ships. Only in 1815, after the end of the War of 1812, did the United States take effective action. A strong naval force was sent to the Mediterranean, and forced the Dey to make peace. This time he had to pay the United States $10,000. Later in the year the threat from Algiers was ended permanently, when a combined British and Dutch squadron bombarded Algiers and destroyed the Algerian fleet.[16]

The Tripolitan War should have sounded a warning to Jefferson that a nation that sent its ships and goods throughout the world could not avoid situations that might require the possibility of force to back unilateral assertions of neutral rights. The Republicans, however, wanted economy. The only sizeable area of expenditure that could be cut was the military. By March 1802 the regular army had been reduced to just over 3,000 men. In the next few years not even that number was maintained. The navy that had been built and purchased during the quasi-war was largely sold, other ships were laid up, port facilities were reduced. By the end of 1807 there were only two frigates and four smaller vessels in service. In the place of an ocean-going fighting navy, Jefferson was placing his faith in the building of small gunboats for coastal defense. His faith in the usefulness of such vessels had been increased by the problems encountered by American ships in the shallow waters off Tripoli.[17]

Republican administrations based their financial policies on revenue derived largely from English imports, and obtained reductions in expenditure by slashing the army and navy, but after 1807 they pursued policies that cut off or reduced trade with England and ultimately led to war with that country. By 1811 Gallatin could report that he had cut the national debt, even though Louisiana had been purchased, but the country was moving towards war with financial problems and totally inadequate military forces. In 1812, Congress had to authorize loans to meet expenses, and as

16   Samuel F. Bemis, *A Diplomatic History of the United States* 5th edn (New York, 1965), pp.67–8, 107, 176–9; Marshall Smelser, *The Democratic Republic, 1800–1815* (New York, 1968), pp.57–61.

17   Harold and Margaret Sprout, *The Rise of American Naval Power, 1776–1918* rev. edn (Princeton, NJ, 1942), pp.50–61; Stagg, *Madison's War*, pp.130–5.

the country drifted towards war Gallatin urged the readoption of internal taxes.[18] In the years from 1801 to 1812 the Republican philosophy of government was embodied in their financial policies, but these policies did not permit preparations for any large-scale conflict.

While Jefferson was wholehearted in his support of Gallatin's financial policies, he was more cautious in the support he gave to the radical Republicans who were determined to attack the federal judiciary. The radicals had been particularly infuriated by the manner in which the federal judges had enforced the Sedition Act, but there was also concern at the Judiciary Act that the Federalists had pushed through in February 1801, after they had been defeated in the 1800 elections. This 1801 Judiciary Act tackled problems that had emerged in the original Judiciary Act of 1789. That act had provided for a Supreme Court, intermediate courts, and district courts, but the intermediate courts had no justices of their own. They consisted of two Supreme Court justices riding circuit (reduced to one in 1793) presiding with a district court judge. In appeals, the same justices were involved at different levels, and in this age of atrocious communications Supreme Court justices had problems in riding circuit. The Federalist Judiciary Act of 1801 ended dual responsibilities and provided for the appointment of 16 new federal judges to serve on the circuit courts.

It could well be argued that this judicial reform was needed, but the Federalists had passed it when they knew they had lost power, and they proceeded to appoint Federalists to the new positions. In their last months in office they also filled any other judicial positions that were available with Federalists. To cap Republican unhappiness, in January 1801 the departing administration had also appointed the leading Virginia Federalist John Marshall as Chief Justice of the Supreme Court. While Jefferson and other Republican leaders were inclined to be cautious in any attack on the judiciary, there was a good deal of anti-legal feeling among rank and file Republicans. This was not simply a matter of objecting to Federalist appointments or the excesses of Federalist judges, it was also a question of hostility to the legal profession in the aftermath of the Revolution. Many simply did not like lawyers as establishment figures, railed against the complexity and cost of the law, found English common law inappropriate for a republican nation, and favored elected judges.

In 1802 the Republicans in Congress launched an attack on the 1801 Judiciary Act. Not all Republicans thought it was wise to attack what should

18   Balinky, *Gallatin*, pp.128–82; Walters, *Gallatin*, pp.244–7.

have been an independent judiciary, and the Federalists resisted the [1 3 3] Republican onslaught, but early in February the Senate repealed the 1801 Act by a one-vote margin. In the House, where the Republicans had a larger majority, the repeal passed more easily, and in March Jefferson signed it. There was a potential problem. The repeal was not to take effect until 1 July 1802, but the 1801 Act had changed the meetings of the Supreme Court from February and August to December and June. This raised the possibility that when the Supreme Court met in June it would examine the constitutionality of the repeal measure. Any chance of that happening quickly disappeared. Republicans in Congress pushed through a measure abolishing the new June and December meetings of the Supreme Court, and providing for only one term of the court each year – in February. Jefferson signed this measure in April. It meant that the Supreme Court would not meet in 1802.[19]

Republicans had won the first clash, but the court issue was soon to be joined again, and this time it would directly involve the new Chief Justice of the Supreme Court, John Marshall. Like Jefferson, Marshall was a product of the Virginia back country. His active service in the Revolution, in which he had endured the winter at Valley Forge, had helped convince him of the necessity for an efficient federal government. After leaving the army he was admitted to the bar, and in the 1780s served in the Virginia House of Burgesses. In the 1790s he had become a leading member of the Federalist party. While serving in Congress he had opposed the Alien and Sedition Acts. For a brief time in 1800 he was Secretary of State, but gave this up in January 1801 to become Chief Justice. He was to serve in that position until 1835. His influence and power was to be used to defend the supremacy of the federal government over the state governments, and the federal courts over the state courts.

Marshall's opportunity to demonstrate that the Supreme Court was not to be cowed by an unfriendly administration came very rapidly. Even before the Judiciary Act of 1801 had been repealed, Marshall had indicated that he was ready to examine aspects of the conduct of the Republicans in regard to the courts. Among Adams' last-minute appointments were a number of Justices of the Peace for the District of Columbia. The action had been taken so late that when the Republicans assumed power the commissions had been signed by the president and sealed by the Secretary of State, but not delivered. Madison, instructed by Jefferson, withheld the commissions. Four of the appointees, including William Marbury, petitioned the Supreme Court in its

19   Ellis, *Jeffersonian Crisis*, pp. 12–15, 59–60, 111–22, 250–3.

[1 3 4] December 1801 term for a writ of mandamus that would compel Madison to deliver their commissions. Marshall accepted the case. It was still pending when Congress took its action against the Federalist Judiciary Act. The new administration and the Supreme Court appeared to be on a collision course.

Marshall's decision was handed down in 1803. Although a case of landmark significance for the future, Marshall's skilful approach avoided a direct clash with the executive while strongly affirming the powers of the court. In the first part of his decision, Marshall argued that in law Marbury had been appointed when his commission had been signed and sealed. 'To withhold his commission,' wrote Marshall, 'is . . . violative of a vested legal right.' In addressing the question of Marbury's remedy, however, Marshall deflected the course of impending confrontation with Jefferson by arguing that the Supreme Court did not have the power to issue a writ of mandamus in a case of this type. This represented no retreat, for Marshall's reason was that the authority to issue writs of mandamus, which had been given to the Supreme Court by Congress in the Judiciary Act of 1789, was unconstitutional. When Congress conferred that power they were violating the Constitution in the same year in which it had gone into effect. 'It is emphatically the province and duty of the judicial department,' Marshall wrote, 'to say what the law is.' Marshall did not give Marbury what he wanted, but he decisively asserted for the Supreme Court the power of deciding whether or not acts of Congress were constitutional.[20]

The more ardent Republicans were not satisfied simply with the repeal of the Judiciary Act of 1801, they wanted to remove Federalist judges who had particularly offended them. They were most interested in punishing those judges who had enforced the Sedition Law and had made their loathing of the Republicans obvious in their remarks, but the first case they proceeded with was in regard to a judge who was obviously unfit to be on the bench for other reasons. The original Judiciary Act of 1789 had made no provision for removing a judge who became incapacitated, and who would not or could not resign. The Federalist Judiciary Act of 1801 had provided for such a removal, but the repeal of that act left the situation as before. The Republicans decided that the way to proceed was through impeachment. Under article II, section 4 of the Constitution 'the President, Vice President, and all Civil Officers of the United States,' can be removed from office if impeached and convicted of 'Treason, Bribery, or other high Crimes and

---

20 Leonard Baker, *John Marshall: A Life in Law* (New York, 1974), pp.394–413; Herbert A. Johnson *et al.* (eds), *The Papers of John Marshall* (Chapel Hill, NC, 1974–), 6, pp.160–87 (171, 183, quotations).

Misdemeanors.' The power of impeachment had been given to the House of [1 3 5] Representatives, and the Republicans had the majority they needed to obtain a vote for impeachment. A conviction was likely to be more difficult because all cases had to be tried in the Senate, where a vote of two-thirds of those present was needed.

Republicans in the House decided that they would first use the process of impeachment to proceed against Judge John Pickering, the federal district court judge in New Hampshire. In 1794, at the time Washington had appointed him to the position of federal judge, his previously high reputation had already been marred by his service as Chief Justice of New Hampshire's courts. Mental difficulties had brought demands for his removal from this position, but local Federalists had maneuvered to achieve his appointment to a federal judgeship. As a federal district judge his mental difficulties increased, and he also became a drunkard. Impeachment had been intended for use against treason or corruption, not for cases of illness, incapacity, or even the display of strong bias on the bench.

The trial took place in March 1804. It was a sorry affair. Pickering was not in attendance, but the Federalists defended him by arguing that he was insane, and that was not a constitutional reason for impeachment. Ultimately, because of Pickering's obvious unfitness for the bench, the Republicans were able to garner some Federalist support for his removal. Pickering was convicted and removed from the bench.[21]

The impeachment of a man who was clearly ill was unsavory, but it had none of the high drama that was entailed in the subsequent impeachment of Samuel Chase, an associate justice of the Supreme Court. He was not ill, but he was an ardent Federalist who had angered Republicans with the vindictiveness and bias with which he had conducted trials brought under the terms of the Sedition Act. Chase was a major figure, a signer of the Declaration of Independence. His early radicalism had been transformed into an ardent conservatism. He had been appointed to the Supreme Court by Washington in 1796. He had become notorious in the trials of James Callender and Thomas Cooper under the Sedition Act, and he had also presided, with his usual impassioned style, over the treason trial of Pennsylvania German John Fries. Only Adams' pardon had saved Fries from the hangman. In 1803 Chase had harangued a grand jury about the dangers of 'mobocracy' under the Jeffersonians. He had become a judge of the worst type, a man who constantly revealed his personal biases in court, yet it would

[1 3 6]   have been very difficult for a dispassionate observer to believe that he was impeachable under the terms defined in the Constitution. Moreover, the haranguing of juries by judges was common in seventeenth- and eighteenth-century England, and was not uncommon in the revolutionary generation in America.

As soon as Pickering was convicted the House of Representatives proceeded against Chase. The case was primarily carried by John Randolph of Virginia, an impassioned and erratic speaker who was at his best in debate, not in legal proceedings. When the trial began before the Senate in February 1805 Randolph encountered a strong defense led by some of America's most effective lawyers. He also encountered a Senate in which some Republicans, as well as ardent Federalists, were dubious of a proceeding that would strike a major blow against the independence of the judiciary. Chase had acted most unwisely as a judge, but he had hardly been guilty of 'high Crimes.' In March Chase was acquitted. Some Republicans, disturbed at the use of impeachment to attack a judicial opponent, joined with the Federalists in opposition. The most votes that could be obtained was 19 out of 34, and a two-thirds majority was needed.[22]

With the acquittal of Chase the possibility that more extreme Republicans would destroy the independence of the judiciary was ended. There was to be more friction between Marshall and Jefferson, but the three appointments that Jefferson made to the court were moderate Republicans. They did nothing to divert Marshall from the strong course that he was pursuing, although William Johnson of South Carolina, appointed by Jefferson in 1804, was willing to dissent from Marshall's opinions.[23] Marshall's greatest assertions of the powers of the federal government – in McCulloch vs Maryland (1819) and Gibbons vs Ogden (1824) – were to come later in his career, but from the beginning of his service on the bench there was never any doubt about his willingness to defend the powers of both the Supreme Court and of the federal government. With reason the Republicans felt that they had defeated Hamiltonianism at the polls but now had to contend with it in the Supreme Court.

In 1810 Marshall in his decision in Fletcher vs Peck both spoke resoundingly for property rights and at the same time asserted the right of the court to invalidate actions of the states. The case stemmed from Georgia's sale of

22   See Jane Shaffer Elsmere, *Justice Samuel Chase* (Muncie, Ind, 1980); William C. Bruce, *John Randolph of Roanoke, 1773–1833* rev. edn, 2 vols (New York, 1939), 1, pp.200–20.
23   Ellis, *Jeffersonian Crisis*, pp.238–40; Miller, *Wolf*, pp.212–13.

huge areas of her western lands to the Yazoo Companies in 1795. After a [1 3 7] subsequent Georgia legislature had rescinded the grants because of bribery, innocent purchasers from Yazoo resorted to the courts. In his 1810 decision Marshall upheld the sanctity of the contract clause of the Constitution, and argued that 'a grant is a contract executed.' Georgia could not simply reverse itself once this contract had been made. Marshall also made it quite clear that the sovereignty of Georgia was limited. 'She is part of a large empire,' he wrote, 'she is a member of the American union; and that union has a constitution, the supremacy of which all acknowledge, and which imposes limits to the legislatures of the several states.'[24] This was not what the Old Republicans believed or wanted to hear, for Marshall was putting the emphasis on the ways in which the Constitution limited the states, not the ways in which the Constitution limited the powers of the federal government. Marshall's willingness to assert the powers of the federal government brought concern to Old Republicans, and in the coming years it was also to bring increasing concern to southern states that were anxious to protect their way of life.

In shaping a distinctive American republic dedicated to ideals of freedom, white Americans were in the process of confronting the dilemma that their new nation had an extensive slave base. Jefferson had written the Declaration of Independence, and was of world importance in shaping ideals of freedom, but he was also an extensive slave owner. Jeffersonian democracy was in the process of moving the United States towards greater democratization of politics for its white population, but at the same time slavery was becoming more deeply entrenched in the southern states.

---

24 C. Peter Magrath, *Yazoo: Law and Politics in the New Republic: The Case of Fletcher v. Peck* (Providence, RI, 1966), pp.50–84; Johnson *et al.* (eds), *Papers of Marshall*, 7, pp.225–41 (236–7, quotations).

CHAPTER 9

RACE AND SLAVERY

The theoretical view of race that prevailed in revolutionary and early national America was that of the Enlightenment. It emphasized the unity of mankind. All human beings were of one species, descended from Adam and Eve. Races differed because of environment, but all were capable of indefinite improvement. Samuel Stanhope Smith, in *An Essay on the Causes of the Variety of Complexion and Figure in the Human Species* (1787), which was the most important work on race of its generation, argued that all the differences between the races could be accounted for by environmental factors. Color was a temporary not a permanent phenomenon. Although some European writers were already using the increasing interest in scientific classification to begin the process of separating human beings into superior and inferior races, environmentalism dominated American scientific thinking on race in the first years of the new nation. In 1810, when Samuel Stanhope Smith issued his influential book in enlarged form, he had not modified his environmental views.[1]

The political rhetoric of revolutionary America was well in accord with scientific beliefs that all human beings were essentially alike. Jefferson had used the Declaration of Independence to state that 'all men are created equal,' and had emphasized the natural rights shared by all. In practical terms, in the half-century after independence the United States moved towards a democratization of the political process as free, white adult males gained the vote, and the rights of political and religious diversity were emphasized.

Yet the revolutionary generation had to live with the knowledge that the republic they were creating had an extensive slave system. Of the approxim-

---

1 Samuel Stanhope Smith, *An Essay on the Causes of the Variety of Complexion and Figure in the Human Species*, ed. Winthrop D. Jordan (Cambridge, Mass, 1965); Reginald Horsman, *Race and Manifest Destiny: The Origins of American Racial Anglo-Saxonism* (Cambridge, Mass, 1981), pp.48–52; Daniel Boorstin, *The Lost World of Thomas Jefferson* (New York, 1948), pp.59–65, 71–5.

ately 4,000,000 inhabitants of the United States in 1790, some 700,000 [1 3 9] were African American slaves. Slavery had become an integral part of the economic system of the South, and existed throughout the colonies. The revolutionary generation wrestled with this contradiction of slavery in a free republic.

For southerners, however well read, the views of European scientists or philosophers were countered by what they viewed as the practical realities of living in a slave society, and controlling potentially dangerous slaves. They were also countered by pragmatic white views of black difference. Slaves were kept in a debased position, and there was an inclination for those in daily contact with slaves to assume that the characteristics of debasement preceded the slavery. Philosophers might argue that color was a temporary phenomenon produced by environment, but in practice southern whites treated Africans as though they were different in nature as well as in status. In the North, where slaves and African Americans were few, political leaders at least found it comparatively simple to translate revolutionary ideas about freedom into the reality of freeing slaves. In the South, it was quite different. To free slaves in areas with large numbers of African American slaves would mean completely transforming an economic and social system.[2]

Thomas Jefferson was practically alone in the United States in *publicly* questioning the inherent equality of Africans. Jefferson, like many in the Upper South, thought slavery to be an evil, but in his *Notes on Virginia* he suggested that it was quite possible that varieties of the same species 'may possess different qualifications.' He advanced 'as a suspicion only, that the blacks, whether originally a distinct race, or made distinct by time and circumstances, are inferior to the whites in the endowments both of body and mind.' Jefferson was here responding to the prejudices gained as a slave owner in a slave society, not as a thinker imbued with the ideas of the European Enlightenment. He did not, however, use his doubts about the capacity of Africans to justify enslaving them. His plan for the government of the trans-Allegheny West that he put forward in 1784 included a provision for the ending of slavery in the new territories of the United States. The Confederation Congress deleted that provision.[3]

2   See Winthrop D. Jordan, *White Over Black: American Attitudes toward the Negro, 1550–1812* (Chapel Hill, NC, 1968) for the fullest discussion of how the colonists shaped their ideas about African Americans.

3   Thomas Jefferson, *Notes on the State of Virginia*, ed. William Peden (Chapel Hill, NC, 1955), p.143; *Journals of the Continental Congress* 34 vols (Washington, DC, 1904–37), 26, pp.119, 246–7.

[1 4 0]   Ultimately, one important effect of the contradictions of slavery in a society that prided itself on being the freest in the world was that, when the South decided that general emancipation was impossible, southerners were encouraged to justify the continued enslavement of Africans by assertions of innate African inferiority. In order to explain why Africans could not be allowed to share in the blessings of republicanism, more stress was laid on African difference and on their incapability of benefiting from freedom.[4]

While there was anti-slavery activity in the United States before the Revolution, primarily among the Quakers, it was the Revolution itself, with its rhetoric of freedom, that gave the greatest stimulus to the attack on slavery as an institution. In his original draft of the Declaration of Independence Jefferson attacked George III for promoting the slave trade, and most of the American states had prohibited the foreign slave trade by the end of the Revolution.[5] At the Constitutional Convention in 1787 the opposition of representatives from the Lower South prevented a constitutional ban on the importation of slaves, and resulted in the agreement that the federal government would do nothing to prohibit the trade for at least 20 years.

In the 1790s Congress began to receive northern petitions against the trade, and in 1794 it prohibited American citizens selling slaves in foreign markets. It was much easier to enlist support for a ban on the importation of slaves than for an attack on slavery itself. In this generation even many of those who supported slavery were willing to admit that the presence of African American slaves presented a dilemma for the new republic. The end of the 20-year ban on federal intervention quickly brought the ending of the legal importation of slaves. In March 1807 Jefferson recommended to Congress that it should act on the subject of the slave trade. In Congress a move to end the trade passed with ease, and the prohibition took effect on 1 January 1808.[6]

It was possible to get general support for a ban on the importation of slaves because such a ban met the wishes of not only those who had a humanitarian opposition to the trade, but also those who believed that the

---

4   Duncan J. MacLeod, *Slavery, Race and the American Revolution* (Cambridge, 1974), pp.8, 12, 77–93; Duncan J. MacLeod, 'Toward caste,' in Ira Berlin and Ronald Hoffman (eds), *Slavery and Freedom in the Age of the American Revolution* (Charlottesville, Va, 1983), pp.231–3; David Brian Davis, *The Problem of Slavery in the Age of Revolution, 1770–1823* (Ithaca, NY, 1975), p.303.

5   *PTJ*, 1, p.426; Jordan, *White Over Black*, pp.271–6.

6   David Brian Davis, 'American slavery and the American Revolution,' in Berlin and Hoffman, (eds), *Slavery*, pp.266–7; John C. Miller, *The Wolf by the Ears: Thomas Jefferson and Slavery* (New York, 1977), pp.145–6.

African presence in American society, whether slave or free, should be [1 4 1] reduced. To ban the foreign slave trade meant excluding Africans as well as slaves. Moreover, in the Upper South there was a surplus of slaves in these revolutionary years, and that region could meet the needs of the plantation owners in South Carolina and Georgia who were seeking more slaves.

In the years after the Revolution anti-slavery organizations developed in states as far south as Virginia. These groups were not strident. They were able to win reasonably easy victories in the northern states, where the economic and social complications of ending slavery were minimal. By 1804 slavery was coming to an end in all the states north of Delaware. Vermont provided for a constititional ban on slavery as early as 1777, but the usual way of ending it was to provide for gradual abolition, often freeing only the children of slaves. In New York, where slaves were more numerous than in any other northern state, there was resistance to abolition, some claiming it was an interference with property rights. A bill providing for gradual abolition was finally passed in 1799.

The great stumbling block to the abolition of slavery in Virginia, as in the rest of the South, was not simply the economic costs of such a measure but the fears of a large free African American population. In the 1790s an interest developed in the possibility of ending slavery while ensuring the removal of the freed slaves from the state. Those who supported the idea emphasized that it would be impossible to incorporate Africans within the state's population after emancipation. Jefferson hoped that freedom would be followed by blacks leaving the state, and pamphleteers wrote of the possibility of colonizing blacks in Africa, in Spanish America, or in the American West. The Virginia legislature even asked President Jefferson to examine the possibility of finding a location for freed slaves outside of the United States, and passed resolutions favoring the removal of African Americans from the state.[7]

Ideas of removing both slavery and African Americans were challenged by those who saw the impracticality of expelling hundreds of thousands of freed slaves from the territory of the United States. Virginian St George Tucker in his 1796 *Dissertation on Slavery* said it was desirable to end slavery, but that it would have to be done gradually, both for reasons of safety and because of property rights. He argued that it was impractical either to incorporate the freed slaves within the state or to expel them. On the impossibility of incorporation, Tucker cited the authority of Jefferson. 'If it be true, as Mr Jefferson seems to suppose,' he wrote, 'that the Africans are really an inferior

7   Jordan, *White Over Black*, pp.343–9, 400–1, 551–65; MacLeod, *Slavery*, pp.141–2.

race of mankind,' sound policy would advise their exclusion from Virginian society. Incorporation would eventually 'depreciate the whole national character.'

Tucker was equally convinced that deportation was impracticable. To establish a colony within the United States would lead to future wars, to send freed slaves overseas would involve great numbers and great expense. His 'solution' was gradual emancipation, and a policy that would allow Africans to stay while encouraging them to leave. They would not be permitted to vote or hold public office, would not be allowed to be an attorney, juror, or witness, except in cases involving other African Americans, at the most would possess lands only on a 21-year lease, and would not be permitted to marry whites. Tucker stated that he supported gradual emancipation, but he wanted the freed slaves to leave. He hoped that they might go to Spanish Louisiana.[8]

The stimulus that the Revolution gave to the anti-slavery movement had begun to slacken in the Upper South by the 1790s, and even in the North there was a relaxation of effort in the years from 1800 to 1812, particularly after the ending of the legal importation of slaves in 1808. Generally, in the South manumission was again made more difficult, and there was an effort to reduce the number of free blacks. In the years after 1800 even the evangelical religious sects in the South no longer took up the cause of freeing the slaves, and many Quakers began to move north of the Ohio River.[9]

In spite of all the revolutionary rhetoric the number of slaves increased sharply in the United States in the decades after the Revolution. From 700,000 in 1790, the slave population rose to nearly 900,000 in 1800, to over 1,190,000 in 1810, and to over 1,500,00 in 1820. Most of this was a natural increase, but even though the foreign slave trade ended in 1808 African slaves were the largest group of immigrants in the years from the Revolution to 1815. Because emancipation in the North was usually gradual, there were still slaves in the northern states in these years, but the vast majority of slaves were in the South.

Historians of slavery have emphasized that there was no one pattern of enslavement. The great slave owners, with hundreds of slaves, were the exception not the rule. Many slave owners owned few slaves. There were also great differences in the nature of plantation slavery between the Upper

8 St George Tucker, *A Dissertation on Slavery: With a Proposal for the Gradual Abolition of it in the State of Virginia* (1796; rpr, Westport, Conn, 1970), pp.80–93.
9 Jordan, *White Over Black*, pp.347–9; Miller, *Wolf*, pp.120–5.

and the Lower South, and between the Atlantic states and the new frontier [1 4 3]
regions of the Mississippi Valley. The differences in the ways that slave labor
was used also meant great differences in the lives of individual slaves. Life for
a house slave on a Virginia tidewater plantation with a surplus of slaves was
very different from the life of a field hand on a plantation that was being
carved out of new land acquisitions in Georgia, or across the mountains in
Kentucky or Tennessee. Urban slaves lived a very different existence from
rural slaves.[10]

A particular irony in the revolutionary generation was that the Virginians
who took the lead in so many aspects of shaping the new republic and its
freedoms for the white population were also the greatest slave holders. The
percentage of slaves held in Virginia and Maryland as compared to the rest of
the country was gradually diminishing, but in 1810 over 40 per cent of the
African Americans in the United States lived in those two states.[11]

While slaves were numerous in the Chesapeake region, the need for
them was diminishing in the years after the Revolution as planters moved
from tobacco farming to wheat and more general agriculture. The African
American slave population increased more rapidly in these years than the
free white population. One solution for the Chesapeake planters was to sell
slaves to the planters in the Lower South. There the plantation system was
rapidly expanding with the spreading of cotton cultivation from the mid-
1790s. There is no clearer indication that the banning of the foreign slave
trade involved a fear of increasing the number of black Americans as well as
humanitarian objections to the slave trade than the fact that the internal slave
trade was carried on with increasing vigor in these years.

The lack of any pressing need for slaves in the Chesapeake region also
made it easier for those slave owners who wanted to follow the logic of
revolutionary ideology and free their slaves. Between 1790 and 1810 the
free black population in the United States increased from just under 60,000
to over 186,000. Nearly a third of the free blacks by 1810 were in Virginia
and Maryland. By that date over 20 per cent of the black population of
Maryland, and 7 per cent of the population of Virginia, were free.[12]

In Maryland the trend towards manumission continued. By 1850 nearly
half of Maryland's African American population was free. In Virginia the

---

10   See the discussion in Peter J. Parish, *Slavery: History and Historians* (New York, 1989), pp.1–6.
11   Richard S. Dunn, 'Black society in the Chesapeake, 1776–1810,' in Berlin and Hoffman
     (eds), *Slavery*, p.49.
12   Allan Kulikoff, *Tobacco and Slaves: The Development of Southern Cultures in the Chesapeake,
     1680–1800* (Chapel Hill, NC, 1986), pp.118–61; Dunn, 'Black society,' pp.51, 62.

[1 4 4] result of the revolutionary debate on slavery was very different. Revolutionary rhetoric appeared to be winning the day in 1782, when the individual manumission of slaves was made easier, but the same measure demonstrated a fear of having free African Americans as equal citizens within the state. It provided that freedmen who did not pay their taxes could be sold into slavery. African Americans were also prohibited from forming their own schools. The passage of the 1782 Act also produced a backlash from supporters of slavery. In the following years they petitioned the legislature to repeal it. In an age when petitions were often sent by small groups, the proslavery petitions of 1784 and 1785 had over 1,200 signatures. The effort to repeal the act failed, but the legislature was divided on the issue. There was no legislative support at all for a Quaker effort to secure the general freeing of slaves.[13]

Yet the Quaker stand gained support after the Revolution, when the evangelical churches began to take up an anti-slavery position. In the 1780s some of the white Baptists and Methodists began to attack the prevailing southern system. In 1789 the General Committee of Virginia Baptists adopted a resolution condemning slavery. This was more a victory for the strong convictions of one or two vocal opponents of slavery than a general Virginia Baptist position. The Methodists in the Upper South also passed resolutions condemning slavery in the 1780s, and as late as 1809 the Baltimore Conference of the Methodist Church prohibited its members from engaging in the slave trade. There was also religious opposition to slavery across the mountains in Kentucky and Tennessee. In Kentucky, some of the Presbyterians joined in the condemnation of slavery.[14] In general, however, the evangelical challenge to slavery in the South weakened towards the end of the eighteenth century.

Even in their first period of enthusiasm the impact of the Baptists and Methodists was lessened by lack of influential members. The evangelical movement was very much a movement of the have-nots, and the treatment of African Americans as equals sent shudders through the more respectable members of society. In Virginia, rather than encouraging those in authority to move towards general emancipation, the actions of the evangelicals

---

13   Miller, *Wolf*, p.87; Fredrika Teute Schmidt and Barbara Ripel Wilhelm, 'Early proslavery petitions in Virginia,' *WMQ* 3rd Ser., 30 (1973), pp.133–46.
14   Albert J. Raboteau, 'The slave church in the era of the American Revolution,' in Berlin and Hoffman (eds), *Slavery*, pp.197–202; John W. Blassingame, *The Slave Community: Plantation Life in the Antebellum South* rev. edn (New York, 1979), pp.75–7; Sylvia R. Frey, *Water from the Rock: Black Resistance in a Revolutionary Age* (Princeton, NJ, 1993), pp.244–9.

probably helped to persuade the Virginia legislature that it had gone too far [145] in encouraging the individual freeing of slaves.

The rhetoric of freedom that permeated the language of the revolutionary generation increased fears that the holding of slaves presented a danger to white safety. The Revolution had not only spread ideas of liberty throughout the country, it had also brought great disruption to slave life as British armies campaigned in the South. In Virginia and in other southern states slaves had fled behind British lines, most of them never to return. When British armies evacuated the South they took with them thousands of slaves. Not all slaves could be kept from hearing words of freedom, and some had the practical experience of knowing those who had found a means to leave.[15]

The feelings of unease among slave owners increased sharply in the 1790s with the news that slaves and free blacks on the island of Santo Domingo had risen against the French. The ideas of liberty and equality that the French revolutionaries had hoped to confine to white Frenchmen had spread to black African slaves in the colony of Saint-Domingue. France abolished slavery in 1793, but the war on the island raged on. It was a bloody struggle. The French arbitrarily executed large numbers of those in revolt, and the slave rebels burned plantations and killed slave owners. Thousands of whites fled to the United States and the Spanish colonies of Cuba and Louisiana.

In the early years of the new century the situation on Santo Domingo was a constant cause of concern to southerners. The French attempt to retain control of the island was a disastrous failure. Even the death of the great rebel leader Toussaint L'Ouverture had no effect on the eventual outcome. In 1804 the republic of Haiti was created on the French part of the island. It was a black republic. The whites had fled or were killed. The United States generally regarded it as her duty to give moral support to colonial revolts, but Haiti was different. Southern fears meant that the republic of Haiti was not recognized by the United States until the Civil War.[16]

In Virginia the revolt on Santo Domingo was given a special meaning in 1800 when the slave Gabriel Prosser plotted with others near Richmond to overturn white rule. The plot was betrayed, and over 30 slaves were hanged. In Virginia, and in the South in general, the Gabriel plot was interpreted as a

15 Benjamin Quarles, 'The Revolutionary War as a Black Declaration of Independence,' in Berlin and Hoffman (eds), *Slavery*, pp.283–92.

16 Miller, *Wolf*, pp.133–41; Jordan, *White Over Black*, pp.375–87; Charles C. Tansill, *The United States and Santo Domingo, 1798–1873: A Chapter in Caribbean Diplomacy* (Baltimore, Md, 1938), pp.79–85.

[1 4 6]   sign that what had happened on Santo Domingo could happen in the United States. Instances of a slave killing or attacking a master were now interpreted as the signs or general slave unrest.[17]

After 1800 the Virginia impulse that had originally made manumission easier began to fade. Laws were passed that prohibited free blacks from traveling to another county without permission. Finally, in 1806, Virginia reversed the policy it had adopted in its revolutionary enthusiasm, and passed a law making it more difficult for slave owners to free slaves. After 1800 southern states from Virginia to Georgia became far more aware of the dangers presented by their large slave populations, and began to tighten rather than relax the bonds of slavery.[18]

In their relationship to the largest slave population in the nation, Chesapeake whites exhibited to the full the dilemma that beset the new republic. The logic of Enlightenment thought and the Revolution said that slavery should not exist in the new nation. Science said that the differences between races were not permanent, revolutionary leaders said that all human beings had a natural right to freedom. For a time more slaves were freed, and a new egalitarian religion even welcomed Africans as fellow Christians. Yet fears of a society in which there would be hundreds of thousands of freed slaves prevailed. By 1815 slavery was firmly implanted in Virginia, and hopes of general emancipation had disappeared. Dreams of the ending of slavery had evaporated on fears of race.

The southern states, however, could not reverse the effects the turmoil of the last half of the eighteenth century had on the slaves themselves. The events of these years had irrevocably changed African American life in the Upper South. Not only were there more free blacks, both slave society as well as free black society had been profoundly influenced by secular ideas of freedom and by religious ideas of equality before God. Until the second half of the nineteenth century masters had usually prevented their slaves from becoming members of Christian churches or even learning about the Christian religion. Yet, in the evangelical enthusiasm of the revolutionary era, the evangelical churches had great success in winning converts among free blacks and slaves in the Chesapeake. In the first period of enthusiasm black slaves were included in white congregations, black preachers preached to mixed congregations of African Americans and whites, and there were

17   Jordan, *White Over Black*, pp.391–400, 404; Robert McColley, *Slavery and Jeffersonian Virginia* 2nd edn (Urbana, Ill, 1973), pp.107–13; Douglas R. Egerton, *Gabriel's Rebellion: The Virginia Slave Conspiracies of 1800 and 1802* (Chapel Hill, NC, 1993).

18   Jordan, *White Over Black*, pp.399–406, 574–81.

instances of black preachers preaching to white congregations. By 1800 an increasing number of separate black congregations, with their own preachers, were being formed in the Upper South, particularly among the Baptists.[19]

Historians of slavery have argued that many slaves in the South managed to construct a family life even while under the threat of enforced separation, and subject to the vagaries of individual masters. Slave women often had children before marriage, but tended to maintain stable relationships, particularly in the Lower South. Having partners on other plantations, white sexual demands, and the possibility of separation by sale always caused tensions, but great efforts were made to maintain family life. This was somewhat easier before 1815 than after that date, when there was a great increase both in the internal slave trade and in the expansion of slavery into the Mississippi Valley. If slaves lived on small, isolated plantations, they could have difficulty in finding a suitable permanent partner, but on large plantations slaves could gain support from extended families. Nothing, however, could protect them from the whims and brutalities of individual masters, and on some plantations floggings were the rule rather than the exception. In general, however, the development of humanitarian thought in the second half of the eighteenth century, and the challenge to slavery itself, meant that the more generalized brutality of an earlier period was moderated. Slaves also benefited because the Revolution had led to the reduction of extreme punishments among the society in general.[20]

Slavery in the Lower South, in South Carolina and in Georgia, had less ambiguity than in the Upper South. In South Carolina and Georgia slavery was not attacked as it was in Virginia or Maryland, or even in North Carolina. In South Carolina there was a very high percentage of slaves in the politically influential low country region. Even in the first revolutionary enthusiasm there was no strong anti-slavery movement in the Lower South, and few slave owners felt any compelling need to free their slaves by individual action. Yet, in the low country, the high number of slaves in proportion to whites, and the absence of white families in the hot season, meant that, ironically, in an area in which slavery was largely unchallenged, the slaves themselves were often able to keep a greater control of their own lives.

19   Raboteau, 'Slave church,' pp.194–5, 204–8.
20   Mary Beth Norton, Herbert G. Gutman, and Ira Berlin, 'The African-American family in the age of revolution,' in Berlin and Hoffman (eds), *Slavery*, pp.175–87; Mary Beth Norton, *Liberty's Daughters: The Revolutionary Experience of American Women* (Boston, Mass, 1980), pp.65–8; Parish, *Slavery*, pp.85–7. See also Herbert Gutman, *The Black Family in Slavery and Freedom, 1750–1825* (New York, 1986).

[1 4 8]   Unlike Virginia, South Carolina wanted to increase the number of slaves in the years after the American Revolution. Part of this desire came from the rapid development of the South Carolina upcountry in the second half of the eighteenth century, but the desire for slaves was given another great impetus by the development and expansion of cotton cultivation. Georgia, very much a frontier state in the 1780s, also eagerly sought the development of its hinterland in the years before the War of 1812. In the Lower South there was a strong belief that the nature of the plantation system and the climate made slavery a necessity.

In South Carolina the gulf between white and black was greater than anywhere else in the country. In 1810 none of the low country parishes had a population that was less than 80 per cent black, and some were over 90 per cent. A gulf between black and white also existed because a much larger proportion of South Carolina slaves had been born in Africa than in the Upper South. As late as 1790 over 25 per cent of the South Carolina slave population had been born in Africa. This dropped sharply by 1800, but rose again before the next census because of South Carolina's temporary renewal of foreign slave importations. In 1810 one-fifth of South Carolina's slaves were African born, and by 1820 over half of the state's total population was slave.

Before the official ending of the foreign slave trade in 1808 most of the demand for new slaves in the Lower South was met by the traffic from abroad. The importation of slaves was allowed into North Carolina until 1793, into Georgia until 1798, and South Carolina reopened the trade in 1803. As there was also illegal importation of slaves, it is likely that over 200,000 slaves were imported into the United States between 1790 and 1810. After the federal government banned the trade in 1808 the demand for new slaves was increasingly met by traffic from the Chesapeake.[21]

Cotton, with its back-breaking labor, became the most important crop in South Carolina and Georgia in these years, spreading rapidly into the South Carolina back country and advancing westwards into the interior of Georgia. More slaves lived on large plantations than in the Upper South, and this meant that some of the men could develop specialized occupations. But most of the men, and even more of the women, remained as field hands. The rigor of slave life in South Carolina was somewhat tempered by a heightened sense of African identity. The presence of large numbers of slaves born in

21   Philip D. Morgan, 'Black society in the lowcountry, 1760–1810,' in Berlin and Hoffman (eds), *Slavery*, pp.83–92; Alan Kulikoff, 'Uprooted peoples: Black migrants in the age of the American Revolution,' in ibid., pp.146–51.

Africa, the greatest number of them from Angola, meant that African cus- [149]
toms remained stronger than in other parts of the South.[22]

Slavery expanded rapidly in the trans-Allegheny West in these years. The
frontier south of the Ohio River was a slave frontier. A few hundred slaves
were illegally taken north of the Ohio, in violation of the Northwest
Ordinance of 1787, but southerners failed in their hope of establishing slavery in Indiana and Illinois. For many slaves, whether in the Upper or the
Lower South, these were years in which their lives were totally disrupted by
their forced movement into new areas. For the free white settler the movement west represented opportunity and hope. For the slave, it often meant
leaving loved ones on other plantations, and harder, back-breaking work
clearing new lands and building new dwellings.

Between 1790 and 1810 some 75,000 slaves from Virginia and Maryland were taken into Kentucky and Tennessee, and slavery became well entrenched in those states. The acquisition of Louisiana strengthened slavery
in the Mississippi Valley. Slavery already existed in Spanish Louisiana. After
1803 the position of these Spanish slaves was worsened by American rule.
Under Spanish law slaves were granted specific rights, such as instruction
in religion, the prohibition of husband and wife being sold separately, a ban
on children under 14 being sold away from their mothers, and even some
ability to testify in court. These rights ended under American rule. Both in
Louisiana (and in Mississippi Territory when it was created in 1798) the
foreign slave trade was barred, and new slaves were either brought in by
their masters or by the rapidly expanding internal slave trade.[23]

Throughout the South the great majority of slaves worked as field hands,
but for a minority there was considerable diversity of occupation. On the
larger plantations men plied a variety of trades, and women left the fields to
work as domestic servants. In the southern towns, small and few in number
in these years, occupations were even more diversified. Slaves were hired out
into workshops, or to work on the docks in the coastal cities. It was also far
more difficult to keep a strict control over slaves in an urban environment,
particularly when they were hired out away from their owners.

Of all African Americans, the greatest change in the early national period
came to those who were freed. The growth in manumissions in the immediate post-war years, and the natural increase in the free black population
brought a great increase in these years. The free black population in the

---

22   Morgan, 'Black society,' pp.93–141.
23   Kulikoff, 'Uprooted peoples,' p.148; Miller, *Wolf,* pp.143–4.

[1 5 0]   United States rose from nearly 60,000 to over 230,000 in 1820. By 1810, when the free black population had reached 186,000, a clear pattern had emerged in the southern states. The states of the Upper South had large numbers of free blacks while the Lower South remained predominantly slave. In 1810 over 75 per cent of Delaware African Americans were free. The percentages dropped sharply in states farther to the South. Virginia had some 7 per cent, North Carolina less than 6 per cent, South Carolina little over 2 per cent, and Georgian less than 2 per cent. By 1810, some 13 per cent of the total African American population in the United States were free.[24]

For a time, black freedom in the Upper South produced surprising results. At first Delaware, Maryland, and North Carolina did not exclude free blacks from voting. Delaware excluded them in 1792. In that same year a free black in Baltimore ran for a seat in the Maryland House of Delegates. He did not win, and by 1810 Maryland formally prohibited free blacks from voting. The vote was not denied to free blacks in North Carolina during this period, and voting was also allowed in Tennessee. Kentucky, in its new constitution in 1799, specifically excluded free blacks from voting. The federal government also excluded free blacks from voting in Washington, DC in 1802, and in Mississippi and Indiana Territories in 1808.

In general, free blacks in the South found themselves experiencing increasing restrictions in the years after 1800. In Maryland and Virginia free blacks could not serve in the militia. In North Carolina there was no such prohibition until 1812, when entry into the militia was restricted to free black musicians. In the Lower South, South Carolina did not think it necessary to pass formal laws on these matters. Louisiana had a numerous and active free black population in New Orleans. In 1806 the state banned the entry from the West Indies of free blacks over the age of 15, and in the following years banned any immigration of free blacks from abroad.[25]

In spite of all the restraints southern free blacks gained an increasing sense of community in these years. The spreading of evangelical religion by the Baptists and Methodists was of great importance, for it led to the widespread development of independent black churches, in the South as well as in the North. All the southern states participated in this movement, and it encompassed both slaves and free blacks. When the original revolutionary impetus

24   *A Century of Population Growth*: From the First Census of the United States to the Twelfth, 1790–1900 (Washington, DC, 1909), p.80; Jordan, *White Over Black*, pp.406–7.
25   Jordan, *White Over Black*, pp.407–11; Leonard P. Curry, *The Free Black in Urban America, 1800–1850: The Shadow of a Dream* (Chicago, Ill, 1981), pp.84–5; Quarles, 'Revolutionary War,' p.130.

Plate 1.
George Washington
(1732-1799), painted by
Gilbert Stuart

Plate 2.
John Marshall
(1755-1835), portrait
after crayon drawing by
Saint-Memin

Plate 3.
Alexander Hamilton
(1755/7-1804), painted
by John Trumbull

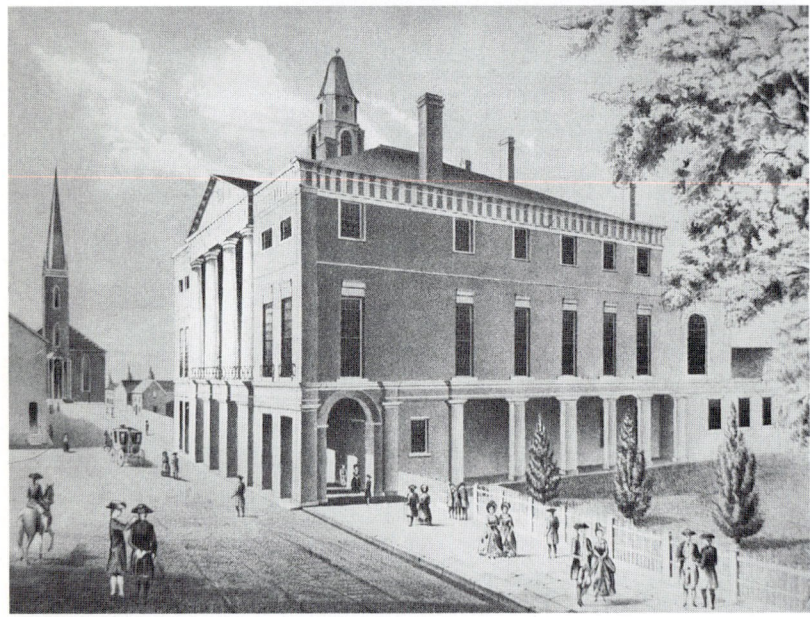

Plate 4.
City Hall, Wall Street New York, 1790

Plate 5.
Thomas Jefferson
(1743-1826), painted by
Rembrandt Peale

Plate 6.
James Madison
(1751-1836)

Plate 7.
18th Century Tobacco Plantation

Plate 8.
Samuel Slater's Massachusetts Cotton Mill, c.1800

Plate 9.
Believed to be Tecumeseh
(c.1768-1813), portrait
by an unknown artist.

Plate 10.
Andrew Jackson
(1767-1845), painted by
Thomas Sully.

Plate 11.
Burning of Washington, D.C., British troops in the city, August 1814

Plate 12.
President's House, Washington, D.C., burned by the British in 1814, rebuilt and painted white, sketch by Benjamin Latrobe

Plate 13.
Constitution defeats *Java,* 29 December 1812, painted by C.R. Patterson

Plate 14.
Battle of Lake Erie, September 10, 1813. Commodore Oliver Hazard Perry transfers his flag

Plate 15.
Battle of Queenston Heights, 13 October 1812

Plate 16.
Andrew Jackson at the battle of New Orleans, January 1815, painted by
Charles McBarron

of white Baptists welcoming blacks into their churches died away after [1 5 1] 1790, African Americans founded numerous churches. These churches were to have a particular vigor in creating a sense of community among free blacks in northern cities, but they also reached African Americans throughout the South.[26]

In southern towns it was possible for free blacks to gain a greater sense of community than in the rural areas. In 1800 nearly half of Baltimore Methodists were African Americans, and both the Sharp Street Methodist Church and the African Methodist Church had established schools before 1810. In Charleston some 4,000 slaves and free blacks belonged to African Methodist churches in the years before 1815. There was also the development of black self-help organizations, into which members paid dues to provide some security in the event of sickness, unemployment or death in the family. The Brown Fellowship Society was established in Charleston in 1790. One of the primary purposes of many African American organizations was also to provide schools for African American children. Three more self-help societies had been established in Charleston by 1813.[27]

In the major northern cities the free black communities made rapid strides in developing a sense of social cohesiveness. Gary Nash has pointed out that in the 50 years from the eve of the American Revolution what had been a population of 4,000 slaves and a few hundred free blacks living in the cities of Philadelphia, New York, and Boston had increased to nearly 22,000 free blacks and some 500 slaves. Complete freedom was slow in coming. In New York, where the gradual abolition of slavery was not provided for until 1799, there were still nearly 3,000 slaves in 1800, more than in any other city in the United States except Charleston.

Most of the slaves who were freed in the northern cities remained there, and their numbers were swelled by the movement of African Americans from rural areas in the Upper South and in the North. For black men the particular attraction of these ports was the opportunity for maritime occupations. The occupation of merchant seaman was of vital importance of freed blacks, and they also worked in various occupations on and around the docks. A few were able to become artisans. Black women often worked as domestic servants.[28]

26 Nathan O. Hatch, *The Democratization of American Christianity* (New Haven, Conn, 1989), pp.102–13; Frey, *Water from the Rock*, pp.284–96.
27 Curry, *Free Blacks*, pp.156, 180–1, 197–9; Quarles, 'Revolutionary War,' p.297.
28 Gary Nash, 'Forging freedom: the emancipation experience in the northern seaport cities, 1775–1820,' in Berlin and Hoffman (eds), *Slavery*, pp.4–10, 14–18; Curry, *Free Blacks*, pp.2–7. For African American seamen, see W. Jeffrey Bolster, *Black Jacks: African American Seamen in the Age of Sail* (Cambridge, Mass, 1997).

[1 5 2]   The evangelical churches and African American ministers served as cata-
lysts for these growing communities, and their sense of cohesiveness helped
to attract other free blacks from rural areas. The first developments of independent churches were in Philadelphia, where free blacks began to find
themselves unwelcome in mixed churches that had developed in the years
of evangelical enthusiasm. In 1794 African Americans broke away from St
George's Methodist Church, and established St Thomas' African Episcopal
Church and the Bethel Methodist Church. These churches were immediate successes, and they acquired large memberships. By 1810 the Bethel
Church had some 1,300 members. By far the most support was given to
the Methodists, but the free blacks had a separate Presbyterian church in
Philadelphia by 1807, and a separate Baptist church was established in
1810. Boston and New York also developed independent black churches
in the first decades of the young republic.[29]

One of the primary objectives of the new black communities emerging in
northern cities was the education of their young. This was made necessary
because in most cases free black children were excluded from white schools.
In Philadelphia the black communities were able to build on the earlier work
of the Quakers. Since before the Revolution the Quakers had engaged in
the education of African Americans, and this activity continued in the post-
war years. They were joined in the 1790s by the Pennsylvania Society for
Promoting the Abolition of Slavery, which in 1794 established a school of
its own. By 1800 it was giving some support to two free black schools, and
there were increased educational opportunities for free black children in the
following years. In New York the New York Manumission Society spon-
sored schools, and in 1812 free blacks in the city organized a society to promote education. Boston provided free schools for whites, but blacks were not
admitted. Free blacks had to arrange for their own education. In 1812 the
city appropriated $200 to help support a free black school. Resources were
limited, but great efforts were made to provide education.[30]

Self-help societies became a prominent feature of free black communities
in northern cities. Also, occasionally, better-off free blacks formed societies
to help support the destitute. In Philadelphia the first self-help organization
dated back at least to the Revolution, but the major growth in such societies
was after 1790, often connected with the churches. Two early organizations
in Philadelphia in the 1790s were the Female Benevolent Society of St

29   Hatch, *Democratization*, pp.107–13; Curry, *Free Blacks*, pp.174–89.
30   Curry, *Free Blacks*, pp.153–4, 156, 158, 161, 165; Quarles, 'Revolutionary War,' p.299.

Thomas and the male African Friendly Society of the same church. Several [1 5 3] more societies were founded in the following years. Philadelphia had 11 by 1811. The 1790s also brought the formation of similar societies in New York, and in Providence, Rhode Island. Some free blacks also found a sense of community in forming Masonic organizations. An African American Masonic lodge was formed in Boston in the 1780s. As they could not get a charter from the white Masons in Massachusetts, they secured one from England. In turn, in the 1790s, the Boston lodge authorized lodges in Providence and Philadelphia. The Providence lodge did not succeed, but Freemasonry became of importance among the free blacks in Philadelphia. Several more lodges were founded in these years. One founded by black seamen in 1798 obtained its charter from Germany. New York received authority to establish a lodge in 1812. Like other African American fraternal organizations, the Masons provided help for their members in time of need.[31]

The research of Gary Nash has shown that once the blacks in northern cities obtained freedom it was at first difficult for them to establish separate households. A sizeable proportion of free blacks continued to live in white households. This situation began to change in the first two decades of the nineteenth century. By 1820 only 16 per cent of Boston's free blacks and 25 per cent of those in Philadelphia lived in white households. In New York, where slavery was only slowly being abolished, 36 per cent still lived with whites. At first free blacks who left white households often lived with other blacks, but by 1820 in Boston, Philadelphia, and New York most free blacks lived in nuclear black households with an adult male and an adult female. Children were fewer than in white households, presumably both by choice and because of higher death rates among free blacks than among whites.[32]

The emerging black communities in northern cities very much had to depend on their own resources, and on the few abolitionist groups that helped them, because northern society did not greet them with open arms. Prejudice was rampant. In these early years, however, free blacks did exercise some political rights that they were later to lose. In both Massachusetts and New York free blacks exercised the right to vote, and had an impact on some of the elections. There was also some free black voting in Pennsylvania. Free blacks at times showed the independence of spirit on national concerns that they had demonstrated during the Revolution. In 1799 74 African

31   Curry, *Free Blacks*, pp.208–9, 211; Quarles, 'Revolutionary War,' p.298.
32   Nash, 'Forging freedom,' pp.21–42.

[1 5 4]   Americans from Philadelphia and its surrounding area petitioned the federal government to end the importation of slaves, and to change the fugitive slave law so that it would be more difficult to kidnap free blacks. The petition was rejected by the House by a vote of 85 to 1.[33]

For African Americans the revolutionary era brought both promise and disappointment. Slavery was coming to an end in the northern states, and all over the United States many more were now free. But by 1808, at the time the foreign slave trade ended, it was also clear that slavery was firmly entrenched and expanding in the South. Among both slave and free blacks a distinctive African American culture was emerging, with African elements stronger in the regions of the Lower South that had large majorities of slaves in their population. In northern cities with growing populations there was the development of a distinct sense of community.

This sense of community was revealed not only in Philadelphia or New York, but even far away on Dartmoor in England. The prison built originally to house French prisoners of war was used in the War of 1812 to house American sailors, mostly captured on the privateers that sailed the oceans in their hundreds to harass British shipping. Some 6,500 prisoners were admitted to Dartmoor during the war; about one-seventh of them African Americans. At first all the prisoners were mixed together, as they had to be on the ships, but in 1814 white prisoners asked that the blacks should be segregated. Eventually, they were all moved to No. 4 barracks.

In the winter of 1814–15 the African American barracks housed some 800 prisoners; there were a few whites who, for various reasons, were given refuge when they had to flee from other barracks. No. 4 became a flourishing African American community, led by the towering 'King Dick,' probably Richard Crafus, who settled in Boston after the war under the name of Richard Seavers. He had the greatest influence of any prisoner in Dartmoor, black or white.

The black barracks played a key role in most areas of prison life. It was a main source of ready-cooked food, and beer that was smuggled into the prison was sold from the stalls set up by black prisoners. White prisoners went to No. 4 to be taught fencing, boxing, dancing, and music; visiting British officers were irritated when the band from No. 4 played 'Yankee Doodle.' White prisoners also went to No. 4 to gamble; the tables there were the best patronized in the prison. The black barracks was also the place to go for religion. On Sunday a black Methodist preacher attracted whites as well

33   Curry, *Free Blacks*, pp.217–21; Quarles, 'Revolutionary War,' p.300.

as blacks, and a British minister came each Thursday to preach in No. 4. One diarist argued that it was the black choir that attracted so many whites to the barracks every Sunday, but from other diaries it is evident that at least two whites were converted by the black Methodist preacher and moved into No. 4. There was also a theatre in the loft of No. 4, with mostly black actors (there was another theatre in No. 5 with all white casts). Among the productions staged in No. 4 were *Othello* and *Romeo and Juliet*, along with a variety of other productions.

At the end of the war, when the British began to repatriate the prisoners, many of the African Americans were not eager to return to the United States. They would not accept repatriation on a ship bound for a southern port. By June 1815 only about 900 prisoners were left in Dartmoor, of which about half were African American. All the prisoners were now confined in No. 4 barracks.[34] For black Americans the prison of Dartmoor in royal England had advantages that they could not get in the republican United States.

34 Reginald Horsman, 'The paradox of Dartmoor prison,' *American Heritage* 26 (1975), pp.12–17, 85.

CHAPTER 10

LOUISIANA AND THE POLITICS
OF EXPANSION

In his *American Geography* of 1789 Jedidiah Morse described Louisiana as a Spanish province, bounded on the east by the Mississippi River, on the south by the Gulf of Mexico, on the west by New Mexico, and running indefinitely north. It was huge, and it was difficult to describe.[1] Much of it was unexplored. Before 1763 the European powers had acknowledged the region as belonging to France. Her explorers and fur traders knew some of it, but there was no precise boundary separating it from the possessions of Spain in the Southwest. France had ceded the region to Spain in 1763. Spain, France, and the United States all ignored any Indian right to territorial sovereignty over the region; the best the Indians could hope for was some acknowledgment of their right of soil.

In the late 1790s the French had become interested in the possibility of reacquiring some of the North American possessions they had lost to the British and Spanish in 1763. The center of the French empire in the New World was in the West Indies, but they desired a mainland possession that could supply their sugar-rich West Indian colonies with provisions. In September 1800, by the secret treaty of San Ildefonso, Spain promised to return Louisiana to France. The actual transfer depended on France securing a kingdom in Italy for the son-in-law of the Spanish king. The treaty did not specify exact boundaries. It stated that Spain would return the territory to France with the same boundaries as it had when France had owned it.[2] This vagueness ultimately allowed the United States to try to stretch her limits to encompass territory that Spain believed she had retained.

When Jefferson became president in March 1801 he did not know that France was about to regain Louisiana. His instinct was to be favorably inclined towards France, because he believed that Great Britain, not France, presented the greatest threat to American republicanism. He appointed

---

1   Jedidiah Morse, *The American Geography* (1789; rpr, New York, 1970), p.477.
2   Alexander DeConde, *This Affair of Louisiana* (New York, 1976), pp.57–97.

Robert R. Livingston, known to be friendly to the French, as minister to [1 5 7] France. Within two months Jefferson had heard rumors of the treaty of San Ildefonso. He wrote to James Monroe late in May that there was 'considerable reason to apprehend' that Spain had ceded Louisiana and the Floridas to France.[3]

The Floridas referred to the area on the Gulf of Mexico south of the 31st parallel and east of the Mississippi River. East Florida was roughly the modern state, and West Florida consisted of the southern parts of modern Alabama and Mississippi. Part of West Florida immediately east of the Mississippi had belonged to France before 1763, the remainder of the Floridas had belonged to Spain. The treaty of San Ildefonso dealt with the province of Louisiana west of the Mississippi, not with the Floridas to the east of the river.

In April 1802, when Jefferson became convinced that Spain had ceded Louisiana and the Floridas to France, he wrote to Livingston that although France was the '*natural friend*' of the United States, the cession of Louisiana and the Floridas had completely changed the diplomatic situation. There was one spot on the globe, he wrote, whose possessor is 'our natural and habitual enemy' – New Orleans. The produce of three-fifths of American territory had to pass through that city. Spain he thought was harmless, and might soon have yielded possession, but powerful France was quite different. 'The day that France takes possession of N. Orleans,' wrote Jefferson, 'we must marry ourselves to the British fleet and nation.'[4]

On the face of it, this was a remarkable reversal. Since the Revolution Jefferson had consistently warned his friends and countrymen that Great Britain and her navy presented the greatest threat to the young republic. His political arguments throughout the 1790s had been shaped by a belief that English influence was insidiously worming its way into American politics and American society, and that everything possible should be done to break the dependence on British trade. When he wrote to Livingston of an American marriage with the British fleet and nation, he was most likely making absolutely sure that Livingston would impress the French with the serious consequences of any step to take occupation of New Orleans rather than expecting an actual alliance with Great Britain. Throughout the Louisiana crisis Jefferson did everything possible to convince the French that the

3 Jefferson to Monroe, 26 May 1801, in *WOTJ*, 9, p.260 (26 May 1801).
4 Jefferson to Livingston, 18 Apr. 1802, ibid., 9, pp.364–5. See also Jefferson to Du Pont de Nemours, 25 Apr. 1802, in Dumas Malone (ed.), *Correspondence Between Thomas Jefferson and Pierre Samuel du Pont de Nemours, 1798–1817* (Boston, Mass, 1930), p.47.

[1 5 8] consequences of France controlling the Gulf of Mexico would be to push the Americans into the arms of the English. Jefferson was hoping that the threat of this alliance would make it unnecessary.

Jefferson's primary fear was for American exports through the Gulf. He wanted to continue a free flow of goods down the Mississippi, but he also wanted free access to the Gulf through the rivers of West Florida. The farmers who were pressing on across the Mississippi Valley had to have access to markets. Jefferson had written to James Monroe in November 1801 that he looked forward to distant times when the American population will 'cover the whole northern, if not the southern continent,' but it was the rivers into the Gulf of Mexico and American exports, not land beyond the Mississippi, that were central to Jefferson's thoughts in this crisis.[5]

The Louisiana problem worsened in October 1802 when local Spanish authorities suspended the American right of deposit at New Orleans. This was on orders from Spain, and the order was reversed in March 1803, but the Americans assumed that this was directly as a result of the impending transfer of the region to France. There was an immediate public outcry. In February, Jefferson told Livingston that the suspension of the right of deposit had thrown the country into 'a flame,' particularly in the West.[6]

The Federalist opposition, always ready for a break with France and happy to try to embarrass Jefferson, pressed for prompt action. The Federalists had none of the enthusiasm of the Republicans for a rapid advance across the Mississippi Valley, but they recognized the economic importance of the rivers into the Gulf of Mexico. In the late 1790s Federalist Secretary of State Timothy Pickering had stated that any attempt by France to regain control of Louisiana should be resisted, and during the crisis with France Hamilton had expressed his desire for a military occupation of the Gulf region.[7]

Jefferson preferred peace to war, and he knew that his desires both for inexpensive and reduced regular forces and for decreasing the influence of Great Britain would be harmed by a war with France. He also believed that to seize New Orleans would be counter-productive; its seizure, he wrote later, would simply have produced a blockade of the river by a superior naval force. Instead of military action, Jefferson asked Congress to provide an initial $2,000,000 to be used to buy New Orleans and the Floridas. Congress

---

5 *WOTJ*, 9, p.317 (24 Nov. 1801).
6 Ibid., 9, p.441 (3 Feb. 1803); DeConde, *This Affair*, pp.119–25.
7 Pickering to King, 20 June 1797, in Charles R. King (ed.), *The Life and Correspondence of Rufus King* 6 vols (New York, 1894–1900), 2, p.192; John C. Miller, *Alexander Hamilton: Portrait in Paradox* (New York, 1959), pp.495–9.

gave him the money, and the Senate confirmed Jefferson's friend and protégé [1 5 9] James Monroe as a special envoy to France. In March 1803, when Monroe sailed to join Livingston, he took their instructions with him. They were authorized to pay not more than 50,000,000 *livres* (under $10,000,000) for New Orleans and the Floridas. If they could only get part of what they wanted, the Floridas were thought to be worth one-quarter the value of New Orleans, and East Florida half the value of West Florida. To obtain New Orleans and the Floridas the envoys were given authority to guarantee everything west of the Mississippi to France. If France would not sell, and the Mississippi was closed, the envoys were authorized to make an alliance with Great Britain.[8]

By the time Monroe arrived in France the crisis was nearing a solution. Napoleon was now in power, and the decision regarding Louisiana was in his hands. It was based on events in the West Indies and Europe, not on the situation in the United States. France wanted Louisiana to supply her sugar islands in the West Indies. The key island was Santo Domingo, whose slaves had been in revolt since the 1790s. Napoleon had sent an army but, wasted by disease, it needed reinforcements from Europe. They were to leave in the fall of 1802, but bad weather prevented them from sailing before winter set in. By the next spring the political situation had changed. France and England were about to renew their war. When war broke out it would be difficult to send reinforcements to Santo Domingo, and any French occupation of Louisiana would be made problematical. Napoleon needed troops and money in Europe. He decided to sell Louisiana. The area was still under the control of Spain, and in the summer of 1802 France had promised Spain that she would never sell it, but Spain was in no position to resist French power. The French asked Livingston what the United States would give for the whole of Louisiana.[9]

This was an age when envoys could not phone home or fly back for additional instructions, but if they kept Napoleon waiting he might well change his mind. When Monroe arrived the two envoys agreed to buy the whole of Louisiana for some $15,000,000; a quarter of this was to be for the spoliation claims of American citizens against France. The $15,000,000 total was 50 per cent more than the envoys had been authorized to spend. They had also bought the whole of Louisiana, which was not covered in their instructions.[10]

8   Madison to Livingston and Monroe, 2 Mar. 1803, *ASP, FR*, 2, pp.540–4.
9   E. Wilson Lyon, *Louisiana in French Diplomacy, 1759–1804* (Norman, Okla, 1934), pp.191–219.
10   DeConde, *This Affair*, pp.162–72.

[160]   In July 1803, when news of the purchase reached the United States, both Jefferson and his Secretary of State James Madison were delighted. Not only had the United States obtained access to the Gulf via the Mississippi River, the size of the country had been doubled by the unexpected purchase of the whole of Louisiana. Madison wrote to Monroe that the purchase of Louisiana, though not expected 'is received with warm, &, in a manner universal approbation.'[11]

Although the Republican party, and most Americans, agreed that to double the size of the country without war was indeed a triumph, there were some problems with the purchase. One that had to be dealt with immediately was that Jefferson thought it was unconstitutional. He was also very disappointed that the Floridas were apparently not included. He busily set about interpreting the treaty and history in a way to include them. The Federalists were furious at the purchase. They approved buying New Orleans, but they objected bitterly to the purchase of the vast Louisiana region west of the Mississippi.

In mid-July, when Jefferson presented the agreement to his cabinet, he raised the problem of constitutionality. He said he wanted to send the fullest possible information to Congress, because Congress would have to prepare a constitutional amendment to bring Louisiana into the Union. Even before Monroe had left for France, Jefferson had felt doubts about what he expected to be a much smaller purchase. The basic problem was whether the Constitution allowed the acquisition of foreign territory and its incorporation into the Union. In his letters Jefferson consistently stated that he saw no such power in the Constitution. The cabinet listened to Jefferson's qualms, agreed to call for a special session of Congress to meet in October before the six-month period for ratification expired, but most cabinet members tried to dissuade Jefferson from seeking a constitutional amendment.[12]

In writing to one of his political allies, John Breckinridge, Jefferson stated that in seizing a chance for the good of the country he had 'done an act beyond the Constitution.' In July Jefferson drafted a constitutional amendment to provide for the admission of the Louisiana area within the bounds of the Union. Members of the cabinet still thought it would be a political mistake to admit to an unconstitutional act. Moreover, an amendment to the Constitution would need not only the approval of Congress but the concurrence of three-quarters of the states.[13]

11   *WJM*, 7, p.60 n. (30 July 1803).
12   DeConde, *This Affair*, pp.181–3.
13   Jefferson to Breckinridge, 12 Aug. 1803, in *WOTJ*, 10, pp.5–7 n.; also, ibid., pp.3–12.

In August Jefferson decided that expediency, and the obvious advant- [1 6 1]
ages of the purchase, should be put above principle. He heard from Europe
that if the ratifications were not completed within six months Napoleon
might change his mind. He wrote again to his Congressional ally John
Breckinridge, and asked him not to mention his earlier constitutional qualms
about the purchase. He also told Madison that the least said about constitutional difficulties the better. The amendment was quietly shelved. When Congress assembled on 17 October 1803 Jefferson's message said nothing about
the constitutional doubts that had worried him throughout the year. Within
three days the Senate gave its approval by a vote of 24 to 7. Of the nine
Federalists in the Senate, only one voted in favor. Another – John Quincy
Adams – would have, but he did not take his seat until the following day.[14]

Jefferson very much hoped that the treaty could be interpreted to mean
that at least the part of West Florida west of the Perdido River that France
had owned before 1763 had been bought by the United States. He was not
dissuaded by the fact that both Spain and France disagreed with this interpretation. He reasoned that whatever power held the land east of the
Mississippi became the 'natural enemy' of the United States.[15]

Jefferson's first effort to include West Florida in the Louisiana purchase
was a rather blatant bluff. In February 1804, by the Mobile Act, his party
allies in Congress authorized him, when he thought it expedient, to establish a customs district at Mobile. As the Spanish still occupied Mobile, and
had no intention of relinquishing it, Spain objected to the Mobile Act. James
Monroe was now ordered to proceed to Spain to join the American minister
there to try to obtain the Floridas by negotiation. The negotiations failed.
Jefferson was to raise the whole question again in his second term.[16]

In the summer of 1803 the Federalists were furious that the man who
throughout the 1790s had lectured them on strict construction of the
Constitution had ignored it to double the size of the nation. The Federalists
had little strength in the existing states of the Mississippi Valley, and this
purchase not only promised an expansion that would increase the strength
of the Republican party, but also meant that the original states of the Union
were in danger of being swamped by newly created states in the West.
Federalist Senator William Plumer of New Hampshire expressed his fear

14   Jefferson to Breckinridge, 18 Aug. 1803, to Madison, 18 Aug. 1803, in ibid., 10, pp.7–8 n.,
     10–11 n.; DeConde, *This Affair*, pp.184–7.
15   Jefferson to Du Pont de Nemours, 1 Feb. 1803, in Malone (ed.), *Correspondence of Jefferson and
     Du Pont*, pp.75–6.
16   *AC*, 8th Cong., 1st Sess., Appendix, pp.1253–8 (24 Feb. 1804); Isaac Cox, *The West Florida
     Controversy, 1798–1813: A Study in American Diplomacy* (Baltimore, 1918), pp.100–38.

that Louisiana was 'a *world*' in itself; when admitted to the United States it would at a single stroke destroy the whole weight and importance of the eastern states. It would also enhance the power of the presidency through the patronage of new appointments. For Plumer not even a constitutional amendment would be enough to allow the admission of states from territory that was not part of the United States when the Constitution was written. Such new states would need the approval of each original state. The United States, he believed, had the right to conquer or buy foreign territory, but the territory would have to be given a military or colonial government.[17] Plumer's private thoughts demonstrated the degree to which some leading Federalists were becoming out of touch with much of American opinion.

On the day after proclaiming the ratification of the Louisiana treaty Jefferson asked Congress to implement the purchase of Louisiana, and over the next four months the purchase became a subject of Congressional debate. There was never any chance of the wishes of the administration being denied, because this became very much a party question. Democratic–Republicans, from whatever section, rallied behind the president, while Federalists for the most part attacked plans for expansion into the trans-Mississippi West. But the Federalists could easily be outvoted in both the House and the Senate. Their impotence increased their vehemence, and increased their alienation from the general American population. Increasingly the Federalists were becoming a northeastern, even a New England party.

The House immediately took up the bill to enable the president to take possession of Louisiana, and to rule it until Congress provided for its government. The Federalists argued that the vast territory west of the river was ungovernable. American population would be scattered, a sense of community lost, the balance of power between eastern and western states destroyed, and the power of the president enhanced. They warned that all great empires, whether monarchies or republics, had broken apart. Gaylord Griswold of New York raised in the House some of the same constitutional questions raised in private by Jefferson. In discussing the admission of new states, he argued that the Constitution referred only to the territory of the United States existing in 1787.[18]

---

17 Everett S. Brown (ed.), *William Plumer's Memorandum of Proceedings in the United States Senate, 1803–1807* (1923; rpr, New York, 1969), pp.6–13. See also Lynn Turner, *William Plumer of New Hampshire, 1759–1850* (Chapel Hill, NC, 1962), pp.109–13.

18 *AC*, 8th Cong., 1st Sess., pp.432–3 (Griswold); see also pp.456, 459–61; Henry Adams, *History of the United States during the Administrations of Thomas Jefferson and James Madison* 9 vols (New York, 1889–91), 2, pp.94–100.

The Federalists were particularly angered that the Republicans were using [1 6 3] arguments they had condemned just a few years before. John Randolph of Virginia, one of the key Republican members in the House, led the way in defending a broad interpretation of constitutional powers. As was so often the case, in the nineteenth century or later, most politicians found reasons to support the president of their own party, even if it meant modifying or reversing previous stances. In the case of Louisiana they had little difficulty in doing this, for the advantages of the purchase were so obvious, and it was of general popularity in the country. The bill quickly passed the House. The Democratic–Republicans were solidly in support. The only opposition came from 25 Federalists, most of them from New England.[19]

The Federalists found themselves in a frustrating position. They feared that the power of the presidency had been enhanced, but believed that Louisiana should be ruled as a colony because it would be unconstitutional to create states from an area acquired since 1787. The underlying fear of the New England Federalists was revealed when Uriah Tracy of Connecticut argued that absorbing this vast area would make the northern states 'insignificant in the Union.' The Republican leaders defended expansion. John Breckinridge of Kentucky argued that a republic should be extensive, because 'the more extensive its domain the more safe and more durable it will be.' With the Republicans dominating the Senate, the bill easily passed. William Plumer's comment was that if such a bill had been passed by the Federalists it would have been regarded as '*monarchal*; but when enacted by the *exclusive friends* of the people, it is pure *republicanism*.'[20]

The most divisive debate about the Louisiana acquisition came over the subject of how the region would be governed, for this involved Republican as well as Federalist objections. In the bill introduced into Congress at the end of December the whole area was divided into two units. The apparently limitless region north of the 33rd parallel, which was still practically all Indian country, was separated from the region south of the parallel. This southern area, which was to become the state of Louisiana, was named the Territory of Orleans. Its government was to be a modified version of the first stage of the American territorial system. Although the territory already had a population of more than 40,000 it was to have no local legislature. It was believed that the French and Spanish 'monarchists' that had been brought

19 *AC*, 8th Cong., 1st Sess., pp.406–10, 434–40, 456–7, 488–9; DeConde, *This Affair*, pp.189–92; Adams, *History*, 2, p.104.
20 *AC*, 8th Cong., 1st Sess., p.58 (Tracy), p.60 (Breckinridge), p.73; Brown (ed.), *Plumer's Memorandum*, pp.26–7 (Plumer).

[1 6 4] within the United States could not be trusted to participate in a republican system until after a period of adjustment. The president was empowered to appoint a governor, a secretary, a 13-member executive council, and the judicial officers.[21]

Debate on the Orleans government bill occupied Congress from January to March 1804, and in its course strict party lines dissolved. They usually returned when the key votes were taken. The difficulty for the Republicans was that many of them, particularly in the House, thought that the American republic was being too autocratic in dealing with the French and Spanish residents of the new territory. The difficulty for the Federalists was that the administration argument that the inhabitants of the region were as yet unfit to receive the blessings of a free government simply confirmed them in their belief that the nation was being expanded to include elements that would destroy its homogeneity.

Some of the western Republicans were particularly angry at the autocratic features of this bill. In the Senate, Joseph Anderson of Tennessee said it was a 'system of tyranny,' and Thomas Worthington of Ohio said it was a 'military despotism.' Federalist John Quincy Adams, who within a few years was to leave his party, agreed with them. He said that this was 'a Colonial system of government.' In the House, Republican George Washington Campbell of Tennessee said the bill established 'a complete despotism.' John Boyle of Kentucky said that he admired Jefferson but this bill set a dangerous precedent; were Jefferson 'an angel, instead of a man, I would not clothe him with this power.' In this case, Federalists were not united against the plans of the administration, for some of them believed that if the United States was to have possessions beyond the Mississippi they should be ruled so as to discourage settlers from going there. This position even gained the support of some eastern Republicans. As western states increased in number, sectional self-interest affected voting on questions of encouraging or discouraging western settlement.[22]

While the bill easily passed the Senate, the debate in the House led to amendments to liberalize the provisions for the government of the territory. These passed the House, but were rejected in the Senate. In the eventual compromise the House yielded and the only concession given to those who believed that the governmental system was despotic was that the measure

---

21   *AC*, 8th Cong., 1st Sess., pp.1293–1300; Adams, *History*, 2, pp.120–2.
22   Brown (ed.), *Plumer's Memorandum*, p.111 (Anderson), 134 (Worthington), 145 (Adams); *AC*, 8th Cong., 1st Sess., p.1063 (Campbell), 1076 (Boyle); Adams, *History*, 2, pp.123–5.

was limited to one year. This was not enough to win the support of all the [1 6 5] disaffected Republicans, and the bill only passed the House by the close vote of 51 to 45.[23]

The reaction of the old French and Spanish political leaders in New Orleans was that they had enjoyed more practical rights under the royal government of Spain than under the republican government of the United States. They were joined in their protests by Americans who now began to move into Louisiana in increasing numbers. In February 1805 three agents from the territory visited Washington to express the discontent, and to ask for admission as a state. This request was not granted, but in the following month the government of the territory of Orleans was modified by the addition of a territorial legislature. The Territory of Orleans was admitted to the Union as the state of Louisiana in 1812.[24]

The whole Louisiana affair had demonstrated that maintaining strict constitutionality was as difficult for Jefferson as it had been for Hamilton. Hamilton had interpreted the Constitution in such a way as to allow the creation of a national bank; Jefferson had let his belief in the unconstitutionality of the Louisiana purchase be buried because of its obvious advantages for the nation. The purchase had shown that under the pressure of expansion presidential power would be enhanced, and republicanism modified to suit what were considered to be the weaknesses of non-homogeneous peoples. It also demonstrated that party allegiance had reached the point where a popular president could win party support for measures distrusted by many of its individual members.

Many northeasterners viewed the Louisiana purchase as a disaster. Not only had Jefferson and his Republicans ridden roughshod over the Constitution, they had gained increased popularity by doing so. Some northeasterners were also disturbed because the areas of the Louisiana purchase that seemed most likely to gain population and become states were those that already had a slave system, or clearly would be suitable for it. For many this was objectionable not because of strong moral objections to slavery, but because the three-fifths compromise in the Constitutional Convention had given the slave states additional seats in the lower House. It was common in these years for northeastern Federalists to bemoan a compromise that gave southern states more representatives.

23   *AC*, 8th Cong., 1st Sess., pp.256, 1191–4, 1196–9; 1201–2, 1206–8, 1229–30.
24   Clarence E. Carter (ed.), *The Territorial Papers of the United States* (Washington, DC, 1934–), 9, pp.242–3, 245–8, 261, 304–5; Thomas P. Abernethy, *The South in the New Nation, 1789–1819* (Baton Rouge, La, 1961), pp.266, 364–6.

[166]   While many younger Federalists worked hard to try to develop a larger popular base for their party, some of the old guard now looked towards a more radical solution. Some of the more extreme New Englanders began to talk and write of a separate northeastern confederacy. This group of separatists was small, and was to be frustrated by the lack of general support in New England, but it was no lunatic fringe. In the winter of 1803–4 Senator Timothy Pickering of Massachusetts, who had served as Secretary of State in the 1790s, and Representative Roger Griswold of Connecticut took the lead in attempting to shape a movement that would provide for the separation of the Northeast from the Union. They had a variety of complaints about a 'southern government,' but at the heart of their despair was a belief that westward expansion, culminating in the Louisiana purchase, was destroying northeastern commercial interests by placing the region in a permanent political minority.

    The small group of Federalists in the Senate felt particularly frustrated at their political impotence, and of the six New England Federalist senators four – Pickering, William Plumer of New Hampshire, and Uriah Tracy and James Hillhouse of Connecticut – thought separation had become necessary. In the House, along with Griswold of Connecticut, Calvin Goddard of the same state and Samuel Hunt of New Hampshire supported this move. The tone of their objections was well expressed by one of Pickering's sympathetic friends, Stephen Higginson. 'The Virginia faction have certainly formed a deliberate plan to govern and depress New England,' he wrote, 'and this eagerness to extend our territory and create new States is an essential part of it.'[25]

    Late in January 1804 Pickering tried to influence George Cabot to support separation. Cabot, he hoped, would be able to influence what survived of the old 'Essex Junto,' a group whose influence on New England politics had become slight, but which still carried the weight of influential New England names. Pickering said he did not believe in the practicability of a long continued union. He told another of his correspondents that the northern states could not resist the power that the South had gained from the three-fifths compromise. Cabot gave Pickering no support for separation. There was no popular backing for it. For all the perceived evils of the

---

25   Higginson to Pickering, 22 Nov. 1803, in 'Letters of Stephen Higginson, 1783–1804,' in *American Historical Association, Annual Report*, 1896, vol. 1 (Washington, DC, 1896), p.837; Turner, *Plumer*, pp.133–42; Hervey P. Prentiss, *Timothy Pickering as the Leader of New England Federalism, 1800–1815* (1934; rpr, New York, 1972), pp.23–30; Winfred E. Bernhard, *Fisher Ames: Federalist and Statesman, 1758–1808* (Chapel Hill, NC, 1965), pp.339–42.

southern and western domination of government, the evils of disunion seemed greater. Cabot told Pickering that separation was impractical at that time, though the situation might change if the government should have a war with Great Britain.[26] [167]

Pickering, who seemed the least willing of the disaffected to abandon plans for a separate northeastern confederacy, now tried to influence New York politicians in his plans. He asked Rufus King how, without separation, the northeastern states, would ever 'rid themselves of negro Presidents and negro Congresses.' King had far too much respect for the Union to go along with Pickering.[27]

With influential leaders in his own party declining to go along with his plans Pickering hoped that he might be able to work through Republican Vice-President Aaron Burr. In 1804 Burr was trying to recoup his political fortunes by running for governor of New York against Morgan Lewis, the choice of the state Republican establishment. Burr's unwillingness to withdraw gracefully from the tied presidential contest with Jefferson in 1801 had alienated many within his party, his career as a national figure in the Republican party appeared to be in ruins, and he had a reputation for unscrupulousness. To win in New York he was willing to accept Federalist support.

Any hopes that the conspirators or Burr might have had in New York were dashed when Alexander Hamilton refused to support him. Hamilton had long distrusted Burr, and to make sure he would not become president Hamilton had thrown his support behind Jefferson in the tied presidential race of 1801. His low opinion of Burr, and his attacks on Burr's character, were common gossip, and appeared in the press. Burr felt he had suffered from Hamilton's attacks for too long, and challenged him to a duel. Dueling was still common in the United States during the early republic, and, in spite of efforts to stamp it out, remained a feature of public life for several decades into the nineteenth century. To avoid New York laws the duelists went to Weehawken, New Jersey, and on 11 July 1804 Burr shot and mortally wounded the great intellectual leader of the Federalist party, the man who had done more than any other to shape the earliest policies of the American government under the Constitution.[28] He died the next day.

26 Henry Adams (ed.), *Documents Relating to New-England Federalism, 1800–1815* (Boston, Mass, 1977), pp.338–49; Prentiss, *Pickering*, pp.25–6; David H. Fischer, 'The myth of the Essex Junto,' *WMQ* 3rd Ser., 21(1964), pp.191–25.
27 King (ed.), *Life and Correspondence of King*, 4, pp.360–6.
28 Milton Lomask, *Aaron Burr* 2 vols (New York, 1979–82), 1, pp.333–55.

There was no doubt now that Burr's career as a national politician was over, but there was no law against dueling in New Jersey, and Burr completed his term as vice-president of the United States. In some areas beyond the Alleghenies he was admired for what he had done. His last major duty as vice-president was to preside over the impeachment trial of Associate Justice Samuel Chase of the Supreme Court. Before that happened Jefferson had been re-elected, and a new vice-president had been chosen.

The election of 1800, with its tied electoral vote for Jefferson and Burr, had convinced leading politicians that the Constitutional provision that elected both president and vice-president on the same ticket had to be changed before the next presidential election. Congress agreed on a revised plan in its 1803–4 session, and the states approved it in time for the 1804 election. Electors would now vote on a separate ticket for the vice-president. It was also agreed that should no presidential candidate obtain a majority of the electoral votes, the House of Representatives, with each state delegation casting one vote, would choose from the three with the highest number of votes.[29]

A Congressional caucus of the Republicans unanimously nominated Jefferson for re-election. For his running mate, the Republicans kept their strong Virginia–New York alliance by nominating George Clinton. The Federalists faced major difficulties. The transition from a Federalist government to that of the Republicans had occurred without any of the disasters that the Federalists had prophesied. There was still an effective federal government, but it was a government that was much more attuned to the popular will than that of the Federalists. Many Americans held the sentiment expressed by 'A Mechanic' in a New York newspaper: 'We mechanics and plain men are never noticed by federalists except at and about the election.'[30]

Jefferson had enjoyed a lucky first term. A key factor was peace in Europe from 1801 to 1803. In spite of all the Republican railing against trade with Great Britain, trade was flourishing in these years. American revenues from tariffs on imports increased, so that the Jeffersonians could both cut taxes and decrease the national debt. The Louisiana purchase also greatly helped the Republican party. Jefferson had been able to double the size of the country by peaceful negotiation. The general mood in the country was that this was a great addition to the nation. Not only had the Republicans secured permanent access to the Gulf, they had also provided the land for future

29 Marshall Smelser, *The Democratic Republic, 1801–1815* (New York, 1968), pp.74–5.
30 *NYCA*, p.81 (11 Apr. 1807).

generations. In their intense opposition to the Louisiana purchase the Federalists were ignoring the wishes of the many Americans who were looking to the Mississippi Valley, not to the Atlantic.

Westward expansion was continually weakening the Federalists. The new states – Kentucky, Tennessee, and Ohio – were overwhelmingly Democratic–Republican. The Federalists continued to have strength in New England, but even there the old elite was too often out of touch with the desires of the mass of the population. In the 1804 election, in an effort to broaden their appeal in the South, the Federalists threw their support behind Charles Cotesworth Pinckney of South Carolina, a state that had a strong Federalist party in the 1790s. The Federalist effort to broaden the base of the party was a sad failure. The election was a crushing victory for Jefferson. He obtained 162 electoral votes to just 14 for Pinckney. Pinckney's votes came from Connecticut (nine), Delaware (three), and Maryland (two). Only Connecticut and Delaware had a majority for Pinckney, for Maryland also gave nine electoral votes to Jefferson. Even Massachusetts had more popular votes for Jefferson than Pinckney.[31]

As Jefferson and George Clinton took office in the spring of 1805, Aaron Burr was following the ruinous course he had taken since tying Jefferson in the 1801 electoral vote. In the years following the killing of Hamilton Burr engaged in a conspiracy whose details are still difficult to interpret; difficult because Burr told different stories to different people, and perhaps because he was engaged in an opportunist plunge rather than a coherent plot. At times the whole affair has more the atmosphere of a bad novel than an epic conspiracy.

After his duel with Hamilton in July 1804 Burr went to Philadelphia, and while there talked to the British minister Anthony Merry. Merry reported to England that Burr had talked of the possibility of separating the West from the Union. After Burr's term as vice-president ended he again talked to Merry. He now told him that the Territory of Orleans wanted to leave the Union. In the winter of 1804–5 Burr had met a delegation from New Orleans that was in Washington to protest the autocratic nature of American rule. Burr told Merry he needed a large loan, and a British squadron at the mouth of the Mississippi. It is, possible, however, that Burr was more interested in gaining the money for other purposes. Others, particularly westerners, were to hear from Burr of plans for the invasion of Spanish territory, and Burr was later to claim that his object in the West was land speculation.

31 Manning Dauer, 'Election of 1804,' in S&I, 1, pp.159–82.

[1 7 0]   In 1805 and 1806 Burr twice traveled into the Mississippi Valley. His main recruit was a wealthy Irish immigrant, Harman Blennerhassett, who was enlisted with vague promises of adventure and money. Burr was warmly welcomed in Kentucky, Tennessee, and New Orleans, stayed with Andrew Jackson, met Henry Clay, and also talked with General James Wilkinson. In the early 1790s Wilkinson had managed to combine service in the American army with payments from the Spanish in New Orleans. Though Wilkinson was eventually to escape unscathed, he seems to have been involved with whatever Burr was doing from almost the beginning.

Burr was quite indiscreet, but his talk was more of invading Spanish territory than separating the West. The removal of the Spanish from the Gulf had long been of interest to the westerners. In 1797, Senator William Blount of Tennessee had been expelled from the Senate for secretly trying to secure British aid for a filibustering attack on Spanish Louisiana and the Floridas.[32] Burr, who was more interested in recouping his fortunes than in any specific territorial aim, believed that he could even involve the Spanish in his plans. When he returned east he secretly approached the Marqués de Casa Yrujo, the Spanish minister in the United States. As with the British, he broached the plan of western separation. This time he also introduced an outlandish plot of men in disguise seizing the president, and possibly taking over the Washington Navy Yard before sailing to New Orleans and establishing an independent country. Like the British, the Spanish provided no money.

Rumors that Burr was engaged in devious maneuvers had by this time even reached Jefferson, but it all sounded so unlikely that nothing was done. In the summer of 1806 Burr again went west. As his strange schemes began to unravel, they became more outlandish. Blennerhassett, who unlike the British and the Spanish gave Burr a lot of money, understood Burr was going to invade Mexico, become king, and confer titles of nobility. A variety of rumors flew, newspaper articles were printed (Blennerhassett even wrote some), and letters of warning were sent to Washington. Jefferson at last acted. In October 1806 he warned that Burr should be watched, sent an agent to discover what he was doing, and ordered that if Burr committed any overt act he should be arrested.

In November Burr was brought before a Grand Jury in Kentucky. He was freed, but everything now unraveled. Blennerhassett talked to Jefferson's agent, and Wilkinson, deciding the time had come to desert Burr, wrote to warn Jefferson of a conspiracy to take New Orleans and invade Spanish

32   William H. Masterson, *William Blount* (New York, 1954), pp.302–23.

territory. Late in the month Jefferson issued a proclamation warning citizens [1 7 1]
to withdraw from any conspiracy against Spain. Burr did actually meet up
with some recruits for his expedition (less than 100), but warrants were out
for his arrest. He eventually surrendered in Mississippi Territory, where a
Grand Jury rejected the charges against him. Burr traveled east, but was
arrested again.

As the conspiracy had happened within the Virginia district of the federal
courts, Burr's trial was before Chief Justice John Marshall in Richmond,
Virginia. Burr was prosecuted by the Attorney-General, Caesar Rodney,
and had some of the best lawyers in the country to defend him. The initial
proceedings were before a Grand Jury to decide if Burr and Blennerhassett
should be charged with treason for plotting to separate parts of the West
from the Union. Marshall, at the request of Burr, issued a subpoena to
Jefferson, but Jefferson ignored it. Wilkinson appeared as a witness, and the
Grand Jury agreed that charges should be brought. The trial began in August
1807. Jefferson very much wanted a conviction, and it seems possible that
Marshall had decided not to give him what he desired. By the Constitution,
two witnesses to the overt act were needed. As Burr had not been present at
Blennerhassett's Island in the Ohio when the expedition set out, Marshall
found reasons to give a charge to the jury that resulted in his acquittal. The
government now tried Burr on the charge of levying war against Spain.
Again he was acquitted.[33]

Burr's public career had, of course, ended. He lived until 1836. A few
years earlier, at the age of 77, he had married a rich widow. She was just
obtaining her divorce from him on the grounds of adultery as he died.[34] If
Burr had graciously deferred to Jefferson in the tied vote of 1801, he could
well have become president in 1809. For Jefferson, the problems caused by
Burr were only a small part of the trials he suffered in his second term. The
generally good fortune he had enjoyed in his first years as president was succeeded by foreign policy problems that left him longing to leave office by
the end of his second term.

---

33   See Thomas P. Abernethy, *The Burr Conspiracy* (New York, 1954); Abernethy, *South in the
     New Nation*, pp.261–96; Leonard Baker, *John Marshall: A Life in Law* (New York, 1974),
     pp.447–518.

34   Lomask, *Burr*, 2, pp.395–403.

CHAPTER 11

FOREIGN TRIALS

After the renewal of the European war in 1803, American foreign trade continued to flourish. Since Jay's Treaty, the British had treated American neutral commerce with moderation, and American shippers were growing rich on the profits of the re-export trade, primarily from the West Indies. The British government had abandoned its earlier insistence that the Americans should not engage in a trade that they were banned from in peacetime, and American shippers had been allowed to ship goods from the French West Indies to France by means of the 'broken voyage;' American ships first called at an American port before proceeding to Europe. This boom period for America was to end not simply because of far more intrusive policies by the European belligerents but because of the way that the Democratic–Republican administrations chose to respond to British and French policies.

After 1803 the war in Europe became far more a life or death struggle for both England and France. To achieve his larger continental ambitions, Napoleon was determined to defeat Great Britain, the country with the resources to back the coalitions that resisted his plans. Immediately after 1803 it seemed likely that he would invade England. As he massed his barges and his invasion forces, the British placed their trust in their naval power, fitting out and manning all the warships they could muster. Even after the danger of invasion vanished, the British believed that naval strength was essential for the defeat of Napoleon.

The new intensity in the European struggle was first felt in the United States because of the British practice of impressment. In time of war, the British manned their ships by seizing merchant seamen and forcing them to serve in the regular navy. British merchant or fishing vessels returning to port were in constant danger of being stopped by a warship and having members of their crew removed. Press-gangs also roamed the port towns, visiting the grog shops and brothels, to find their recruits for the Royal Navy. Conditions in the regular navy were brutal, and not surprisingly desertions were frequent. For ships in American waters, a favorite destination for deserters was the United States. The American merchant navy offered much better pay and conditions, and the American freedoms that attracted persecuted British radicals also proved a draw to British sailors.

To dissuade others, the British navy ardently sought its deserters. After war had broken out in the 1790s, British seamen from American ships in British ports were seized by press-gangs and at times Americans were also taken. This issue was complicated by the British doctrine of inalienable allegiance (which meant that those born in Great Britain were never freed from their obligation to serve), by the presence of American sailors on British ships, and by the ease with which deserters could obtain false papers. A British sailor who had legitimately emigrated to the United States after the Revolution might be seized. There was also the additional difficulty that seamen paid off from one ship in a foreign port might well sign up on a ship of another nation. Some Americans who were impressed might have actually deserted from a British ship. A much greater problem, however, was that press-gangs needing seamen often did not bother to distinguish between British and American seamen, and many American seamen were impressed into the British navy.

Before 1801 the British navy had been reasonably cautious in the ways that its impressment had infringed on American rights, but in the crisis situation after 1803 caution was soon abandoned. In 1804 and 1805 it became a regular practice for British warships to stop American merchant vessels on the high seas to search for deserters. They would also routinely do the same thing when they stopped ships in the course of the various blockades that were enforced in these years. The American government claimed that from the renewal of the European war in 1803 to April 1806 some 2,800 seamen were impressed; more than in all the war years of the 1790s.[1] From 1803 to 1812 impressment became a source of aggravation to American political leaders and to the American public. Ironically, the least vociferous were often American shipowners and maritime interests. Their profits from trade were such that they were willing to take, or were willing that their seamen should take, the risks that it entailed.

In June 1804 maritime aggression reached the shores of the United States when British warships arrived off New York. They were at first interested in French ships that were anchored there, but they caused an uproar when they

---

1   The figures are from James F. Zimmerman, *The Impressment of American Seamen* (New York, 1925), p.263.

entered the harbor itself to impress 14 seamen from a British merchant ship, and when they remained off the port to stop and search scores of American ships.[2] Jefferson was still absorbed with his plans for the acquisition of the Spanish Floridas, and actions that at a different time would likely have inspired him to an ardent attack on British arrogance hardly stirred him. He wrote in mid-September that the English administration was 'entirely cordial,' and that there had never been a time when the American 'flag had been so little molested by them in the European seas.' The British recalled one of their captains for violating an American port, but his career was unhurt. In the following year he was promoted to command a ship of the line.[3]

In the winter of 1804–5 the impressment problem began to bring some tentative reactions both in the cabinet and Congress. At the beginning of the new year James Monroe, who had succeeded Federalist Rufus King as the minister to Great Britain, was instructed by Madison to press for a convention that would deal primarily with impressment, but would also try to obtain British agreement on some of the American interpretations of her rights of trade in time of war. In Congress, a bill was introduced to give the president the power to prohibit the provisioning of any ship that had been engaged in impressing seamen from American vessels. The British delayed action on any convention, but as yet there were few signs that the American leaders were prepared to take any strong stance. In March Madison informed Monroe that a Congressional bill regarding impressment had been postponed, that conciliation appeared to be the object, and that 'the present administration in Great Britain appears more liberal and cordial towards the United States than any preceding one.'[4]

The impressment issue was soon to be compounded, however, by major American concerns about British restrictions on American commerce. The British administration of William Pitt that had taken office in the spring of 1804 was determined to pursue the war against Napoleon with greater vigor, and a major concern of the government was the degree to which English naval power was nullified by American ships replacing the French ships that the British had swept from the seas. British fears involved more than simply the current war effort. The British shipping interest feared

---

2   George L. Rives (ed.), *Selections from the Correspondence of Thomas Barclay* (New York, 1894), pp.162–205; Captain Basil Hall, *Fragments of Voyages and Travels*, new edn (London, 1842), pp.46–9.

3   Jefferson to Levi Lincoln, 16 Sept. 1804, in *WOTJ*, 10, p.104; *IBM*, p.209, n.18.

4   Madison to Monroe, 8 Mar. 1804, *Letters and Other Writings of James Madison* 4 vols (Philadelphia, 1867), 2, pp.200–1.

that American shippers were using the war to challenge their supremacy. They pointed out that the Americans were hindering the struggle against Napoleon by engaging extensively in a carrying trade between the French West Indies and France, and that they were also being allowed into the British West Indies in violation of the British Navigation Laws. The shipping interest, and their many supporters, argued that as British naval supremacy and British power itself depended on the continued supremacy of the British at sea, steps should be taken to curb the expansion of American trade.[5]

The first real indication that the British were preparing to check American trade with France came in the summer of 1805 when a British appeals court issued the *Essex* decision. The British were no longer prepared to look leniently on the American trade between the French West Indies and France. In the *Essex* decision, the British court decided that the 'broken voyage,' by which American ships evaded British restrictions by first calling at an American port, did not legalize the trade unless a proper import duty was paid; what was important was the ultimate destination of the goods. In enforcing this policy the British did what they had done at the very beginning of the wars with France in 1793; they began seizing American ships before officially informing the Americans of the decision. Throughout the summer and fall extensive seizures were made. The days of easy profits from the European wars were over.[6]

Yet, when Congress assembled in the fall of 1805, Jefferson's mind was still on the Floridas. As Spain was allied with France, Jefferson thought that British naval power could serve to help rather than hurt the United States. His preoccupation, first with Louisiana in general, and then with the Floridas, meant that his reaction to changing and more severe British policies was delayed. Jefferson at this time was far less pro-French and anti-English than he had been ten years earlier. A key element in this was the coming to power of Napoleon, and his assumption of the title of Emperor in 1804. Jefferson hated monarchy and emperors and military adventurers. Napoleon's course of action after 1803 did much to sour Jefferson on the French. The Louisiana crisis also made Jefferson very aware of potential dangers from a revived, aggressive France.

Jefferson tried to obtain the Floridas by making use of some of the techniques by which he had sought Louisiana. He suggested, as he had during

5   Reginald Horsman, *The Causes of the War of 1812* (Philadelphia, 1962), pp.31–8.
6   Bradford Perkins, *The First Rapprochement: England and the United States, 1795–1805* (Philadelphia, 1955), pp.177–80.

his preparations for the purchase of Florida, that it might be necessary to seek an alliance with Great Britain if Spain did not prove more agreeable. He was concerned that Spain's refusal to yield to American pressure stemmed from her renewed closeness to France. Since December 1804 Spain had been at war with England, and in August 1805 Jefferson suggested to Madison that they should consider proposing a treaty of alliance with England, to come into force when war took place with France or Spain. 'I am strongly impressed,' Jefferson wrote to Madison, 'with a belief of hostile and treacherous intentions against us on the part of France.'[7]

In the summer and fall of 1805 Jefferson appeared to take the possibility of an alliance with England much more seriously than he had at the time of the Louisiana negotiations. He seemed to believe that he could secure a temporary alliance with England for the purpose of securing the territorial aims of the United States on the Gulf. In suggesting this he had to ignore the increasingly rigorous English policies towards the United States at sea, his own constant warnings that the United States would be harmed by close ties to Great Britain, and the likelihood that England would require substantial commitments from the United States if she were to help the United States secure her territorial objectives against the Spanish. Madison pointed out to Jefferson that England would not commit herself to aiding the United States without something in return.[8]

Jefferson's annual message was warlike in its references to Spain, but he followed it with a secret, more peaceful message to Congress that indicated that negotiation might secure American objectives. He had learned from Europe that it might be possible to use French influence to obtain West Florida from Spain. Congress proved willing to provide $2,000,000 for negotiations, but only after an acrimonious debate. When it was realized that Jefferson's underlying object was to use the money to persuade France to pressure Spain, Virginian John Randolph, who had been one of the Republican leaders in the House of Representatives, objected to Jefferson's maneuvering, and began the process that was to estrange him completely from the administration. In the following years he was to pursue his own course, often railing at the policies pursued by both the Jefferson and the Madison administrations, while completely rejecting the Federalists. Randolph's revolt, and Federalist opposition, delayed the voting of money. By the time the measure passed Congress in February 1806 the administration found

7   Jefferson to Madison, 4, 7, 25 Aug. 1805, JP.
8   Madison to Jefferson, 1 Sept. 1805, JP.

that it could not enlist French help in obtaining Spanish territory. Napoleon [1 7 7]
had lost interest in the proposal.[9]

Jefferson never gave up his hope of obtaining the Floridas, but it
remained for the Madison administration to begin the process of actually
acquiring them. Jefferson's interest in the Floridas was primarily to make
sure that American farmers had access to the Gulf for their exports, but he
also believed that the corrupt, decadent monarchy of Spain should be expelled
from a continent that was destined for the expansion of republicanism.

Randolph was not the only Republican who was becoming disillusioned
with the actions of the party. In the years after 1801, as the Republican
administration demonstrated a willingness to make a broad use of federal
power, other party members began to have qualms about the administration
policies. They were not as vituperative and extreme as Randolph, but the
'Old Republicans' gradually came to believe that the party was betraying the
principles upon which it had been founded in the 1790s. The Senate also
developed a small group of Republican dissidents who often disagreed with
administration policies, and at times even sided with the Federalists. The
most vocal, particularly after Jefferson left the presidency, were William
Branch Giles of Virginia and Samuel Smith of Maryland. Although Republican factionalism caused much difficulty in the Madison presidency, the
impact of Republican dissidents was weakened by the imbalance between
the two national parties. Even with its dissidents not giving steady support
the Republicans had enough of a majority over the Federalist opposition to
pass what they wanted.[10]

The process by which the European war between England and France
became one of blockade and counter-blockade increased rapidly in 1805
and 1806. After Nelson's victory at Trafalgar in October 1805 the seas
belonged to England. United States shipping still encountered French privateers, and American ships that found their way into French ports might
suffer from Napoleonic whims, but England was now able to begin plans for
a general blockade of the continent of Europe. The necessity of taking this
step was increased for England by the remarkable success Napoleon was
achieving in his campaigns on land in 1805 and 1806. Napoleon defeated

9   *MO&P*, 1, pp.384–5 (3 Dec. 1805); *WOTJ*, 10, pp.198–205 (6 Dec. 1805); Clifford Egan,
    Neither Peace Nor War: Franco-American Relations, 1803–1812 (Baton Rouge, La, 1983),
    pp.47–66.
10 See Norman K. Risjord, *The Old Republicans: Southern Conservatism in the Age of Jefferson* (New
    York, 1965), pp.2–145; Robert A. Rutland, *The Presidency of James Madison* (Lawrence, Kans,
    1990), pp.11–17.

[1 7 8] the Austrians at Ulm, the Russians at Austerlitz, and the Prussians at Jena and Auerstadt. With England supreme on the sea and France supreme on the land, the two countries tried to fight each other by economic means; England by blockading France and her possessions, France by closing the continent to English trade.

For England and France the United States was a weak, little power, far away across the Atlantic. What the United States thought was unimportant. As the most important commercial neutral, the United States still had great opportunities for profit, but trade would only be carried on under severe restrictions and harassment. Merchants were prepared to endure this, but the American government and the American public wanted respect as well as profit.

In London, the American minister James Monroe saw at first hand England's determination to use every effort to defeat Napoleon, and was also made fully aware of the resentment the British shipping interest felt at the profits of American shippers. He wrote to Jefferson in November to warn him of British hostility, and suggested the possibility of strengthening the American navy and militia and commercial discrimination against Great Britain.[11]

In the winter of 1805–6, as the American Congress was discussing the contentious Florida issue, it also turned to deal with the impact of the *Essex* decision on American commerce. American merchants were irate at the change in British policy, and Secretary of State Madison had reacted by writing a long pamphlet examining British policy towards neutral trade. At the beginning of the year members of Congress received copies of Madison's pamphlet, *Examination of the British Doctrine*. It was a long attack on the British efforts to prevent neutrals trading with enemy colonies.[12]

In late January, when Congress took up the question of retaliation against Great Britain, Andrew Gregg of Pennsylvania introduced a measure calling for a ban on the importation of British goods until the United States grievances about impressment and the seizures of ships under the British Rule of 1756 had been resolved. This measure was too extreme for many, and Joseph Nicholson of Maryland suggested limiting non-importation to goods that could be obtained elsewhere or made in America. Both Jefferson and Madison supported Nicholson's resolution. It was the type of discrimination

11 Monroe to Jefferson, 1 Nov. 1805, JP.
12 Madison to Monroe, 24 Sept. 1805, MADP; Madison to Jefferson, 5 Oct. 1805, JP; Anthony Merry to Mulgrave, 30 Sept., 1805, 2 Feb. 1806, FO 5/45, 5/48.

against British commerce that they had pressed for in the early 1790s, and they both had great faith in commercial discrimination as a way to force a change in British policy. In the Congressional debate most of the support was for partial rather than total non-importation, but John Randolph poured scorn on those who thought they could challenge the might of Great Britain at sea. He drew a distinction between carrying the products of American agriculture abroad and the re-export trade from the West Indies, a trade that had simply developed as a result of the European war. He did not think that the United States should risk war with England to defend the special wartime profits of the American shipping interest.[13]

The Non-importation Act for selective non-importation against Great Britain was finally given approval by the Senate in April 1806. Its long list of prohibited articles included hemp, flax, and some woolen goods.[14] Ultimately, however, it was not to be enforced until near the end of 1807. The reason for the delay was that Jefferson and Madison were now extremely confident that they could achieve a satisfactory settlement with England, and that the threat of non-importation could be used to speed the negotiations. The optimism was the result of news from England that Prime Minister William Pitt had died in January, and that a Whig ministry, led by Lord Grenville and Charles James Fox, had been formed. Jefferson much admired Charles James Fox, and had great hopes for his friendship for America. The Americans were soon to discover that while a Whig ministry was more conciliatory it did not end the seizures and blockades that infuriated American opinion.[15]

In the spring of 1806 the administration sent William Pinkney of Maryland to join James Monroe in London to negotiate an agreement with Great Britain. Impressment and problems of neutral trade were to be the main objects of the negotiations, but the envoys were also to discuss replacing the commercial sections of Jay's Treaty that were expiring in 1807. The instructions displayed an unwise confidence that the British would accept the American position on several vital issues. Madison told the envoys that England would have to give up impressment, restore the treatment of neutral trade to the situation existing before the *Essex* decision, and pay for spoliations that resulted from it. Jefferson told Monroe that he thought the changes in the British government were 'assuring us a just settlement of our

13   *AC*, 9th Cong., 1st Sess., pp.412–13, 537–823.
14   Ibid., pp.240, 1259–62.
15   See Jefferson to Thomas Paine, 25 Mar. 1806, *WOTJ*, 10, p.248; Jefferson to Monroe, 4 May, 1806, MONP.

[1 8 0] differences,' but Madison had more doubts than Jefferson that England would agree to American demands. Jefferson might have been less confident if he had known that the British minister in the United States, Anthony Merry, was advising his government that resistance to the American demands 'will only be attended with the Salutary Effect of commanding from this Government that Respect which they have nearly lost towards Great Britain.'[16]

Even before Pinkney reached England in June there were signs that negotiations would not be as easy as Jefferson expected. Whoever was in power in England, the navy in wartime was hard to control. In late April there was an outcry in America when British ships operating directly outside the port of New York went too far in their efforts to stop and search American shipping. In firing a warning shot, the *Leander* killed a seaman. The body was laid out for citizens to see, and a New York mob seized provisions that were intended for the British ships and burnt a British flag. Memories and stories of the Revolution were vivid for many Americans, and deaths from British action stirred popular emotions.[17]

Jefferson's hopes that the new Whig ministry of Grenville and Fox would be more friendly towards the United States were, in part, realized. Much Whig support came from the manufacturing interests, and the manufacturers very much depended on the American market. The anti-American British shipping interest gave its support to the Tories. A major problem for the Americans was that in this whole era the Whigs only held office from early 1806 to early 1807. The Whigs made some gestures towards friendship with the United States. The anti-American and often obnoxious British minister Anthony Merry was recalled and replaced with the pro-American David Erskine, who had an American wife. Also, the new government, against vocal opposition from the Tories and the British shipping interest, pushed through the American Intercourse Bill. For the duration of the war, this gave neutrals the right of limited trade with the British West Indies. This trade, which was officially prohibited, had been going on sporadically since 1793 because the British West Indies had a desperate need for American supplies. West Indian governors had allowed goods in under the excuse of emergency, and the British Parliament had regularly passed acts of indemnity. The Whigs decided to make this wartime violation of the Navigation Laws legal.

16   Jefferson to Monroe, 16 March, 4 May 1806 (quotation), MONP; Madison to Monroe and Pinkney, 17 May 1806, *ASP, FR*, 3, pp.119–24; Merry to Charles James Fox, 4 May 1806, FO 5/49.

17   Rives (ed.), *Barclay Correspondence*, pp.230–41.

The Whigs were prepared to accept American trade with the British West [1 8 1] Indies because it was in the British as well as the American interest, but no one who wished to defeat Napoleon could argue that the American re-export trade in the produce of the French West Indies was anything but profitable for the United States and France. Fox, however, was looking for compromise with the United States, and in May 1806 the British government somewhat modified the *Essex* decision by issuing what became known as 'Fox's blockade.' This declared a blockade of the European coast from the Elbe to Brest, but it would only be enforced strictly from Ostend to the Seine. Neutral vessels could trade outside this area, provided they were not carrying contraband, and providing that they had not come from, or were not sailing to, an enemy port.[18]

For the Americans, however, Fox's blockade was simply another cause for complaint. In defining neutral rights, the United States objected bitterly to the idea of a 'paper blockade.' For a blockade to be legal the Americans insisted that ships had actually to hover off the port or stretch of coast that was being blockaded. In these years both the British and the French frequently declared that whole long stretches of coast or whole countries were in a state of blockade. Such a blockade was enforced against American shipping by simply stopping and searching ships wherever they could be found – off the American coast, in the Atlantic, or in the Channel. The Whigs viewed Fox's blockade as a moderate measure, far more moderate than the measures that the Tories wished to pursue, but to the Americans it was simply another example of British arrogance towards neutral trade.

Monroe and Pinkney decided that they would have to ignore the American government's insistence that the British renounce impressment in any treaty. The most that the British negotiators would agree to was a statement that they would be careful not to impress American citizens. The treaty that was signed on 31 December 1806 was the best that the American negotiators could obtain. Like John Jay in 1794, they had discovered that the British would not give up their maritime rights in order to appease the United States. Yet, because this was an English Whig, rather than Tory, ministry there was an attempt to reach a compromise on the question of the American re-export trade from the French West Indies. It was stated that the American vessels could bring the produce of the enemy colonies to the non-blockaded ports of France and Spain, and return with goods to the colonies, if the 'broken voyage' was carried out, and a very modest duty paid

18   Horsman, *Causes*, pp.69–80.

[182] in American ports; 2 per cent on the trip to Europe, and 1 per cent on the return.[19]

The Whigs wanted American trade, particularly keeping the United States as the main market for British manufactured goods, but ultimately the United States was a minor consideration when compared to the war against Napoleon. In December, before the treaty with the United States was signed, the British received news that Napoleon's land victories of 1805 and 1806 were to be followed by commercial warfare against Great Britain, commercial warfare that would be directed against American as well as British shipping. The Berlin Decree of 21 November 1806 declared a blockade of the whole of Great Britain, and prohibited any trade in British goods. This meant that French warships and privateers that could escape the British blockade of France would seize any neutral ships trading with Great Britain, and, more significantly, any ships coming from British ports were banned entry to continental ports controlled by France (at a time when France was beginning to control much of Europe). Monroe and Pinkney were informed that, unless the United States resisted the French decree, England could not promise to uphold the terms of the treaty that had just been signed.[20]

It is almost certain that if there had been some swift means of communication between the American negotiators and the American government no treaty would have been signed. Jefferson's reaction to the earlier news that the British negotiators were insisting on retaining the right of impressment had been that, without a renunciation of this right, it would be better to have no treaty. Both Jefferson and Madison found both the treaty, and the accompanying note regarding the British reaction to Napoleon's Berlin Decree, unacceptable. Jefferson quickly made the decision that he would not submit the treaty to the Senate for ratification.

To compare the reception of the Monroe and Pinkney Treaty by Jefferson and Madison to that of Jay's Treaty by Washington and Hamilton is also to compare the very different approach of the Federalists and the Republicans to American foreign policy. Hamilton had convinced Washington that above all else the United States needed to avoid a break with Great Britain. Although Jefferson was now disillusioned with France, and had even toyed with the idea of an alliance with England to obtain Spanish territory, he believed that commercial ties with England were less important than

---

19 Horsman, *Causes*, pp.83–92; Donald Hickey, *The War of 1812: A Forgotten Conflict* (Urbana, Ill, 1989), pp.13–16.
20 *ASP, FR*, 3, pp.151–2.

American neutral rights. He ignored the reality that his administration's [1 8 3] financial policies, national solvency, and American commercial prosperity in an era of general European war depended on trade with Great Britain and on some British acquiescence in American trade to Europe. He also ignored the reality that the sharp reductions in support to the army and navy made any policy but close ties with Great Britain extremely dangerous. The Federalist reaction to British infringements of American rights was to swallow pride, and to remember the balance sheets; Jefferson's was to assert what he believed were the rights of the young republic.

Yet, while the Federalists had been far more willing than the Republicans to reach an accommodation with Great Britain, they also enjoyed the advantage that in the 1790s American trade was not burdened with the extreme regulations and vagaries of policy that it faced in Europe from 1806 to 1812. The *Essex* decision and Napoleon's Berlin Decree were only the beginning. The European powers were to ignore American sensibilities in their efforts to work out systems of blockade and counter-blockade that would enable them to win the war. Even an administration that was more concerned about balance sheets than abstract rights would have had trouble reining in Congressional and public opinion in the face of the extreme policies of both England and France.

Monroe and Pinkney were told that ratification was impossible, but that negotiations should continue. If the treaty could not be put into an acceptable form – which to Jefferson meant a British renunciation of the right of impressment – the American negotiators were told to back out of the negotiations while trying to preserve a 'friendly understanding.'[21] A Republican ally of Jefferson wrote to Monroe that Jefferson would not accept the treaty because of impressment and the British reaction to the Berlin Decree, and as the president enjoyed great popularity 'his will is that of the nation.'[22]

The initial British reaction to the Berlin Decree was moderate only in relation to what was to come later. In January 1807 the Whig government issued an Order in Council that banned all neutral coastal trade between ports in the hands of the enemy. This would affect American ships that frequently dropped off their cargo in one port and then went to others to pick up goods for the return voyage. In England, however, the Tories launched an attack on the government for the feebleness of its response, accusing it of

---

21   Jefferson to Monroe, 21 Mar. 1806 (quotation), MONP; Madison to Monroe, 20 Mar. 1806, MADP.
22   Joseph H. Nicholson to Monroe, 12 Apr. 1807, MONP.

[1 8 4] adopting a weak policy of commercial retaliation against France out of fear of offending the United States. In March 1807 the Whig administration fell, and the Tories resumed power.[23]

The Tories intended to carry out an economic war against Napoleon by all possible means, and they also believed that measures to reduce the growth of American shipping would have benefits for England even beyond defeating Napoleon. In the spring and summer of 1807 the new Tory government began to draft plans for a general blockade of Napoleonic Europe. With Jefferson insisting on defending American neutral rights, the United States and Great Britain were on a collision course.

The crisis that arrived initially came from the practice of impressment, not from the tightening restrictions on trade. In 1806 and 1807 British ships continued to hover off the American coast. They found this an excellent station both for intercepting French ships that took refuge in American ports, and for stopping and examining American merchant vessels. In spite of the friction this caused they also sent boats ashore to obtain provisions and water. The proximity to the American shores gave British seamen many opportunities to desert, and they took advantage of them.

In the early months of 1807 a British naval squadron was waiting in Chesapeake Bay for two French ships. Desertions reached a peak in March, when sailors stole a boat and rowed to shore. They joyfully paraded in Norfolk, Virginia, and some of them enlisted on American ships. It was said that some had even enlisted on one of the few frigates in the regular American navy – the *Chesapeake*. This caused complications because the British had never claimed the right to impress seamen from the warships of a foreign power; that was viewed as an infringement of national sovereignty. The British officers tried to get their deserters back by official appeals to the American authorities, but these produced no results.

When the British naval commander-in-chief at Halifax heard of these events he issued an order that if the *Chesapeake* was encountered she should be stopped and searched. On 22 June the *Chesapeake*, under the command of Commodore James Barron, sailed. When hailed by the British ship *Leopard* she hove to. A British lieutenant came aboard, and said that the ship had to be searched for deserters. Baron refused, and the British returned to their ship. When the *Chesapeake* got underway again the *Leopard* first fired a shot across her bows, and, when she still proceeded, fired into her, killing 3 and wounding 18. The American ship, which was leaving on a long cruise to the

23 Horsman, *Causes*, pp.95–100.

Mediterranean, was in no way prepared for action, and she struck her colors. [1 8 5] The British boarded and searched her, and took off four men that they claimed were British deserters.

While the diplomatic and economic results of the *Chesapeake* affair were to be momentous, on a human level the incident well illustrates the complications of the whole impressment question. The four seamen who were taken from the American ship had deserted from British ships, but three of them were American citizens. Of these, two were African Americans who had been impressed on to a British ship. William Ware, one of the African Americans, was a freedman, the son of a Maryland female slave of mixed ancestry and a white man. The other, Daniel Martin, was a Massachusetts free black, who had been brought into the state from Buenos Aires as a boy. The one actual British subject, a volunteer, was court martialed, found guilty, and hanged on board the ship from which he had deserted. William Ware died in hospital in Halifax in 1809. The other two men were finally freed in 1812.[24]

While the seized seamen suffered, Anglo-American relations reached boiling point. The *Chesapeake* returned to Norfolk, and there was uproar. All communication with British ships was forbidden, and their water casks were destroyed. As news reached other parts of the United States there was a popular outcry against the British. Throughout July protests, public meetings, and threats to the British occurred in all parts of the country. The British minister, David Erskine, reported that the United States was in ferment. Thomas Barclay, the British Consul-General in New York, wrote that 'the lower order of the Americans are much irritated and inclined for violent measures.'[25]

Jefferson was in a dilemma. This was the kind of British disregard of American rights that he had long warned about, yet his instincts were to avoid war. He might talk or write of it, as he had done in the Florida negotiations, but for Jefferson threats of military alliance or action were typically an accompaniment to a peaceful solution. There was also the obvious problem that the United States militarily was completely unprepared for war. Both the navy and the army were much weaker than when the Republicans had assumed power. Since the revolutionary era Jefferson had believed that

24   *ASP, FR*, 3, pp.6–18; John L. Emmerson, *The Chesapeake Affair of 1807* (Portsmouth, Va, 1954), pp.5–9, 17, 21–3, 76–7; Castlereagh to Foster, 4 Mar. 1812, in *IBM*, p.349; Spencer C. Tucker and Frank T. Reuter, *Injured Honor: The Chesapeake–Leopard Affair, June 22, 1807* (Annapolis, Md, 1996).

25   Erskine to Canning, 2, 4, 17, 31 July 1807, FO 5/52; Rives (ed.), *Barclay Correspondence*, p.264.

[1 8 6] the United States had the power to achieve its ends against Great Britain by economic means. Secretary of State Madison also had great faith in the power of economic coercion.

In the months following the *Chesapeake* incident Jefferson acted cautiously. He ordered British armed vessels to leave American waters, but instead of calling Congress into special session he decided to wait and see if the British would disavow this act of aggression. Monroe was instructed to seek this disavowal, reparations, and the return of the four seamen. If the instructions had stopped at this point, at least a partial solution might have been achieved reasonably quickly. The British would not hand over the actual British-born deserter among the four, but the American citizens were a different matter, and the British did not claim the right to impress from American ships of war. A quick solution was made impossible, however, because Monroe was also asked to obtain a disavowal of impressment. The British had already made it clear in the Monroe–Pinkney negotiations that they were not prepared to yield on the general impressment issue. This part of the instructions meant that the unredressed *Chesapeake* affair would remain a source of grievance in the years preceding the War of 1812.[26]

Historians are not in complete agreement about Jefferson's intentions in 1807, but it appears most likely, from both his actions and his statements, that he was hoping for peace. Given the slowness of early nineteenth-century communications, his decision to ask for redress of grievances, rather than calling Congress into emergency session for immediate action, meant that there would now be a three-month period for public passions to cool. The extent of the eventual reaction would be determined both by England's actions during the summer and Jefferson's thoughts on what would be the most effective way to produce a change in British policies. Congress would assemble late in 1807, and Jefferson had enough Congressional support for any action that he decided to take against Great Britain.

26   Madison to Monroe, 6 July 1807, in *WJM*, 7, pp.454–60.

CHAPTER 12

THE FAILURE OF ECONOMIC COERCION

By the time Congress assembled in October 1807 Jefferson had reached the conclusion that there was little chance of Britain giving the concessions he wanted. Even worse, there were strong rumors that the Tory government was about to enact even stronger measures against neutral commerce. The possibility of war had to be addressed by the administration, and in July Secretary of the Treasury Gallatin presented cost estimates. He expected to have to provide money to protect the coasts against British attack and to pay for the invasion of Canada. Jefferson, who just two years before had thought that he might have to ally with Great Britain to combat French support for Spanish possessions on the Gulf of Mexico, now reluctantly wished success to Bonaparte, pointing out that Britain was as tyrannical on the sea as Napoleon was on land. He was hoping that Napoleon's victories on the continent would again allow him to mass his armies in the Channel ports, and force the British to use all her ships far away from American waters.[1]

Jefferson still believed that impressment from American ships was the great stumbling block, but there was not the slightest sign from England that they were prepared to make concessions on this vital question. As the time neared for Congress to meet, Jefferson became increasingly concerned that this would mean that war might become necessary. Yet Jefferson and his cabinet members knew that the United States was ill prepared for war. When Gallatin read the draft of Jefferson's annual message he thought it was too hostile in its references to Great Britain, and told Jefferson that if there was a chance of agreement it would be best not to ruin it. The American public, he argued, would support a war if it came because of a British refusal to make reparation for the *Chesapeake* affair, but not a war because Britain would not give up the right of impressment. The United States needed more time for

---

1 Jefferson to Madison, 20 Aug. 1807, to Thomas Lieper, 21 Aug. 1807, JP; Raymond Walters, Jr, *Albert Gallatin: Jeffersonian Financier and Diplomat* (New York, 1957), pp.196–7; J. C. A. Stagg, *Mr Madison's War: Politics, Diplomacy, and Warfare in the Early Republic, 1783–1830* (Princeton, NJ, 1983), pp.136–7.

[1 8 8] preparations. The administration assumed that as Britain had supreme power at sea, war could only be waged by an invasion of Canada.[2]

Jefferson had no desire to use his influence to urge the country to war. He thought it might eventually have to come, but he still had faith that commercial retaliation could change British policies. It was in this mode of thinking that Jefferson turned towards embargo and economic coercion rather than to a fiery message that would inspire Congress to declare war. His opinion of Congress, a view also revealing of his own thoughts, was that the members appeared disposed for peace. He thought they were more inclined to combat British impressment by a non-importation act than by force of arms. He was still worried, however, that this might eventually lead to war. The initial advantage of an embargo was that in preventing American ships sailing it would reduce the number of American vessels at sea, and if war should come there would be fewer losses to British naval power. In mid-September Madison had suggested an embargo to Jefferson as a particularly effective means of forcing other nations to respect American rights. He believed that such a measure would particularly hurt the British West Indies.[3]

In the middle of December the Non-importation Act against selected British products, which had been passed and deferred in the previous year, was at last put into effect. Almost immediately news arrived of a new British proclamation, issued on 16 October, that ordered all British seamen serving on foreign vessels to return to England, and ordered the British navy to impress those who were serving on foreign merchant ships. It also stated that citizenship granted by foreign powers did not release British seamen from their obligations to Great Britain. The proclamation was a direct challenge to the American position on impressment.[4]

On 18 December the administration recommended to Congress that because of the dangers to American ships and seamen a measure should be passed to keep American vessels in American waters. Although the Federalists were appalled at this act, the Senate passed it on the same afternoon by a vote of 22 to 6. The House took a little longer, but by 22 December the president signed the embargo. The measure prohibited all American vessels sailing for foreign ports. They could engage in coastal trade, but would have to post bond. Foreign vessels could leave, but only in ballast. Many imports were directly prohibited by the Non-importation Act directed

---

2   Gallatin to Jefferson, 21 Oct. 1807, JP.
3   Jefferson to Randolph, 26 Oct. 1807, JP; Stagg, *Madison's War*, p.22.
4   *ASP, FR*, 3, pp.25–6; James F. Zimmerman, *The Impressment of American Seamen* (New York, 1925), pp.149–50.

against Great Britain, but other imports would now sharply diminish as [189] there presumably would be no American ships to carry them, and foreign ships would hardly find it worth their while coming to the United States as they could not carry American goods away.[5]

Any doubts Jefferson might have had about the necessity for the embargo ended soon after it was issued when news arrived that not only the British but also the French had enacted sweeping new regulations against neutral commerce. In November Great Britain had issued Orders in Council that placed all of French-controlled Europe in a state of blockade. Trade with French possessions, and trade in French goods was prohibited, except that ships could proceed to France if they were given a British license. This meant that all American ships trading with French-occupied Europe could be seized unless they were given permission by the British. This last provision was needed because even in time of war the British were continuing to trade with the enemy – they wished to sell their goods.[6]

Napoleon replied to the British in the following month by issuing the Milan Decree. By this decree Great Britain and ports occupied by British troops were blockaded, and any neutral ship that obeyed British regulations would also be liable to seizure.[7] The European belligerents were trying to crush each other economically. The British wanted to use their naval power to control all trade to French Europe, Napoleon wished to use his continental system to deprive the British of a market for their goods, and end the prosperity that enabled them to finance the war. Both sides, however, would trade with the other when they thought it would be to their advantage. In theory, American ships could now legally trade only with the limited regions in Europe that were not under French or British control, but there were many chances for evasion. The British did not have enough ships to blockade the entire coast of French Europe, and they were prepared to allow trade in British goods under license. The French would frequently allow neutrals into their ports even if they had obeyed British regulations, for they needed some of the imported goods. For neutral ships that managed to avoid British or French seizure the profits of the carrying trade could now be even higher, but American ships had been forbidden to sail to Europe.

From 1807 to 1815 the American economy first labored under self-imposed restrictions and then under a crushing British blockade. The embargo was only to last until March 1809, but was to be succeeded by

5   *M&P*, 1, p.433; *AC*, 10th Cong., 1st Sess., pp.50–1, 1217–23.
6   *Hansard*, 1st Ser., 10 (1808), pp.131–48.
7   *ASP, FR*, 3, pp.290–1.

other methods of economic coercion and ultimately by war. In the pre-war years the embargo was by far the most severe of the self-imposed restrictions, although because of the surpluses built up in the years immediately prior to the embargo both the government and the general economy were able to survive it better than they did the steady economic attrition from 1809 to the end of the war.

The most immediate impact of the embargo was on those areas of the country that depended on maritime activities, and on the regions of northern New York and northern New England that, because of communication difficulties, depended on trade with Canada. The noisy, bustling ports of New England that had boomed in the years of growth since the mid-1790s suddenly fell silent. It was not only the shipowners and seamen that suffered, but also those involved in a host of subsidiary activities. Unemployment plagued these areas. The New England merchants and those who had invested in foreign commerce had the profits from previous years to sustain them, but the thought that the American government, not foreign blockades, had destroyed American foreign trade infuriated the Federalist opposition.

The Republican victories in the elections after 1800 had left the Federalists strongest in the Northeast, in the very areas that were hurt most by the embargo. They were angered that the president who had lectured them in the 1790s on the misuse of federal power was now using that power to stop them from trading. They were also frustrated that, though the embargo enabled them to revive their political fortunes in maritime areas, they appeared to be in a position of permanent inferiority nationally. For the next eight years many Americans were to feel no qualms about breaking the law. Ships that were abroad were told to stay abroad to violate the embargo, and there was extensive smuggling.

Evasion was so widespread that the government found it necessary to pass supplementary enforcement acts in January and March 1808, and in January 1809. In New York and Vermont the militia were called out to combat the smuggling. Yet, law breaking continued throughout the embargo. There was extensive evasion on Lake Champlain, along on the St Lawrence, and on the borders of Nova Scotia. Flour and other farm produce went north, and British-manufactured goods came south. Coastal vessels claimed that damage or the weather forced them to put into British ports. There was also smuggling in the South along the border of Spanish Florida.[8]

---

8 Burton Spivak, *Jefferson's English Crisis: Commerce, Embargo, and the Republican Revolution* (Charlottesville, Va, 1979), pp.113–15, 141–2, 163–77; Stagg, *Madison's War*, p.139.

For all their complaints, northeasterners had advantages not present in [191] much of the country. Merchants who could not invest in foreign trade were able to use the profits of previous years to give infant manufacturing a boost. In these years of restriction there was an increased demand for American goods. In Philadelphia the shift to manufacturing proceeded so successfully that while those directly connected to maritime activities suffered, others prospered, both from new manufacturing and from extensive construction.[9]

The rural areas in the South and West, from which Jefferson drew so much of his support, suffered greatly under the embargo. The tobacco and cotton growers, who depended on the English market, were hurt badly, as were the farmers and plantation owners of the trans-Allegheny West. They did not have the surplus capital that was available in the Northeast. Fortunately for the Republicans, they turned their anger against the British and their blockades rather than against the American government and its policies of economic coercion.[10]

Because most of the income of the American government came from duties on imports, revenue dropped precipitately when the United States turned to economic coercion. It declined from over $17,000,000 in 1808 to less than $8,000,000 in 1809. This did not cause an immediate crisis, for the booming economy of the previous years and strict economy in government had enabled Secretary of the Treasury Gallatin to amass a surplus. This situation was to change sharply for the worse when economic restriction continued, and when the United States eventually went to war. American exports declined from $108,343,000 in 1807 to $22,430,000 in 1808. Imports fell from $138,000,000 to $56,990,000.[11]

For Jefferson the tragedy of the embargo was that it did not produce a sudden desire in Great Britain for concessions to the United States. He faced the major difficulty that British restrictions on trade with French Europe had been imposed with the argument that they were essential to defeat Napoleon. British manufacturers and their employees might suffer from a lack of American raw materials and a lack of a market for British-manufactured goods, but the government was able to contend that this was necessary for the war against the French. There was also the major problem

9   Louis M. Sears, 'Jefferson and the embargo: 1808,' in *American Historical Association, Annual Report*, 1920 (Washington, DC, 1925), pp.253–63.
10 Louis M. Sears, *Jefferson and the Embargo* (Durham, NC, 1927), pp.73–252.
11 Davis R. Davis, *Financial History of the United States* 9th edn (New York, 1924), pp.123–6; Emory R. Johnson *et al.* (eds), *History of Domestic and Foreign Commerce of the United States* 2 vols (1915; rpr, New York, 1967), 2, p.20.

for Jefferson that his embargo was most injurious to the British manufacturing interests that generally backed the Whig party. The Tories were in power, and the Tory shipping interest was delighted that the Americans appeared to be ruining their own shipping. In imposing the embargo the American government was effectively achieving what the British government had sought in issuing the Orders in Council.

A final blow for Jefferson's hopes that the British could quickly be brought to grant concessions was that British exports in 1808 were greatly helped by uprisings in Latin America. In the fall of 1807, after the French invaded Portugal, the Portuguese royal family fled to Brazil. Brazilian trade was opened to British merchants. In early 1808 the French invasion of Spain and the deposing of the Spanish royal family led to a Spanish revolt against the French. This opened the trade of Spain and her colonies to British ships. William Pinkney reported to Madison from England that there was great enthusiasm for the Spanish in England, and that the Orders in Council and the embargo were 'thrown into the shade by it.' The drop in British exports to the United States in 1808 was made up by the increase in exports to the rest of the American continents.[12]

The British showed no willingness to respond to the main American complaints about impressment or blockades, and the Americans complicated any resolution of the *Chesapeake* affair by insisting that discussions on that matter should be linked with the general question of impressment. British envoy George Rose, who arrived in the United States in December 1807, was given authority to disavow the attack on the *Chesapeake* and to offer reparations, but only if the United States would also disavow the actions of the commander of the *Chesapeake* in encouraging desertions from the British service. Discussions failed, and in three months Rose left for England. Relations with France were equally bleak. In April 1808 Napoleon issued his Bayonne Decree, which ordered the seizing of American ships in French harbors on the grounds that as the embargo was in operation these vessels must have been working for the British.[13]

It was in the depressing atmosphere produced by the embargo that the United States in 1808 entered the contest for president. Jefferson had made it clear that he was longing to return to Monticello, and it appeared that James Madison was the logical candidate to succeed him. The brilliant

12   Pinkney to Madison, 2 Aug. 1808, MADP.
13   Instructions to Rose, 24 Oct. 1807, in *IBM*, pp.235–41; Irving Brant, *James Madison: Secretary of State, 1801–1809* (Indianapolis, 1953), pp.404–18; Reginald Horsman, *The Causes of the War of 1812* (Philadelphia, 1962), pp.138–42.

Madison, however, never could command the personal following and love [193] that Jefferson inspired, and he had a particular problem in that the volatile John Randolph disliked him. Randolph had become increasingly disillusioned with what he viewed as the abandonment of Republican principles. He had broken with Jefferson on the issue of Jefferson's efforts to obtain the Floridas through France, and had bitterly attacked Madison in regard to the complicated issue of the Georgian Yazoo land claims. Supposedly innocent purchasers of these lands, hurt when the Georgia legislature had revoked its sale, had eventually appealed to Congress for relief. Madison had been a member of a committee that had recommended setting aside land to recompense the petitioners, and Randolph had attacked Madison and the others as conniving at the earlier corruption.[14]

Randolph thought that James Monroe would be the best candidate to succeed Jefferson, and Monroe himself had ambitions in that direction. Some New York Republicans thought that George Clinton, the vice-president, deserved support. The Republican caucus easily overrode the opposition, and supported Madison for president with George Clinton to continue as vice-president.

The Federalists had regained some support as a result of the embargo, but they were still a minority and largely a sectional party, with their main strength in New England. Attempting to gain more national support, they nominated Charles Cotesworth Pinckney of South Carolina for president and Rufus King of New York as vice-president. Any hope the Federalists had for the future rested in the younger Federalists, who had ignored the separatism and bitter opposition of many of the old guard in the party in order to try to appeal more directly to the electorate. Learning from the success of the Republicans, who had organized to beat them in the late 1790s, the younger Federalists set up state organizations to attempt to get out the vote.[15]

Even the disruptions of the embargo could not produce a major Federalist revival. In the fall 1808 election Madison received 122 electoral votes to Pinckney's 47. Although the Federalists gained in the House of Representatives they still held little more than a third of the seats. In many areas of the Northeast they increased their vote, but they had been so far behind that they could not get majorities. This was the case in New York City, where the embargo caused great problems for those connected to maritime activities.

14 C. Peter Magrath, *Yazoo, Law and Politics in the New Republic, The Case of Fletcher v. Peck* (Providence, RI, 1966), pp.35–6, 39–49; Brant, *Madison*, pp.234–40.
15 David H. Fischer, *The Revolution of American Conservatism: The Federalist Party in the Era of Jeffersonian Democracy* (New York, 1965), pp.91–109.

[1 9 4] The elections in these years of economic coercion were closer, but the Republicans still won.[16]

When he took office in March 1809 Madison inherited a divided country that was less prosperous than it had been in 1807, but he did not inherit the embargo. As Jefferson neared the end of his second term he realized that the embargo had been a failure. Although British manufacturers had suffered from it, it had helped the Tory government achieve its aim of cutting American trade with France and damaging the American shipping industry. Napoleon had simply made it an excuse to seize American shipping. The embargo had failed, but there was little support for war. National divisions were deeper in 1809 than they had been in 1807, and the United States was in no way prepared for a war against Great Britain.

Just before he left office Jefferson decided to replace the embargo with a Non-intercourse Act directed against both Britain and France, which was approved on 1 March 1809. In one sense this measure was more severe than the embargo, in that it banned all trade with the two countries, imports as well as exports. In reality, however, the Non-intercourse Act was an admission of failure. It was well known that once American ships were freely allowed abroad, even if they were not supposed to trade with Britain and France, those countries would indirectly, or at times directly, benefit from American trade. The president was empowered to suspend the act for either England or France if one of them repealed its edicts against American commerce.[17] The nation had already used the strongest possible method of economic coercion, and it had failed. There appeared not the slightest reason to think that the Non-intercourse Act would change the policies of either Great Britain or France.

The early years of Madison's first administration were dominated by a sense of national impotence and frustration. More experiments in economic coercion, a far less prosperous nation, and an inability to influence the policies of Great Britain and France brought considerable dissatisfaction both inside and outside of Congress. It also led to increased Republican factionalism. The group sometimes known as the 'Invisibles' were often in opposition to Madison's policies, and particularly disliked Albert Gallatin, who continued as Secretary of the Treasury and became Madison's main advisor. This faction included William Branch Giles and Wilson Cary Nicholas of Virginia, Michael Leib of Pennsylvania, and Samuel Smith of Maryland.

16 Irving Brant, 'Election of 1808,' in S&I, pp.185–221; *NYCA*, p.91.
17 *AC*, 10th Cong., 2nd Sess., pp.911–12, 1437–41, 1443–1536, 1539–41.

Madison had hoped to choose Gallatin as his Secretary of State, but the [195]
opposition of Giles and others led him to appoint Robert Smith, Samuel's
brother. For Secretary of War he named revolutionary war surgeon William
Eustis, and South Carolinian Paul Hamilton became Secretary of the Navy.
Hamilton's drinking was to mar his performance in what was to become an
important position. Madison's effort to stem the factionalism did not work.
Republican dissent in Congress was to cause him difficulty, and Robert
Smith was a disruptive force in his cabinet.[18]

To add to Madison's problems, his administration began with a blunder
on the part of the British minister to the United States that caused Madison
great embarrassment. David Erskine, a friend of the United States, had been
appointed as minister by the short-lived Whig ministry, and had never been
recalled by the Tories. His friendly attitudes towards the United States were a
poor representation of the views of the country he was serving. He wanted
an agreement with the United States, and he wanted Great Britain to remove
its Orders in Council because he feared they would lead to war. His instructions from British Foreign Secretary George Canning made it clear, however,
that the Orders in Council could only be removed if the United States
committed itself to stop trading with France and her colonies, and agreed
that British ships could capture American ships that tried to evade any such
prohibition.[19]

In his eagerness to achieve an agreement, Erskine, in negotiations in April
1809 with the new Secretary of State Robert Smith, accepted an arrangement by which the British would remove the Orders in Council of January
and October 1807 in exchange for the Americans removing the Non-
intercourse Act. He obtained no specific pledge from the Americans that
they would not trade with France or its colonies, nor did he gain an acceptance of the idea that British ships could seize American vessels that did
engage in that trade. He accepted the American contention that the same
purposes would be served by leaving the Non-intercourse Act in force
against the French. Open trade between the United States and Great Britain
would be renewed in June.[20]

In the months immediately following the Erskine agreement American
optimism soared. Ships left in large numbers to trade with Britain, and
Madison was praised on all sides. It appeared that the embargo had won a

18   Stagg, *Madison's War*, 48–50; Robert A. Rutland, *The Presidency of James Madison* (Lawrence,
     Kans, 1990), pp.31–3.
19   *IBM*, pp.261–6.
20   *ASP, FR*, 3, pp.295–7.

[196] belated success, and that Madison would preside over a contented country. By June the optimism was cooling. First news arrived that the British had indeed changed the Orders in Council, but it was not the repeal that the American government had expected. On 26 April the British government issued a new Order in Council declaring a strict blockade all the way from the Ems River in the north to Pesaro and Orbitello in Italy. This meant that all trade with Holland, France, and Napoleon's kingdom of Italy was prohibited. Ports outside this area were opened to neutral commerce, with the significant exception that American shipping could not trade with the French colonies.[21]

News of this order arrived in the United States in the second week in June. Writing to Jefferson, Madison commented that he found it 'curious.' In his reply, Jefferson went beyond curious to say that it gave him 'great anxiety.' Jefferson found the new Order in Council to be in direct opposition to the Erskine agreement. Erskine tried to explain it all away by saying that the British government had issued it because they had not expected the agreement he had signed, but even Madison now found that explanation 'extraordinary.' In the following month the apparent contradiction was made clear when news arrived that the British government had repudiated the Erskine agreement. Erskine had misinterpreted his instructions. He was recalled to England.[22]

On 9 August Madison renewed non-intercourse against Great Britain, and Americans fumed at what was regarded as British perfidy. From this time war became much more likely. Jefferson commented that if Napoleon had the sense to correct his injustices towards the United States war with England was 'inevitable.' From South Carolina to Kentucky there were public meetings deploring the British action and supporting Madison in the renewal of non-intercourse. In Kentucky it was suggested that American merchant ships should be armed, and a resolution drafted in Charleston, South Carolina, promised support for any measures of the government, including war.[23]

The new British minister to the United States, Francis James Jackson, only worsened the situation. The instructions he received from British Foreign Secretary Canning indicated Canning's contempt for the United States. They contained the remarkable argument that the American government,

21 Horsman, *Causes*, pp.149–52.
22 Madison to Jefferson, 12, 20 June 1809, Jefferson to Madison, 16 June 1809, MADP; *ASP, FR*, 3, p.303; *IBM*, pp.270–6.
23 *M&P*, 1, p.473; Jefferson to Madison, 17 Aug. 1809, Resolutions of Washington County, Kentucky, 28 Aug. 1809, Resolutions of Charleston, South Carolina, 5 Sept. 1809, MADP.

not Erskine, was at fault because it should have realized that the British [1 9 7] government could not possibly have sanctioned such an agreement. Jackson was only prepared to sign an agreement if the United States would agree to all British demands regarding the cessation of trade with France or her colonies.

Jackson himself was the antithesis of the amiable Erskine, and his stay in the United States was brief. The American government could not accept Jackson's argument that it was responsible for the Erskine débâcle. Jackson arrived in Washington in September 1809. By the beginning of November the American government broke off all negotiations with him. Although he was recalled by the British in April 1810, he stayed on through the summer. He visited Federalist strongholds in New England, and complained about the American government. On their part, leading Federalists feted a man who was obnoxious to a majority of Americans.[24]

The Congressional session of 1809–10 revealed a confused and largely impotent Congress. It was agreed that the Non-intercourse Act was not an effective measure, but there seemed little agreement on what policies should replace it. For many the one bright spot was the appearance in the Senate of fiery young Henry Clay from Kentucky. He was serving out the unexpired term of another senator. When he arrived in Washington Clay quickly brought passion to the debates. In February he delivered a scathing speech, attacking the vacillation and timidity of government policies. Arguing that peaceful resistance to Great Britain had failed, he declaimed that he was for 'resistance by the *sword*,' and that the British could be attacked by an invasion of Canada.[25] As yet Congress, fully aware of the pitiful weakness of American military forces, was still looking for peaceful solutions, but Clay's speech represented an increasing feeling in the country that the attempted British destruction of American trade would have to be resisted.

As Americans began to consider the possibility that war might be necessary, the situation was much complicated by the continued hostility of Napoleon. Consumed by his European ambitions, Napoleon conducted a strange and erratic policy towards the United States. It was in France's interest to encourage American friendship, for the French needed American shipping and trade, but in his attitude towards the United States Napoleon often settled for temporary gains while ignoring the long-term effects of his policies on French interests. In March 1810, when the United States was becoming

---

24   *IBM*, pp.276–87, 302–3; *ASP, FR*, 3, pp.309–19.
25   *AC*, 11th Cong., 2nd Sess., pp.579–82.

[1 9 8]   increasingly disgusted at the course of British policy, Napoleon issued his Rambouillet Decree. He ordered the confiscation of American vessels and their cargoes on the grounds that the United States had prohibited all trade with France. A clear sign of widespread violations of the Non-intercourse Act by American shipping was that Napoleon was able to seize property to the value of $10,000,000 in this way.[26]

In looking for a substitute for non-intercourse, the Republicans were hurt by their increasing factionalism. Gallatin had a plan for excluding British and French ships from American ports while allowing the importation of their goods in American ships, but attempts to get the measure through Congress foundered on the objections of Gallatin's enemies. Ultimately, a committee headed by Nathaniel Macon, which had failed to get the Gallatin plan through Congress, came up with the bill that was given the name Macon's Bill No. 2. This bill removed all restrictions on American trade, but promised that should either Britain or France lift its restrictions against American commerce before 3 March 1811, then the American government would reimpose non-intercourse against the country that had not acted. This bill passed into law on 1 May 1810.[27]

Macon's Bill No. 2 offered nothing new to Great Britain. The British government had already turned down the Erskine agreement by which the Orders in Council were removed in exchange for the removal of non-intercourse. For Napoleon, however, it offered the opportunity of turning the Americans more firmly against the British while allowing him to proceed as he wished against American commerce. The key for Napoleon was that there was no need for him actually to end his actions against American commerce. All he had to do was say that he had removed his restrictions.

In August 1810 the French Foreign Minister, the Duc de Cadore, informed John Armstrong, the American minister in France, that the Berlin and Milan Decrees would be revoked as of 1 November 1810. This had no real meaning for French policy. In the next year and a half the American government began to realize that the French were still seizing American ships. In response to Cadore's letter Madison announced early in November that, unless the British lifted their restrictions against American commerce by 1 February 1811, the United States would renew non-intercourse against Great Britain. Britain did not act, and Madison ordered non-intercourse against

---

26   Eli F. Hecksher, *The Continental System: An Economic Interpretation* (Oxford, 1922), p.140.
27   *AC*, 11th Cong., 2nd Sess., pp.2582–3; Marshall Smelser, *The Democratic Republic* (New York, 1968), pp.196–7.

Great Britain while allowing open trade with France and her possessions. [199]
Secretary of State Robert Smith, whose relationship with Madison was
becoming increasingly strained, opposed this act on the grounds that the
French had not really abandoned their decrees.[28]

Although Napoleon was not changing his policies towards the United
States, Macon's Bill No. 2 and the French response solved a major American
dilemma. It was clearly ludicrous for the militarily weak United States
to contemplate war against the two major European powers, but since 1803
Britain and France had been treating American commerce with equal
disdain. In destroying the French republic Napoleon had alienated many
Americans, but for the Republicans the main enemy was always Great
Britain, not France. Both countries might scorn American neutral rights,
but the British had the naval power to cause far more trouble for American
shipping than the French. Also Britain was the old colonial enemy, and to
the Republican leadership had always represented a major threat to infant
American republicanism. Cadore's letter was a lie, but its result was logical in
view of Republican attitudes since the early 1790s and their policies since
they had assumed power.

Writing to his Attorney-General Caesar Rodney in September 1810,
Madison revealed his thinking on the results of Macon's Bill No. 2. He said
that what had happened had at least extricated the United States 'from the
dilemma of a mortifying peace, or war with both the great belligerents.' He
was not sure what Great Britain would do, but whatever she did in the short
run, 'it is probable we shall ultimately be at issue with her on her fictitious
blockades.'[29]

The frustrations that Madison experienced in dealing with the British,
and the inability of the United States to affect the course of European events,
undoubtedly made him all the more ready to take action in an area over
which the United States did have some control. The worsening state of relations with Britain convinced Madison that, in the event of war, Britain
should be prevented from using Spanish possessions on the Gulf of Mexico
as a base for attacking the United States. Since 1807 Governor W. C. C.
Claiborne of the Territory of Orleans had been suggesting that Jefferson's
long-desired objective of obtaining West Florida was attainable. In 1810,
after a visit to Washington, he became actively engaged in encouraging
separatism in that region, particularly among Americans who had moved

28   *ASP, FR*, 3, pp.386–7; *M&P*, 1, pp.481–2; Stagg, *Madison's War*, p.57.
29   Madison to Rodney, 30 Sept. 1810, Caesar Rodney Papers, LC.

into the Baton Rouge area. Madison was ready to advance American interests in the Southwest.[30]

When in late September a partially American-inspired uprising occurred in part of West Florida, the rebels quickly offered the area to the United States. Madison was anxious to accept, but he realized that there were constitutional problems. He wrote to Jefferson that he was worried that if he acted quickly, when Congress was about to come into session, the action might be viewed as 'premature & disrespectful, if not of being illegal.' He said he was leaning towards action because the original Congressional law that had authorized Jefferson to take possession of Louisiana had covered territory east of the Mississippi River as far as the Perdido. Madison took the position that as Congress had legislated for the area he could annex it to avert any danger of it passing into the hands of a third party – in this case, Great Britain.[31]

On 27 October Madison issued a proclamation annexing West Florida to the Perdido River. He emphasized to Governor Claiborne that there was to be no use of force. Claiborne occupied Baton Rouge in December 1810, and in the following year placed the area to the Pascagoula River under American control. In December, when the Congressmen assembled and Madison informed them of his action, they debated giving Congressional approval. Those who supported Madison argued that it had been necessary for him to act because of the pressing nature of the problem. They argued that the control of West Florida was vital to the safety of New Orleans, and that if the president had not acted the rebels might have sought the protection of a foreign power. Henry Clay defended the president, arguing that any power that controlled Cuba and Florida controlled all that part of the United States that had to export its goods through the Gulf of Mexico.[32]

The Federalists objected strongly to the president's actions. Senator Outerbridge Horsey of Delaware argued that the Constitution had given Congress the exclusive power of making laws and declaring war, and the president had illegally done both by occupying West Florida and by adding the area to the Territory of Orleans. Europe might be barbarous, he argued, but that was no reason for the new republic to make use of force to achieve

---

30 Abraham D. Sofaer, *War, Foreign Affairs and Constitutional Power: The Origins* (Cambridge, Mass, 1976), pp.292–7; Jared W. Bradley, 'W. C. C. Claiborne and Spain: foreign affairs under Jefferson and Madison, 1801–1811,' *Louisiana History* 12 (1971), pp.297–314, 13 (1972), pp.5–26.

31 Madison to Jefferson, 19 Oct. 1810, in *WJM*, 8, pp.109–12.

32 *AC*, 11th Cong., 3rd Sess., pp.55–64; John A. Logan, *No Transfer: An American Security Principle* (New Haven, Conn, 1961), pp.114–17; Sofaer, *War*, pp.297–300.

its ends. As in the case of Louisiana, party allegiance proved vital in judging [201] the president's actions. In January 1811 Congress voted along party lines to give a strong endorsement to Madison and the occupation of West Florida up to the Perdido River. Going even further, Congress agreed that the president could occupy territory east of the Perdido, if it became necessary to prevent the area passing from Spain to another power.[33]

This victory on West Florida was one of the few consolations for Madison during the acrimonious and largely ineffective 1810–11 session of the 11th Congress. Congress continued to be confused about how to challenge British policies, and made the financing of any war more difficult by failing to recharter the Bank of the United States. In its brief period of existence the bank had become the cornerstone of the American financial system. It had provided credit for American economic growth while acting as a restraint on the wilder excesses of the rapidly proliferating state banks. As the original charter of the bank was only for 20 years, it was due to expire in 1811 unless Congress rechartered it.

Since the early 1790s, when Jefferson had led his followers in a passionate attack on Hamilton's Bank of the United States, many Republicans had changed their views. Secretary of the Treasury Albert Gallatin was convinced of the bank's worth, and as early as 1809 had recommended the renewal of the charter. No action was taken at that time, but Gallatin had the support of Madison, and the charter came up for renewal in this 1810–11 session of Congress. The situation was confused politically. The Republicans were badly divided. While some were now convinced that the bank was essential, others still regarded it as a key element in the Federalist policy for America. Some agrarian Republicans simply disliked the whole idea of banks, while proponents of state banks were happy to have the competition and the restraints of the United States Bank removed. Opponents stressed Jefferson's original argument that the bank was unconstitutional. The Federalist opposition supported the renewal.

The renewal bill aroused passions in the different states, and some of them sent instructions to their senators on how to vote. Both Virginia and Massachusetts instructed their senators to vote against the renewal bill. The bill was debated in the House in January, and in the Senate in February. In both bodies there was an almost equal division. In the House the bill failed by a vote of 65 to 64. In the Senate, where it failed by a vote of 18 to 17, Madison's Vice-President George Clinton cast the deciding negative vote,

---

33   *AC*, 11th Cong., 3rd Sess., pp.44–5, 47, 53–5, 374–80; Logan, *No Transfer*, pp.118–20.

opposing the desires of Madison and Gallatin. The Bank of the United States went out of business. The main office in Philadelphia was sold, and became a private, unincorporated bank. The branches were taken over by state-chartered banks.[34]

Gallatin was so disgusted by the failure of the recharter, and by the constant attacks of his Republican opponents, that in March he offered to resign. He eventually stayed on, but Madison, urged by some of his supporters to exercise leadership, decided that he would strengthen his cabinet by removing one of the main malcontents, Secretary of State Robert Smith. When he would not accept the position of minister to Russia, Madison removed him. James Monroe succeeded him as Secretary of State.[35]

Before Congress adjourned in March 1811 it had to give its approval to Madison's renewal of non-intercourse against Great Britain. In the debate there was much concern that Madison had been taken in by Napoleon, for there was little evidence that he had actually repealed his decrees. The 11th Congress was a dispirited body, but there were signs that some members were reaching the end of their patience. When the Non-intercourse Act was eventually passed, with the provision that it would not be removed until England took off the Orders in Council, there was a minority Republican move to insist that England would also have to give up impressment.[36] This was defeated, but among the Republicans the opinion was growing that American honor required a stronger response to British policies and British disdain. These arguments were to become much stronger when a new Congress assembled in the fall of 1811.

---

34   Bray Hammond, *Banks and Politics in America: From the Revolution to the Civil War* (Princeton, NJ, 1957), pp.209–26; Curtis B. Nettels, *The Emergence of a National Economy, 1775–1815* (New York, 1962), p.301; Stagg, *Madison's War*, p.62.
35   Stagg, *Madison's War*, pp.62–5; Rutland, *Presidency of Madison*, pp.68–70, 74–5.
36   *AC*, 11th Cong., 3rd Sess., pp.357–8, 1033–96.

CHAPTER 13

THE COMING OF WAR

The ineffectiveness of American foreign policy in the years from 1807 to 1811 had become a source of disgust to many Americans. It was quite clear that neither Great Britain nor France had respect for the young republic. The United States and the two European belligerents had totally different interpretations of the status of neutrals in wartime. The British believed that neutrals had no basis for objection when Britain used her naval power to defeat the French. Deserters could not be allowed to leave with impunity and sail on American ships. Also, if American vessels were aiding the French by carrying goods to and from French possessions, then the British government felt justified in using every possible means to stop them. American distinctions between real and paper blockades were looked upon as quibbles. The British felt justified in scouring the seas for ships that were aiding the enemy, and if neutral ships were aiding the enemy then they were fair prey.

The French were less oppressive in dealing with American shipping because they were weaker at sea, and because their true interest lay in encouraging neutral shipping to replace those French ships that British naval power kept from the seas. Yet the French realized that Britain was greatly helped by its extensive trade with the United States. They also realized that the war against them was financed by the British ability to sell goods throughout the world. Napoleon wished to keep those British goods he did not need out of French-occupied ports. He was also ready to seize American ships when he had the opportunity.

For the American government and its citizens all this was intensely frustrating. Since the beginning of the Revolution they had argued that the seas should be free in war and peace. With a large merchant marine it would, of course, have been very much to America's advantage to be able to trade everywhere without restriction. In wartime, there were great profits to be made. The American shipping interest were prepared to accept the risks of wartime trading, because it was worth it, but the Republicans believed that

[2 0 4] the European powers, particularly Great Britain, should stop arbitrary interference with American ships and the seizure of American seamen.

Economic coercion had seemed logical because both Jefferson and Madison had faith in peaceful means of redress. But economic coercion had failed. The methods chosen had hurt the United States more than Great Britain. The frustrations of the previous years had convinced the American administration, and most of the Republican members of Congress, that even war was preferable to continued ineffectiveness. When war was debated in 1811 and 1812, talk of the valor of revolutionary forebears was often on the lips of those who urged military action. War against Britain was made easier because England had been the revolutionary enemy, and to some it seemed necessary that the republic should now be defended for a second time.

There was to be strong resistance from the Federalists, because it seemed certain that if the United States went to war she would be able to carry out less trading, not more. If profit had been the sole consideration, the United States would have ignored impressment and the seizures of ships and cargoes, and simply kept on trading. This is what much of the maritime interest wanted.

In the months between the adjournment of the 11th Congress in March 1811 and the meeting of the first session of the 12th Congress in November, Madison and his cabinet had little hope that non-intercourse would move the British or that any peaceful solution would be found. Since Francis James Jackson's recall in April 1810, the British ministry in the United States had been run by a Secretary of Legation who had no power to negotiate. Because of this, and the lack of any progress in his negotiations, William Pinkney, the American minister in England, informed the British in January 1811 that he was returning to the United States. This moved the British to send Augustus J. Foster as a new minister. Foster's only achievement was a settlement of the *Chesapeake* affair. Great Britain agreed to pay reparations and to hand back the two seamen who were still alive. The United States did not achieve its aim of tying the *Chesapeake* question to the general issue of impressment. Madison told Jefferson that Foster's mission was merely for delay and deceit. The British 'Cabinet,' he wrote, 'is inflexible in its folly and depravity.'[1]

The growing American feeling that war was the next step was reflected in the reversal of the usual pattern in the encounters between British and American ships off the American coast. Paul Hamilton, the Secretary of the Navy, had long been disgusted at what he considered to be the feeble

---

1 *ASP, FR*, 3, pp.408–14, 435–70; Madison to Jefferson, 19 Apr. 1811, MADP.

American response to British aggression, and since at least the spring of [205]
1810 had argued that a stronger American reaction was necessary. In July
of that year, writing in frustration to Caesar Rodney, the Attorney-General,
he said that all his naval officers were Federalists and far too reluctant to
respond to threats from British vessels.[2]

In the spring of 1811 Hamilton's desire that his ships should be more
active in protecting American merchant vessels produced results. In May the
American frigate *President* was ordered to sea to protect American shipping,
and later in that month fired on the British sloop *Little Belt*, killing British
seamen. Madison's view was that this might well be followed by more such
incidents, and possibly an open rupture.[3]

In the fall, as the time approached for Congress to assemble, many now
assumed that war was the next step. Matthew Lyon, the famous victim of the
Sedition Act, wrote to James Monroe in September that he was concerned
about the 'approaching war.' The war, he wrote, could only have the purpose
of protecting American maritime rights, and punishing the British for their
encroachments. He once had believed this could be accomplished by the
invasion of Canada, but now thought that this would be a very difficult
task. He was also concerned that help would be given to 'a Tyrant so dangerous to the liberties of the World as Bonaparte.' A Tennessean, writing of
the departure of Tennessee's Congressional delegation for Washington, said
that he thought Madison's first message would be the most important state
paper since the Declaration of Independence. He said there was now no
alternative but war, submission, or permanent embargo. He favored a little
blood-letting.[4]

A peculiarity of the early American political system was the long delay
that ensued between the election of a new Congress and its presence in
Washington. When the 11th Congress expired in March 1811, its successor
had already been chosen in the previous year. It did not take office until
November 1811. Among the men elected in 1810 were a core of some 20 or
30 who came to Washington prepared to ask for an end to vacillation and
a reassertion of American rights against Great Britain. The most prominent
of them were from the southern and western regions of the nation, and

2 Hamilton to Rodney, 23 May, 27 July, 1810, War of 1812 Papers, Indiana University,
   Bloomington, Indiana.
3 Bradford Perkins, *Prologue to War: England and the United States, 1805–1812* (Berkeley, Cal,
   1961), pp.271–3.
4 Lyon to Monroe, 26 Sept. 1811, MONP; Anthony Butler to Jackson, 12 Oct. 1811, Jackson
   Papers, LC.

they were all Democratic–Republicans. They later became known as the War Hawks. They took the lead in persuading their fellow party members that war was the only means of redeeming American national honor and defending the American right to trade without danger to her ships or to her seamen.[5]

Congress was sharply split. The Federalist minority was adamantly opposed to war, and the Republicans themselves were divided on what was necessary to make the war possible. The movement towards war was slowly carried forward both by President Madison and the War Hawks. Madison was no dynamic war leader. He had reluctantly arrived at the decision that English policies had left him no choice but to ask Congress to prepare the nation for war.

The predominant concerns of those who supported war preparations, and ultimately war itself, were the British policies at sea. Although the Embargo and American economic coercion had done more than the British and French to disrupt American commerce, the War Hawks and their supporters placed the blame squarely on Great Britain. In the Congressional debates of 1811–12 the Republican Congressmen defended military preparations and war by arguing that all peaceful means had failed and blockades and impressment had to be resisted by force. There was a particular emphasis on Britain's blocking of the direct trade – the exports of the United States. Joseph Desha of Kentucky, and others, said they would not fight for the carrying trade, but they would fight for the right to export America's own products. Otherwise, said Jonathan Roberts, the United States would be yielding to 'absolute recolonization.' By refusing to fight, Clay argued, the nation would lose its 'commerce, character, a nation's best treasure, honor!' Like Desha, Clay insisted that the United States was claiming the right to the direct trade – 'the right to export our cotton, tobacco, and other domestic produce to market.'[6]

The United States, it was argued, had shown forbearance in attempting to change the policies of the European powers by peaceful means. These efforts had been rejected, American rights and American honor had been trampled upon, and the only choice that remained was to show, as their revolution-ary forefathers had shown, that oppression would be resisted. In the early nineteenth century the War of 1812 was often called the Second War for

---

5 Reginald Horsman, 'Who were the War Hawks?' *Indiana Magazine of History* 60 (1964), pp.121–36.
6 *AC*, 12th Cong., 1st Sess., p.487 (Desha), p.503 (Roberts), pp.599–601 (Clay).

Independence. It was an apt name. Congressmen favoring war believed that [2 0 7] not even a successful Revolution had freed the young republic from the tentacles of British power.

Memories of the Revolution also echoed in discussions of the American Indians and Canada. After long recitals of how America's right to export her crops had been denied, and how ships and seamen had been seized, Congressmen pointed out that the British had returned to their old practice of inciting the Indians in 'savage warfare' against the American settlers.

Relations with the American Indians had deteriorated rapidly in the previous years. When the Indians of the Old Northwest realized that the 'permanent' line of the 1795 Treaty of Greenville was only temporary, and that the American government would support its settlers in demanding larger areas beyond the Ohio River, Indian resistance stiffened. After 1805, Tecumseh and his brother Tenskwatawa urged resistance to the Americans. Tecumseh attempted to enlist tribes from the whole region south to the Gulf into his cause.[7]

From the time that Tenskwatawa and Tecumseh began to recruit Indians to resist American demands, western officials were quick to blame the British in Canada rather than American policies for the Indian reaction. Governor William Henry Harrison of Indiana Territory constantly linked Indian difficulties with British incitement. After 1807 he had some reason for his fears of British influence, for from that time the British in Upper Canada tried to take advantage of this situation, as they had done in the years before 1795. The trigger for this renewed activity was the crisis in Anglo-American relations in the aftermath of the *Chesapeake* affair. British officials in Canada feared that, if war came, Canada would be invaded, and they authorized agents at the British post at Amherstburg, across the river from Detroit, to remind the Indians that the British were their friends, that the Americans were seizing their lands, and that in the event of war Indians would be needed to fight alongside the British. To the British in Canada this was a prudent defensive maneuver, to Americans with memories of combined British–Indian attacks in the Revolution it was a provocation.[8]

Governor Harrison decided that the village established by Tecumseh on the Tippecanoe River in northern Indiana was a threat to American settlement. In the fall of 1811 he took advantage of the absence of Tecumseh on a

---

7 See R. David Edmunds, *Tecumseh and the Quest for Indian Leadership* (Boston, Mass, 1984), and *The Shawnee Prophet* (Lincoln, Neb, 1983).

8 Reginald Horsman, *Matthew Elliott: British Indian Agent* (Detroit, 1964), pp. 157–73.

recruiting expedition in the South to lead a force north from Vincennes to the vicinity of the village. Tenskwatawa tried to pre-empt any American attack by sending his warriors to attack the American encampment. The resulting battle was evenly fought, but the Indians dispersed. Harrison burned their village. When Tecumseh returned, he joined his warriors in seeking British aid. Unrest flared along the frontiers of the Old Northwest.[9]

Since the time of the *Chesapeake* crisis Americans had assumed that if war came the main way in which it would be fought would be by the invasion of Canada. This was the only area in which the British appeared to be vulnerable. The Americans would have liked to free the seas for their exports and to protect American seamen, but Britain could not be defeated at sea. In the debates leading to war Joseph Anderson of Tennessee said that the invasion of Canada had always been talked about whenever there had been the prospect of war against Great Britain. An attack on Canada was the way to strike back, and where the United States could obtain 'some small reparation for the many losses and injuries, which have been sustained from the depredations committed upon the honor and interests of the nation.'[10]

The Americans had desired Canada since the earliest years of the Revolution. An invasion might mean the end of British power on the North American continent, and it would remove British support for Indian resistance. If British disregard for American rights at sea finally made war necessary, Canada could be more than the means of fighting the war. It might also become the prize to provide redress for years of British insults and intransigence.[11]

More than anyone else, Henry Clay of Kentucky led the nation towards war. Clay was young and dynamic, and he had reached the conclusion that British policies had left the United States no choice but war. In November 1811, on his very first day as a member of the House of Representatives, he was elected speaker. This gave him great power in the organization of the standing House committees, and he made use of it to place those who supported war preparations in essential positions. The nine-man Foreign Relations Committee had a majority of War Hawks. It was chaired by Peter B. Porter of New York, and supporting him were Joseph Desha from Kentucky, Felix Grundy from Tennessee, John A. Harper of New Hampshire, and John C. Calhoun of South Carolina. Calhoun was serving the first of his

9   Edmunds, *Tecumseh*, pp.161–6; Edmunds, *Prophet*, pp. 94–116.
10   *AC*, 12th Cong., 1st Sess., p.60; Reginald Horsman, 'On to Canada: Manifest destiny and United States strategy in the War of 1812,' *Michigan Historical Review* 13 (1987), pp.9–14.
11   Horsman, 'On to Canada', pp.1–14.

many years in Congress. At this stage of his career he was a nationalist, keen to avenge the offenses to American honor and to protect his state's right to export its products. The South Carolinian delegation was strongly represented among those who favored war; David R. Williams chaired Military Affairs and Langdon Cheves Naval Affairs. Less prominent, but equally prepared to ready the nation for conflict, was Massachusetts Republican Ezekiel Bacon, who chaired Ways and Means. Others who gave strong support to Clay were Richard M. Johnson of his own state, William Lowndes of South Carolina, and George M. Troup of Georgia. The lack of accommodation in Washington meant that Congressmen were crowded together in boarding houses, and helped to give cohesion to Clay's forces. Clay stayed in the same house as Grundy, Calhoun, Lowndes, and Cheves.[12]

Madison was not a man to utter a ringing call to arms, and his annual message simply asked for war preparations. After pointing out that the British had shown 'hostile inflexibility in trampling on rights which no independent nation can relinquish,' Madison said that 'Congress will feel the duty of putting the United States into an armor and an attitude demanded by the crisis.'[13]

The House Foreign Relations Committee acted swiftly to prepare an answer to the president's call. In late November the committee gave its report. In its private discussions the committee reached the conclusion that war was necessary, but believed that first there was a need for preparations. Madison promised his cooperation. The report urged Congress to end submission to the British. Asserting, against the evidence, that the French decrees had been removed, the committee attacked British maritime policies, and asserted that the United States should be able to export her products without losing ships and men. The committee recommended that the regular army should be brought up to its officially authorized strength, 10,000 more men recruited for three years, a volunteer force of 50,000 men raised, the militia embodied, the merchantmen armed, and warships not in service outfitted for war.[14]

The Republicans had reached the point of deciding that war against Great Britain was necessary, but they were ill prepared for it. The difficulty partially stemmed from the hope that economic coercion would work, and

---

12 *AC*, 12th Cong., 1st Sess., pp.330, 333; Reginald Horsman, *The Causes of the War of 1812* (Philadelphia, 1962), pp.226–7; Bernard Mayo, *Henry Clay: Spokesman of the New West* (Boston, 1937), pp.402–3.
13 *M&P*, 1, p.494 (5 Nov. 1811).
14 *AC*, 12th Cong., 1st Sess., pp.373–7.

war would not be necessary. But this assumption was accompanied by a Republican desire for frugality, by a deteriorating financial situation after 1807, and by the Republican distrust of standing military forces. From the time the Republicans had assumed power they had saved money by cutting the military forces. As a result, the military forces were totally inadequate at the time Congress began its discussions leading to war.

By an act of March 1802 the army had been reduced to two regiments of infantry and one of artillery, a total of just over 3,000 officers and men. By early 1805 the total numbers were little more than 2,500. After 1807 there had been a slow increase. Legislation in 1808 authorized an army of nearly 10,000 men, but there was great difficulty in bringing enlistments up to the authorized total. In the fall of 1811 the regular army was well below its authorized strength, and there was a critical shortage of trained personnel.[15]

There had been no American navy until Congress had authorized the construction of a handful of frigates in the mid-1790s, and the Navy Department had not been created until the crisis with France in 1798. During that crisis the Federalists had put together a navy of more than 50 vessels. They had even planned to build six ships of the line. All of this came to an end when the Republicans came to power. Even the naval war with Tripoli had not saved the navy from reduction to the bare bones of a force.

A desire to save money was at the heart of the Republican reduction of the navy, although fears of regular forces and a wish to reduce a military establishment much favored in Federalist areas also entered into Republican calculations. In the aftermath of the Tripolitan War Jefferson placed his faith in gunboats, small vessels that could operate in shallow coastal waters. They could be sailed or rowed, and carried only one or two cannon. They were also very cheap, and had the advantage that they could easily be laid up when not needed. Several hundred were built. In the meantime the number of other vessels was reduced, and most of those retained were put into dry dock. Even in the years of crisis following the *Chesapeake* affair there were only two frigates and four smaller ships in actual service. This was the situation that confronted Congress as it contemplated war against the greatest naval power in the world.[16]

15 James R. Jacobs, *The Beginning of the US Army, 1783–1812* (Princeton, NJ, 1947), pp.244–79, 342–86; J. C. A. Stagg, *Mr Madison's War: Politics, Diplomacy, and Warfare in the Early Republic, 1783–1830* (Chapel Hill, NC, 1983), pp.131–2, 164.

16 Harold and Margaret Sprout, *The Rise of American Naval Power, 1776–1918* rev. edn (Princeton, NJ, 1944), pp.58–63; Craig L. Symonds, *Navalists and Antinavalists: The Naval Policy Debate in the United States, 1785–1827* (Newark, Del, 1980), pp.105–47.

The possibility of resisting any strongly mounted British blockade of the [2 1 1] American coast was hopeless, but the Americans could contemplate harassing the British merchant fleet. In time of war, ships of the American merchant navy could easily be converted into privateers: private vessels licensed by the government to raid enemy shipping. If war came, the American carrying trade would be crippled, along with American exports, but shipowners could outfit hundreds of vessels as privateers. Even the Federalist New Englanders adamantly opposed to war would not miss the chance of the rich pickings that could come from privateering.

In mid-December 1811 the House gave its approval, in principle, to the military recommendations of the Foreign Relations Committee, but once the discussion of the actual measures began there was much disagreement and confusion. Decisions on the regular army were a particular source of frustration because the existing army, which was authorized at a strength of 10,000 men, had only some 5,500 actually enlisted. It was reasonably easy to agree to bring this establishment up to full strength, though more difficult to achieve it, but there was little agreement on what additions should be made. In early December Republican Senator William Giles of Virginia, a frequent critic of Madison and his associates, had introduced an unrealistic bill calling for an addition of 25,000 regulars. It passed the Senate but ran into difficulties in the House. Speaker Henry Clay favored the bill, but the House Foreign Relations Committee tried to reduce the figure to 15,000. Clay prevailed, however, and in January the bill became law. A regular army of 35,000 men had been provided for, but recruitment proceeded at a snail's pace, and when the war began the army had not even reached its official peacetime strength of 10,000.[17]

Once the regular army bill was agreed on, Congress took up the question of raising volunteers. It was realized that the invasion of Canada would largely depend on volunteers and the embodiment of militia units. There was agreement on the figure suggested by the Foreign Relations Committee – 50,000 – but an ominous disagreement on whether these volunteers could be used outside of the territorial limits of the United States. Some argued that volunteers and militia should be used only to defend the country. The bill became law in early February, but there was no agreement on this question of where the recruits could be used. To some degree the question became academic, because it proved extremely difficult to find volunteers. It became

---

17   AC, 12th Cong., 1st Sess., pp.29–30, 35–84, 84, 96–7, 377, 545–8, 565–6, 691, 717–18, 2229–34; Stagg, *Madison's War*, p.164.

clear in the early months of 1812 that Canada could only be invaded if the federal government succeeded in embodying a sufficient force from the state militias.[18]

The Republicans placed great faith in the militia as the best defense of a republic, but it had the disadvantage that it had none of the experience and training of a regular army, and it was not under the control of the federal government. The Constitution gave the power of organizing the militia and appointing its officers to the states. The federal government was given the power to use state militia, but it was not clear what would happen if the states refused to provide militia units desired by the federal government.

The basic militia act had been passed in 1792. Adult, white males between 18 and 45 had the obligation to belong to the militia and arm themselves. All the details were left to the states. At various times arguments were made for a system that would better meet federal needs, but these attempts had not succeeded. In the debates leading to war it became apparent that problems went beyond lack of state coordination. The measures taken in this winter of 1811–12 did not clarify the question of whether the militia could be constitutionally used outside of the country. Even the committed War Hawk Felix Grundy believed that defense was the militia's role. As militia were to be an essential force in the invasion of Canada, this uncertainty boded ill for future years.[19]

Discussions on the navy raised even more problems for the Republicans than those on the land forces. As England's navy was so large, some questioned the use of enlarging a tiny navy. Some Republicans, however, realized that if war came the American coast would be completely vulnerable to British blockade and to coastal depredations. To resist this, the United States would need more than gunboats. The British navy had obligations on the oceans of the world, and while the United States had no way of challenging British naval power as a whole, it could make use of a respectable navy at key points – off Chesapeake Bay or New York, or at other places where the British would send squadrons to stop American trade.

In January 1812 Langdon Cheves, the chairman of the Naval Committee, introduced a bill asking for appropriations to build 12 ships of the line and 20 frigates. Cheves argued that as the United States was going to war to protect her commerce and her neutral rights on the ocean, it was obvious that

---

18   *AC*, 12th Cong., 1st Sess., pp.583, 782–801; Stagg, *Madison's War*, pp.163–70.
19   Lawrence D. Cress, *Citizens in Arms: The Army and the Militia in American Society to the War of 1812* (Chapel Hill, NC, 1982), pp.150–71; Stagg, *Madison's War*, pp.122, 124, 132–3; *AC*, 12th Cong., 1st Sess., pp.782–801.

this could only be done by providing a naval force. To economy-minded Republicans who thought of the navy as a 'Federalist' stronghold, this was not at all obvious. The ensuing debate revealed a deeply divided Republican party. The Federalists, however, while opposing war against Great Britain, were quite happy to see an increased navy.

Most of the western Republicans, including pro-war Tennesseans Felix Grundy and John Rhea, opposed the increase in the navy. From the West, only Henry Clay was prepared to throw his support ardently behind the Cheves proposal. When British minister Augustus Foster dined at Clay's boarding house in February, he commented in his journal that Clay was 'very warlike.' Clay wanted Canada to be invaded as soon as war began, but he realized that the United States would also have to fight at sea. A majority of the Republicans ignored his appeal, and late in January the House rejected the bill to increase the navy.[20]

The Republicans had great difficulty in coming to terms with the costs of war, particularly at a time when the national finances were becoming increasingly precarious. Economic coercion and the reduction in imports had been in effect since 1807, and the reduction in imports had taken a severe toll on the income of the federal government. As customs revenue diminished, Secretary of the Treasury Gallatin had tried to keep his budget balanced by arguing for minimum military expenditure, even as relations with Britain continued to deteriorate. The war preparations of 1811–12 made Gallatin's attempts to meet the problem of reduced revenue by reducing expenditure impossible. He now had to ask Congress to increase tariffs, add new taxes, and authorize loans.[21]

In mid-February Ezekiel Bacon, the chairman of the Ways and Means Committee, brought in proposals to provide the revenue that Gallatin said was needed. The committee recommended doubling tariffs, some direct taxes on individual items, a direct levy from the states, and an authorization for a $11,000,000 loan. Although it was quite obvious that war preparations depended on raising enough money to carry them out, Congress imposed conditions that again weakened the American response. When the bill passed early in March it was with the proviso that the new taxes would only become effective when there was war against a European nation. Yet Madison's reaction to the tax bill passing the House was that this was the

20 *AC*, 12th Cong., 1st Sess., pp.803–46, 909–1005; Symonds, *Navalists*, pp.148–69; Foster Journal, 11 Feb. 1811, Augustus John Foster Papers, LC.
21 Stagg, *Madison's War*, pp.141–3; Raymond Walters, Jr, *Albert Gallatin: Jeffersonian Financier and Diplomat* (New York, 1957), pp. 244–7.

strongest proof Congress had given that it was prepared to stay the course, and fight Great Britain. There was now a general expectation that war would come. In Tennessee, Andrew Jackson issued a call for volunteers, stating that war was 'on the point of breaking out between the United States and the King of Great Britain!' It seemed that only a major British concession would prevent American action.[22]

Ironically, for the first time since American economic coercion had been introduced in 1807 there was now considerable pressure building in Britain for policies that would persuade the Americans to reopen trade. The reason was that in 1811 and 1812 Britain was enduring a severe economic depression. As means were sought to alleviate the distress, one obvious possibility was to restore the lucrative American market. British exports to the United States had been of a value of almost £11,000,000 in 1810, but had dropped to under £2,000,000 in 1811. Northern textile manufacturers were particularly hard hit, and there was widespread unemployment and considerable unrest. Parliament began to be besieged with petitions asking for measures that would help the restoration of trade, and many of these petitions focused on the obvious step that could be taken – a restoration of exports to the United States.

In the spring of 1812 the Whigs were enlisting support for concessions to the United States that would revive trade, and the manufacturing centers of the country joined with them in demanding the repeal of the Orders in Council. As distress and riots swept the industrial centers of the Midlands and the North, Parliament held extensive hearings to delve into the causes of the continuing depression. Manufacturing interests urged the repeal of the Orders and the renewal of commerce with the United States, but British shipping interests and their Tory allies who controlled the government were still determined to hold firm. They argued that both the war against France and the protection of the English merchant marine necessitated a continuation of the Orders in Council and the restrictions on American commerce.[23]

The United States heard of English economic distress, but there was no indication from the British government that it intended to change its policies. In March and April 1812 news from Europe was particularly depressing because it was becoming obvious that the French, in spite of their assertions in 1810 that they had removed their decrees, had not made any

22 *AC*, 12th Cong., 1st Sess., pp.1050–6, 1092–155; Madison to Jefferson, March 1812, MADP; Jackson, Division Orders, 7 Mar. 1812 (draft), Jackson Papers, LC.
23 Horsman, *Causes*, pp.196–200, 245–56.

basic changes in their policies against American shipping. The Federalists [2 1 5] were infuriated that the United States was sliding into war against Great Britain, a country they regarded as essential to American prosperity, while ignoring the insults of France, a country of far less importance to America economically and also, they believed, a threat to the liberties of the world.

On 9 March Madison sent papers to Congress which were clearly designed to increase anger against Great Britain while discrediting the Federalist opposition. The papers, which had cost the government $50,000, concerned John Henry, who in 1808 and 1809 had acted as an agent in the United States for the Governor in Chief of Canada. Fearing war and an American invasion of Canada, the British officials in Canada had employed Henry to gather information on New England opinion, and to encourage any disaffection there. The letters were hardly sensational. There was no evidence of the type of secessionist activity that had been indulged in by Timothy Pickering and others in the aftermath of the Louisiana purchase. Although the Republicans tried to use the letters to stir up opinion against Britain and the Federalists, the Federalists were able to make much of the lack of any hard evidence of treason in the letters, and the way in which the president had used government money in what they said was merely a partisan ploy.[24]

Madison may have stumbled in his efforts to move the nation towards war, but Clay continued to use both his influence as speaker and his powerful oratory to make sure that the faltering drive for war did not stop. In mid-March he recommended to Secretary of State James Monroe that the president should send a confidential message to Congress recommending a 30-day embargo, and that the embargo should be followed by war. The embargo would be a means of making sure that as many American ships as possible would be in port, and out of the reach of the British navy, when war began. Knowing of the difficulties that were being encountered in finding recruits for the regular army or as long-term volunteers, Clay also suggested that the president recommend that provision be made for 10,000 short-term volunteers.[25] It had been quite common in campaigns against the Indians to enlist volunteers for a short period, usually for one campaign. Men who did not want to leave their farms and families for an extended period of time were often prepared to enlist for a brief period.

24 William R. Manning (ed.), *Diplomatic Correspondence of the United States: Canadian Relations, 1784–1860* 4 vols (Washington, DC, 1940–5), 1, pp.183–200; Perkins, *Prologue*, pp.369–72.
25 Clay to Monroe, 15 Mar. 1812, MONP.

[2 1 6]   On 1 April British minister Foster visited the president, and reported in his journal that he was 'very warlike,' but on the same day Madison recommended not a 30-day embargo but one for 60 days. Madison was being cautious. He was still hoping that he might hear something that would make war unnecessary. By a 70 to 41 majority the House of Representatives passed the embargo bill on the same day that the recommendation was received from the president. The Senate was badly divided on the issue, and before passing the measure, by a vote of 20 to 13, took caution a step further by extending the embargo to 90 days. Most of those who supported the measure believed that it would be followed by war.[26]

As war neared, the British Orders in Council rather than impressment dominated the arguments of those who were ready to fight. Impressment was always a running sore in British–American relations in these years, but the only time that it dominated discussion was in the period immediately before and after the *Chesapeake* affair. It had been the decisive factor in the refusal of Jefferson to accept the Monroe–Pinkney Treaty and in the enactment of the 1807 embargo. After four years of disrupted trade, and American attempts to persuade the British that their blockades were illegal, attention was now focused on the right of the United States to export her own products. Impressment was still of great concern, but it seems clear that the United States would not have fought for impressment alone. In early April Madison told Jefferson that the British government preferred 'war with us, to a repeal of their Orders in Council.' George Washington Campbell, a Senator from Tennessee, told Andrew Jackson at the same time that the embargo was regarded by its supporters 'as the precursor of war – There is not the slightest ground to hope that G. Britain will revoke her orders in council.'[27]

In reality, the repeal of the Orders in Council was so close that the British announced the decision to remove them before the United States declared war. Early nineteenth-century communications were such that the war was well under way before news of the repeal reached the United States. If it had happened a month or so earlier, the American administration and Congress would have regarded it as a success for the American policy of preparing for war, and there seems every reason to suppose that the United States would have remained at peace.

---

26   *M&P*, 1, p.499; *AC*, 12th Cong., 1st Sess., pp.187–90, 1587–614, 2262–4.
27   Madison to Jefferson, 3 Apr. 1812, MADP; Campbell to Jackson, 10 Apr. 1812, Jackson Papers, LC.

The English decision stemmed from a political crisis. Throughout the spring the Tory government resisted opposition efforts to force a removal of the Orders in Council, but on 11 May English Prime Minister Spencer Perceval was shot and killed as he entered Parliament. In some distressed English towns the news of his assassination was received with considerable rejoicing. There was great difficulty in shaping a new ministry. Not until early June did Lord Liverpool accept the task of forming a new Tory administration. On 16 June a government spokesman indicated that the orders would be repealed. This action was taken a week later. There were celebrations in the manufacturing towns that depended on exports to America, and ships were readied to take advantage of the expected American repeal of non-intercourse. Instead, news was to arrive that the United States was at war.[28]

In April and May, as the embargo took effect and American ships began to shelter in American ports, British minister Augustus Foster spoke with many of those involved in shaping the move to war. In his journal he noted their opinions and their attitudes. His view was that the Orders in Council and impressment were the reasons for war, and that the United States had reached the point where national honor would not be satisfied unless the country was prepared to fight to defend its rights. Calhoun commented that merchants would put up with any wrong and only talk of gain, but the government was obliged to give protection. Foster wrote to his mother that a great many people in the United States were afraid of being laughed at 'if they don't fight.' He also suggested that young men were taking the lead. Calhoun, he noted, was 'just from College,' and he said that Senator William Giles had returned to Virginia, saying he would not be back, as everything was being given into the hands of boys.[29]

By mid-May the administration had practically no hope that war could be avoided, but it was waiting to see if there was any sign of a thaw in the dispatches expected from Europe. They contained only the news that British policies were unchanged, and the additional problem that there was no evidence that France had removed her decrees. Periodically in the spring the question of war against France as well as England had been raised, and the renewed evidence that France had not repealed her decrees meant that this question was raised again. The matter was kept alive in Congress primarily

---

28   Horsman, *Causes*, pp.256–8.
29   Foster Journal, 15 Apr. 13, 18, 19, 24 May, 13 June 1812, Foster Papers; Foster to Elizabeth, Duchess of Devonshire 18 April 1812, Vere Foster (ed.), *The Two Duchesses* (London, 1898), p. 360.

because the Federalists found it a desirable way to harass the Republican majority.[30]

In late May Madison prepared a war message, and on 1 June sent it to Congress. The message contained a summary of the main American grievances against England from 1803 to 1812, concentrating on impressment and blockades, but also alluding to British activities among the Indians. Madison argued that as the long patience of the United States had not been rewarded by any concessions from England, Congress should take the necessary action to defend the country's rights.[31]

The reasons for the war had been debated since November 1811. The long delay partially reflected the divisions that beset the country, and the lingering hope that England would make concessions, but more than anything else it stemmed from the realization that the United States had reached breaking point with practically none of the necessary military and financial preparation in place. A majority of Congress were now ready to fight, but it was a sadly divided body. A quirk of the American Constitution is that a declaration of war can be passed by a simple majority of both Houses and a signature of the president, while a peace treaty needs a two-thirds vote in the Senate to be approved. If two-thirds had been needed, the declaration of war against England would not have passed. On 4 June the House of Representatives voted for war by a vote of 79 to 49; the Senate followed on 17 June with a vote only 19 to 13 in favor.

The vote for war was very much a party vote, but it also reflected the degree to which the Federalist party had become sectional in the years since 1800. The Federalists were unanimous in their opposition, and most of the Republicans voted for war, although there was resistance from a block of Republicans in New York. The western Republicans from Ohio, Tennessee, and Kentucky cast their nine votes for war (Clay, the speaker, would have added to that vote). The South strongly supported the war. The states from Maryland south to Georgia were for war by a vote of 34 to 14. Pennsylvania was also strongly in favor, 16 to 2. The bulk of the opposition came from the Northeast, the last area of any substantial Federalist strength. From New Jersey northwards, the six states along the coast voted 34 to 14 against war.[32]

30 George M. Bibb to Henry Clay, 24 May 1812, Henry Clay Papers, LC; Foster Journal, 22 May 1812, Foster Papers.
31 *M&P*, 1, pp.499–505.
32 *AC*, 12th Cong., 1st Sess., pp.296–8, 1630–8.

On 18 June Madison signed the declaration of war. He faced a situation in which the region with the most available capital – New England – was the center of opposition to the conflict. Militarily, the country was ill prepared. To declare war against Great Britain in 1812 was a very risky act. It almost resulted in disaster. By 1814 the United States was to need luck as well as fierce resistance to avoid a humiliating defeat.

CHAPTER 14

THE INVASION OF CANADA

When the War of 1812 began the immediate American objective was the invasion of Canada, but the Revolution had shown that waging military operations on the United States–Canadian border was very difficult. Distances were great, roads were practically non-existent, and the large-scale movement of troops was limited to the dry, summer months. The United States was also badly hampered by its lack of careful military preparations and by the sharing of power between the federal government and the states. J. C. A. Stagg has argued persuasively that the United States in this period simply could not effectively organize the nation's resources for war.[1]

The possibilities for invading Canada were determined by geography. The key to Canada was the St Lawrence River, and its two main cities, Quebec and Montreal. In the French and Indian War, the British had conquered Canada from the French by sending troops by sea into the St Lawrence and capturing Quebec. Once Quebec was taken, those to the West were cut off from supplies and reinforcements. Canada fell. In the War of 1812, as in the Revolution, British naval power made it impossible for the Americans to contemplate reaching the St Lawrence by sea. The obvious point of attack by land was Montreal, which was at the head of navigation. Montreal could be reached by marching northwards from Lake Champlain.

If the War of 1812 had been carefully planned, the United States would have been poised in June of that year with a large army waiting on the shores of Lake Champlain to advance north to attack Montreal when it heard of the declaration of war. There could also have been diversionary attacks at Niagara, between Lake Ontario and Lake Erie, which was the other obvious point of entry into Canada, and across the Detroit River against Fort Malden. The latter operation was thought necessary to prevent any repetition in the West of the joint British/Indian attacks of the Revolution.

---

1 See J. C. A. Stagg, *Mr Madison's War: Politics, Diplomacy, and Warfare in the Early Republic, 1783–1830* (Chapel Hill, NC, 1983), pp.503–9.

Coordinated attacks on the three fronts would have prevented the British concentrating their forces to resist the main American attack. Because of the difficulty of moving supplies by land, and to prevent armies being moved to outflank attacking forces, naval control of the Great Lakes was of prime importance. In the years leading up to the war the United States had not made preparations on the lakes, and when the war began the United States did not have the control of the three lakes – Champlain, Ontario, and Erie – that was needed to ensure the safety of armies advancing into Canada.

The American lack of a large, well-trained army was compounded by problems of command. There was no army general staff. The Secretary of War, William Eustis, to a large extent was obliged to act alone. Eustis, a surgeon in the Revolution, was not up to the job. He was only to last until December 1812. Political factors often assumed great importance in military operations as the Secretary of War tried to justify his actions to the president and to other members of the cabinet.

The senior officer in the army was Major-General Henry Dearborn. He was in his sixties and had served in the Revolution, as had the other Major-General, Thomas Pinckney. The smallness of the army in the 30 years since the Revolution meant that there was a great shortage of senior officers ready to take command of armies of the size needed to invade Canada. As the army expanded, there was a serious shortage of officers and trained non-commissioned officers at all levels. There was also a major problem in relations between the regular army and the militia. The militia provided a majority of the forces available for the invasion of Canada, and senior militia officers were appointed by the state authorities, often for political reasons. Experienced regular army officers were frequently outranked by militia officers in combined operations, and such questions of seniority were left unclarified because of the dual nature of militia forces raised and organized by the states before being called into federal service.[2]

Although Congress in April 1812 had authorized the president to call out state militia to meet its military needs, state authority over the militia hindered federal mobilization. In the course of the war the governors of the New England states, except for New Hampshire, maintained that they had the authority to decide whether or not the state militia should be called out, and denied the right of the federal government to put the state militia under the command of regular army officers.

2 James R. Jacobs, *The Beginning of the US Army, 1783–1812* (Princeton, NJ, 1947), pp.383–4.

[2 2 2]   The difficulty began in June 1812 when Secretary of War Eustis instructed Caleb Strong, the Governor of Massachusetts, to provide General Dearborn with militia that he needed for the defense of the coast. Dearborn asked for 27 companies of infantry and 14 companies of artillery. This would allow regular troops to be transferred to the Canadian border. When Strong did not comply, Eustis wrote again, this time invoking the authority of the president. In August Strong replied that he had discussed the matter with his council. They had decided that there was no danger of invasion and therefore no need to meet the general federal requisition for troops; three companies would be sent into federal service at Passamaquoddy on the Canadian border because the people there had requested them.

Strong and his council also asked the Massachusetts Supreme Court for an opinion on whether the states had the authority to decide whether or not state militia should be sent into federal service, and whether the militia could be put under the command of non-militia officers. The court gave the opinion that it was up to the states to decide, and that the militia could not be put under the command of non-militia officers, except for the president himself.

At first the Governor of Connecticut, Roger Griswold, agreed to supply militia, but he reversed his position after he met with his council. Connecticut then declined to provide militia on the grounds that the constitutional requirements for sending the militia into federal service – to execute the laws of the Union, suppress insurrections, and repel invasions – had not been met. In any case, Connecticut would not agree to place the militia under the command of a federal army officer. Eustis tried to get round Connecticut's objection by stating that the president believed that there was a danger of invasion, but he was again turned down. Griswold commented that the cruising of a hostile fleet on the American coast did not constitute a threat of invasion.[3]

These problems in dealing with the New England states were to continue throughout the war. In November 1813 Martin Chittenden, the Governor of Vermont, objected that Vermont militia had gone to the aid of a neighboring state, and had been placed under the command of a United States army officer. He ordered them to return to Vermont, arguing that the military strength and resources of Vermont should be reserved exclusively for its own defense and protection. In this case some of the officers and men refused to

---

3   *ASP, MA*, 1, pp.322–6; Leonard D. White, *The Jeffersonians: A Study in Administrative History* (New York, 1951), p.540; Samuel E. Morison, *The Life and Letters of Harrison Gray Otis, Federalist, 1765–1848* 2 vols (Boston, 1913), 2, pp.56–65.

return, stating that such an attitude would bring disgrace and ruin to the [2 2 3] United States. Even in 1814, with the British massing to invade south from Montreal, Massachusetts and Connecticut retained control of their state militias, and the governor of Vermont refused to order the militia out of the state. The reluctance or refusal of key New England states to provide militia severely weakened the government on the key Lake Champlain front.[4]

Whether they were regulars, volunteers, or militia all American troops in the War of 1812 encountered frustrating problems in obtaining supplies. Until 1812 the tiny regular peacetime army had no Quartermaster-General. The Secretary of War included that function in his own duties. In effect, military agents at the different posts scattered around the country tried to ensure that supplies were available. In the spring of 1812 Congress attempted to provide for the expected war by creating a Quartermaster's Department under a Quartermaster-General. His duties overlapped with the newly created Commissary-General of Purchases, who was responsible for the final review of military purchases. Only a month before the war began Congress created a separate Ordnance Department, under a Commissary-General of Ordnance.[5]

The creation of new departments did not end the system of obtaining subsistence for the army by awarding contracts to the lowest bidder. The resulting food supply was a source of constant complaint, and often it did not arrive at all. There were so many failures in the first year of the war that in March 1813 the president was given the power to appoint special commissioners to find food when the contractors did not supply it. At the same time the Quartermaster General's Department was reorganized, and eight Quartermaster-Generals appointed to serve the different armies, each operating independently of the others. Clothing was also secured by contract, and was under the direction of the Commissary-General of Purchases.[6]

The supply of ordnance was inefficient. During the American Revolution most of the American firearms came from France and the Netherlands, but in the years following the war attempts had been made to make the United States self-sufficient. This was a slow process, and even the comparatively

4 John Brannan, *Official Letters of the Military and Naval Officers of the United States during the War with Great Britain in the Years 1812, 13, 14 and 15* (Washington, DC, 1823), pp.261–4; Henry Adams, *History of the United States during the Administrations of Thomas Jefferson and James Madison* 9 vols (New York, 1889–91), 8, pp.220–1, 235–7.

5 James A. Huston, *The Sinews of War: Army Logistics, 1775–1953* (Washington, DC, 1966), pp.102, 103–4; Erna Risch, *Quartermaster Support of the Army: A History of the Corps, 1775–1839* (Washington, DC, 1962), pp.136–41.

6 Risch, *Quartermaster*, pp.117, 119, 142–6, 152–3.

small needs of the 1790s were often supplied from abroad. The two federal arsenals – in Springfield and at Harper's Ferry – did not produce enough for the army's requirements. In the crisis of 1798 the federal government signed private contracts for the manufacture of some 40,000 muskets. Among the contracts was one to Eli Whitney, who was working out methods for standardizing production by the use of machines.

Beginning in 1808 Congress made determined efforts to supply the money for muskets in the event that there was a war, and agreed to provide $200,000 a year to provide arms for state militias. Both the federal government and some states also signed private contracts. The pace of this increased in 1809–10 when the federal government signed contracts for some 85,000 muskets. Delivery was slow, and only one-third had been delivered by the summer of 1812. The United States army was given most of the weapons that had been received. By 1813 only 26,000 stands of arms had been delivered to the states (a stand included the muskets, bayonet, ramrod, wiper, and screw driver). The government also contracted out for pistols.[7]

The artillery depended largely on private contracts. The cannon were cast in private foundries, although the gun carriages were made at United States armories. The Ordnance Department inspected them as well as superintending the government's construction of gun carriages and its manufacture of ammunition. A year after the war started it was reported that the Ordnance Department was inadequate. It was decided at that time to establish three new arsenals, one near Pittsburgh, one near Albany, and one on the Chesapeake. Each would employ 30 or 40 workmen.[8]

If American preparations had been even reasonably sound, Canada was vulnerable. At the beginning of the war the British had fewer than 6,000 men in the whole of Upper and Lower Canada. In the West, Major-General Sir Isaac Brock proved to be an able and resourceful general, but most of the best British commanders were in Spain fighting the French. Recruitment for the Canadian regiments, the 'fencibles,' was slow, and the British had little faith in the militia; in Lower Canada it consisted mostly of French-Canadians, who had little reason to love either the British or the Americans, and in Upper Canada there were many immigrants from the United States.

---

7 Constance McLaughlin Green, *Eli Whitney and the Birth of American Technology* (Boston, Mass, 1956), pp.100–18, 150–6; Michael A. Bellesiles, 'The origins of gun culture in the United States, 1760–1865,' *Journal of American History* 83 (1996), pp.444–6; Huston, *Sinews*, pp.96–8, 105–7; White, *Jeffersonians*, pp.532–3.

8 Huston, *Sinews*, pp.98–9; White, *Jeffersonians*, p.226; *ASP, MA*, 1, pp.336–7.

Sir George Prevost, the Governor in Chief, assumed he was likely to lose much of Canada, including Montreal. He believed that his best hope was to fortify and defend Quebec, and eventually use it as a base to retake areas occupied by the Americans.[9] His fears were exaggerated.

With an inadequate number of troops, no efficient organization at the center, a lack of cooperation from key states, an inadequate supply system, and a paucity of talented and experienced general officers, it is hardly surprising that the American invasion of Canada in the summer and fall of 1812 was a fiasco. When war was declared the United States had not yet gathered an invasion force on the key Lake Champlain front. The greatest popular enthusiasm for the war was in Ohio, Kentucky, and Tennessee. Those areas were on the alert because of the tensions in Indian relations following the battle of Tippecanoe in November 1811, and the assumption that once war began the region south of the Great Lakes would be subject to attacks by the British and their Indian allies. These dangers were very much over-estimated. The settlement of the region had increased dramatically since the highly dangerous revolutionary years.

On the eve of war William Hull, the governor of Michigan Territory and a revolutionary veteran, was under orders to advance with an army of some 2,000 men out of Ohio to Detroit. If war came, his task was to invade Upper Canada and capture the British post of Fort Malden at Amherstburg. Hull's incompetence, combined with the inadequate preparations, doomed his expedition. While he was advancing by land, he sent his baggage, including his instructions, to Detroit by way of the Maumee River, Lake Erie, and the Detroit River. He did not know that war had been declared. The British did, and his baggage was captured. One of the few competent commanders on either side at the beginning of the war, British Major-General Sir Isaac Brock, now knew Hull's intentions.

In July and August Hull threw away any advantage he might have had by being on the march at the beginning of the war. In the second week in July he crossed into Canada. He could have taken a weak Fort Malden, but when he heard that the British had captured Fort Mackinac, the key fur trading post in the northern lakes, he retreated to Detroit. Mackinac had fallen because American fur trading interests, with a stake on both sides of the border, had passed news of the American declaration of war to the Canadians faster than the American government had sent word into the Mississippi Valley. The Americans in Fort Mackinac learned of the American declaration

9   Reginald Horsman, *The War of 1812* (London, 1969), pp.26–8.

of war when the British asked them to surrender. Hull was fearful that British-led warriors would now come from the northern lakes to attack his force. He was also concerned that his only supply route was by a precarious land link to Ohio. Lake Erie was in the hands of the British. They had only a few vessels, but the American government had not yet built a fleet.

The British crossed the Detroit River in mid-August. Hull was in a well-entrenched position, but when Brock warned him that if he had to attack he could not guarantee holding his Indian warriors in check, Hull surrendered his whole army without a fight. Subsequently he was court martialed and sentenced to be shot, but reprieved on account of his previous record. Both sides of the Detroit frontier now passed into British hands, and with the loss of Mackinac the Americans had lost any influence west of Lake Michigan.[10]

On the Niagara frontier and along Lake Champlain it took the whole summer to gather the men necessary for action. The original American force along the Niagara River was composed of New York militia, but in October it was reinforced with several thousand new troops, including regulars and volunteers. On paper, this was now a reasonably impressive force of some 6,000 men, including 1,600 regulars. But the overall commander was a New York militia political appointee, Stephen Van Rensselaer, and the commander of the regulars, Brigadier-General Alexander Smyth, showed a great reluctance to take orders from him.

With the American forces far outnumbering the British, Van Rensselaer decided to cross the swift-flowing Niagara River and take the dominant position of Queenston Heights. The Americans were so ill coordinated in these attacks on Canada that General Brock was given time after his victory at Detroit to come east and command on the Niagara frontier. Van Rensselaer had no cooperation from Smyth, although he was able to use regulars who were under his own command, and the logistics were hopeless. The first attempt to provide enough boats to take the attacking force across the river ended in complete failure, and the operation was temporarily abandoned. On a second try, in mid-October, troops were ferried across, but the attack depended on the boats returning across the difficult river to pick up more troops, and this led to confusion. The first wave soon met stiff British resistance. General Brock was killed, but the American attack degenerated into near chaos. Many boatmen fled, and some of the militia on the American side refused to cross to Canada. The Americans fought with only a part

---

10   Ibid., pp.34–41; Alec R. Gilpin, *The War of 1812 in the Old Northwest* (East Lansing, Mich, 1958), pp.23–124.

of their total force. The battle of Queenston Heights was another disaster for [2 2 7]
the American forces. They lost 300 killed and wounded, and 900 (half of them
regulars) were taken prisoner. British losses were little more than 100 killed,
wounded, and missing. Van Rensselaer resigned, and Smyth took overall
command, but in November his efforts at attack also ended in confusion.[11]

The American Commander-in-Chief, Henry Dearborn, spent the summer
and early fall attempting to gather an army for an attack on Montreal from
Lake Champlain. The gathering of forces was slow, Dearborn was excess-
ively cautious, and the troops were beset by a variety of illnesses. Finally,
after months of effort, Dearborn had an army of some 6,000 men assembled
on the west bank of Lake Champlain at Plattsburgh. In November they
cautiously moved north towards the Canadian border. It was already too late
in the season for safe campaigning in northern New York. The British had
been given nearly six months to gather forces to protect Montreal. Even
if Dearborn had been a far more dynamic general, his force was probably
too weak to take the city. After some skirmishing on the Canadian border
Dearborn retreated into winter quarters. Most of the militia were disbanded.
The regulars went into winter camp at Plattsburgh and across the lake in
Burlington, Vermont. The troops at Plattsburgh had no huts until December,
and during the winter there were many deaths from the pneumonia that was
epidemic in the northeastern states.[12] The great invasion of Canada had been
an abysmal failure. Nothing had been gained in the east, and the Detroit
region had been taken by the British. The failure had been more a result of
the lack of preparation and the ineptness of the generals than the strength of
British resistance.

For the American public, the only consolation of a dismal summer and fall
was the American performance at sea. Here, however, appearance was better
than reality. At the beginning of the war the regular American navy consisted of 16 vessels. Only seven of these were frigates, the largest three each
rated at 44 guns. The British navy had hundreds of major vessels, including
more than 100 ships of the line, none of which were rated at less than 74
guns. Even with the British using most of their navy in Europe there were
more than enough ships to shatter American foreign trade by a blockade of
the American coast.

11 Horsman, *War of 1812*, pp.43–9; J. Mackay Hitsman, *The Incredible War of 1812: A Military
    History* (Toronto, 1965), pp.77–93.
12 Allan S. Everest, *The War of 1812 in the Champlain Valley* (Syracuse, NY, 1982), pp. 47–66,
    87–97; Reginald Horsman, *Frontier Doctor: William Beaumont: America's First Great Medical
    Scientist* (Columbia, Mo, 1996), pp.27–35.

[2 2 8]   The temporary circumstance that allowed American morale to be boosted by events at sea was the fact that the largest American frigates were the best of their class in the world. The tiny American navy also had the advantage that it had an abundance of excellent captains and seamen. With a large merchant marine and a tiny regular navy, the Americans had none of the problems of the British in spreading talented officers and experienced seamen over too many ships. The British navy also had grown used to success. Captains of English frigates prided themselves that in a single ship engagement they could beat any enemy frigate. They had proved this against the French and the Spanish. Individual British ships would not wait to bring superior force to bear against individual ships of the tiny American navy. British frigates were anxious to find and challenge American frigates to single ship engagements.

By the end of the year three single frigate engagements had taken place, and the Americans had won all of them. In August the *Constitution* (44), commanded by Captain Isaac Hull, defeated the *Guerrière* (38) in the Atlantic, several hundred miles off Nova Scotia. In October the *United States* (44), Captain Stephen Decatur, defeated the *Macedonian* (38) near the Madeira Islands, and in December the *Constitution*, now commanded by Captain William Bainbridge, overwhelmed the *Java* (38). In October 1812 the frigate *Essex* (32) slipped out of the Delaware, eventually went round Cape Horn into the Pacific, and for over a year caused great havoc among British shipping. Not until February 1814 did it strike its colors to a superior force sent from England.[13]

The American frigates were stronger than the British frigates they had defeated, but the British were unused to naval defeat. While the American public feted their victors, the British press asked how the mightiest navy in the world could be losing at sea to a country with a tiny regular naval force. The Admiralty issued orders that British frigates should avoid single ship engagements with American frigates. The best British captains did not follow this order, and in June 1813 the British navy gained some revenge for the defeats of 1812 when their frigate *Shannon* (36) defeated the American frigate *Chesapeake* (38). Even this, however, was used to boost American morale. Captain James Lawrence's dying words – 'Don't Give up the Ship' – were inscribed on banners, and were used to rally public opinion.[14]

13   Horsman, *War of 1812*, pp.52–66, 70, 145–8.
14   ADM 2/1375, pp.365–73 (9 Jan. 1813), ADM 1/503, pp.332–5 (6 June 1813), ADM 2/1377, pp.166–7 (12 July 1813); William S. Dudley *et al.* (eds), *The Naval War of 1812: A Documentary History* (Washington, DC, 1985–), 2, pp.126–34.

In 1812 the initial British shock was increased by the swarm of American [2 2 9] privateers that put to sea to harass British commerce. Individual privateers regularly used favorable winds or dark nights to slip out of port and evade the British blockades. In the first seven months of the war, in addition to the three frigates, the British lost some 500 merchant vessels. This was all a mystery to the British public, and temporarily elated the Americans, but it disguised the reality of the naval war. The British began to provide the force necessary to blockade the American coast, to keep the tiny American regular navy in port, and cripple American trade. Already, in the fall of 1812, the British had three ships of the line, 21 frigates, and 29 sloops, as well as smaller vessels, on the North American station, and they were preparing to send three more ships of the line, ten frigates, and four sloops. In the course of the winter, still more reinforcements were provided.[15]

The isolated victories at sea could not offset the fiasco of the Canadian invasion, and in the summer and fall of 1812 Madison and his cabinet were under attack from numerous critics. Politically, the Republicans were in no danger. The Federalists had lost any chance they might have had of re-gaining their position as a national party by their fervent opposition to the declaration of war, and they were to complete their ruin by their attitude during the war itself. Outside of New England, feelings ran high against those who were anti-war. Popular resistance forced Federalist newspapers in Savannah, Georgia, and Norristown, Pennsylvania, to close, and a few days after the war began a mob in Baltimore, Maryland, destroyed the office of the strongly Federalist *Federal Republican.* In the following weeks violence continued against any who were supposed to have pro-British sympathies. Late in July, when another attempt was made to publish the paper, there was a major riot in which Federalists were brutally beaten.[16]

Although Madison had major deficiencies as a war leader, the Repub-lican Congressional caucus unanimously nominated him for a second term. Elbridge Gerry of Massachusetts was chosen as the vice-presidential can-didate. Disaffected New York Republicans would not support Madison, and nominated DeWitt Clinton for the presidency. The Federalists were at a loss because they knew that they did not have the national support to win the election. Finally, hoping to link New York to their New England base of

---

15 ADM 2/1375, pp.252–9, 365–73 (18 Nov. 1812, 9 Jan. 1813); Edgar S. Maclay, *A History of American Privateers* (New York, 1924), pp.225–8, 506–7.

16 Donald Hickey, *The War of 1812: A Forgotten Conflict* (Urbana, Il, 1989), pp.56–71; Frank A. Cassell, 'The great Baltimore riot of 1812,' *Maryland Historical Magazine* 70 (1975), pp. 241–59.

support, they threw their support behind Clinton, The unpopularity of the war in much of the Northeast was shown by the voting. Clinton carried the seaboard states from Delaware north to New Hampshire, Maryland was split, and Madison carried everything else: all the southern states south of Maryland, all the western states, and Vermont. His victory by 128 to 89 electoral votes reflected the lack of unanimity in the country about the wisdom of the war. Both houses of Congress remained in the control of the Republicans.[17]

Facing widespread criticism, Madison did not keep the same cabinet. Both the Secretary of War, William Eustis, and the Secretary of the Navy, Paul Hamilton, resigned in December. The abysmal failures on the Canadian border made it necessary for Eustis to go, and naval successes could not save Hamilton, whose problems with drink had become ever more obvious. Madison appointed William Jones of Pennsylvania as Secretary of the Navy, but had difficulty finding anyone willing to accept the position of Secretary of War. After several men rejected the position, he appointed John Armstrong of New York. Armstrong exercised far greater leadership than Eustis had done, but his decisions were frequently questioned. It was a thankless job, and was eventually to ruin Armstrong's reputation.[18]

The Congress that assembled in November 1812 was an acrimonious one. The Federalists were obstructive, and the Republicans were divided on how best to prosecute the war. Efforts to increase the military forces were hindered by Gallatin's warnings of major financial problems. Monroe, who acted as temporary Secretary of War until Armstrong took over, suggested that 20,000 one-year volunteers be raised to invade Canada, and that recruitment for the regular army should be encouraged by generous bounties. For financial reasons, Secretary of the Treasury Gallatin objected to this 20,000 being added to the 35,000 already authorized (but not yet recruited). When the bill was passed in January, it authorized the 20,000 for one year's service, but only up to the number of the existing establishment. The Federalists were in solid opposition to the army proposal, although they supported a bill which appropriated $2,500,000 for the navy to build four ships of the line and six frigates. This bill passed, but it divided the Republicans.[19]

17   Norman K. Risjord, 'Election of 1812,' in S&I, pp.249–72; Irving Brant, *James Madison: Commander in Chief, 1812–1836* (Indianapolis, 1961), pp.96–113; Stagg, *Madison's War*, pp.107, 117, 267, 272–3; Robert A. Rutland, *The Presidency of James Madison* (Lawrence, Kans, 1990), pp.117–19.

18   Brant, *Madison*, pp.119–29.

19   Stagg, *Madison's War*, pp.274–81, 290; Adams, *History*, 6, pp.430–58.

In the debate on the army bill the Republicans now had no hesitation in [2 3 1]
arguing that if Canada could be conquered it should be kept. Nathaniel
Macon argued that taking Canada would rid the United States of a bad
neighbor, and that the St Lawrence was needed as the mouth of the
Mississippi had been needed. Other Republicans supported him, while the
Federalists condemned what they said was now becoming a war of conquest.
Daniel Sheffey, one of the last of the Virginia Federalists, argued that 'this
is not a war for the rights of commerce and seamen, but, in fact, a war for
the conquest of Canada.'[20] What was actually happening was that the
Republicans were trying to convince themselves and the country that at least
something could be gained from a war against British maritime policies that
now appeared to be a huge mistake.

Financing the war was becoming an increasing problem. Expenditure was
soaring, income was declining. The United States still depended primarily
on the income from tariffs, because the Republicans resisted imposing the
necessary internal taxes, but imports plummeted. In 1812 expenditure was
over $20,000,000, income under $10,000,000. The only answer Gallatin
had at his disposal was to obtain the authority for loans and a modest issue
of treasury notes. In March 1812 Congress had authorized a loan of
$11,000,000, and this the government was able to obtain. The general pub-
lic and banks were attracted by the 6 per cent rate. The situation became
more difficult in 1813 when total expenditure was over $30,000,000. In
February 1813 Congress authorized a $16,000,000 loan, as well as an addi-
tional issue of treasury notes. The declining trade conditions and the disasters of 1812 had a negative effect. The government found it very difficult
to get subscribers to the loan, and ultimately much of it had to be obtained
on special terms through a syndicate put together by Stephen Girard, John
Jacob Astor, and David Parish.

The Republicans continued to be reluctant to vote sufficient taxes to pay
for the war and secure the loans, and the loan policy also suffered from New
England opposition to the war. The Northeast had most of the available capital in the country, but of more than $40,000,000 borrowed by the govern-
ment by the end of 1814, New England provided less than $3,000,000.
Gallatin had served at the Treasury since 1801. In May 1813 he left it on
leave of absence, never to return. His policies were in disarray. As the revenue

20   *AC*, 12th Cong., 2nd Sess., p.690 (Sheffey, 11 Jan. 1813), p.758 (Macon, 12 Jan. 1813);
      Reginald Horsman, 'On to Canada: Manifest destiny and United States Strategy in the War
      of 1812,' *Michigan Historical Review* 13 (1987),' pp.16–21.

garnered from taxes on trade continued to decline, loans continued to be the main method of financing the war.[21] The Republican administration never resolved the dilemma that it had declared war while not wanting to pay for it. The situation looked bleak for the following year.

At the heart of the financial problems of the United States was the collapse of much of the trade with Great Britain, and the difficulty of carrying on trade anywhere as the number of British ships off the American coast began to increase. In this situation it was particularly frustrating that some of the trade that was being carried on directly benefited the British. Flour and other supplies were being sent to Canada, to the British West Indies, and to the British armies in the Iberian Peninsula. Most of this trade was from New England. To facilitate this trade, the British did not extend their strict blockade to the New England coast, and granted licenses to American ships so that they could avoid seizure by British ships.

In July 1812 the British consul in Boston informed the Commander-in-Chief of the British North American station that he had consulted leading American merchants. They were perfectly willing to carry on a trade in flour and bread stuff to the Spanish Peninsula and to the British West Indies. The consul reported that the war was 'unanimously execrated' in his area, and that he could certainly contract to supply 10,000 barrels a month, or even larger quantities, for delivery at any port. Orders to British naval commanders in American waters were to detain all American vessels, except those carrying licenses. The Commander-in-Chief supplied the consul with a signed draft of a license. He said that anyone wishing to carry on this trade to British areas could be given a copy. The draft included the phrase that the named individual was 'well inclined toward the English interest.' In the following months American ships in large numbers proved willing to carry these licenses. New England was the main source of the trade, but there were many such clearances from New York, and even out of the Chesapeake. They became so popular that ships that wanted to get past the British blockade for other trade made use of forged licenses.[22]

In November 1812 Congress tried to ban the export of flour and bread stuff, but failed, and later the Senate also refused to pass a law stating that American ships could not sail under British license. It was not until July

---

21   Stagg, *Madison's War*, pp.298–300; Alexander Balinky, *Albert Gallatin: Fiscal Theories and Policies* (New Brunswick, NJ, 1958), pp.183–202; Davis R. Dewey, *Financial History of the United States* 9th edn (New York, 1924), pp.132–42; Edward J. Perkins, *American Public Finance and Financial Services, 1700–1815* (Columbus, Ohio, 1994), pp.330–4.
22   ADM 1/502, pp.140, 207, 222–3, 328 (18, 30 July, 4, 5 Aug., 19 Oct. 1812).

1813 that Congress finally prohibited such trade, and even after that measure was passed there was extensive illegal trade out of New England. The British blockade of the American coast south of New England gradually became tighter. While it was impossible to prevent individual privateers sailing from the small ports that existed along the entire American coastline, the British were able to crush most of the American trade that did not benefit Great Britain. Late in 1812 the Admiralty ordered a formal blockade of Chesapeake and Delaware Bays, and this was put into effect in February 1813. In the spring the blockade was extended north to New York and south to Charleston, Port Royal, Savannah, and the mouth of the Mississippi. The Americans also had no way of preventing the strong British naval forces from landing raiding parties on the American coast, and in the spring and summer of 1813 the British frequently sent shore parties to pillage and burn along the shores of Chesapeake Bay.[23]

Major land operations in the North were suspended during the winter months, but such endeavors as the American forces attempted brought further disappointments. William Henry Harrison, who took command of the American northwestern army, attempted to position his forces to regain control of the Detroit area. American troops under General James Winchester were sent to advance on the Maumee, but Winchester unwisely split his forces. He personally commanded nearly 1,000 of them who moved to the River Raisin, quite close to Detroit. In January 1813 a British force, accompanied by several hundred Indians, marched swiftly from the Detroit River. In the battle of Frenchtown they overwhelmed the Americans. The new year had started with another defeat.[24]

In the South major campaigns did not cease in the winter. In that region many Americans were hopeful that they could take advantage of the war to gain more of the Floridas. The United States was not at war with Spain, but Spain was an ally of England in Europe, and it could be argued that the Floridas might be used by Great Britain to attack the United States. Madison, who had already taken part of West Florida in 1810, was also hoping that the war would give him the opportunity for further territorial gains in the area. Tennesseans were eager for the War of 1812, and they knew the value of the Gulf. In the fall of 1812 the Secretary of War asked the Tennessee governor to provide 1,500 militia for the defense of New Orleans and the

23 ADM 2/1375, pp.337–8 (26 Dec. 1812), ADM 1/503, p.109 (6 Feb. 1813), ADM 2/1376, pp.179–81 (26 Mar. 1813); Stagg, *Madison's War*, pp.274–5; Horsman, *War of 1812*, pp.75–80; *ASP, MA*, 1, pp.358–67.

24 Gilpin, *War of 1812*, pp.147–71.

lower Mississippi. It was also anticipated that this force might be used to invade the Floridas. In Tennessee there was none of the resistance of New England: 2,000 rather than 1,500 troops were provided, and under the command of Andrew Jackson they reached Natchez in February.

Madison's hopes of taking the Floridas rapidly evaporated. In January he asked Congress to authorize him to occupy the Floridas, using the argument that there was a danger of the British using the possessions of their European ally to attack the Americans. Congress balked, and only gave permission to occupy the rest of West Florida; in essence this meant moving troops to Mobile. Jackson's army was not needed for that and it was disbanded. In March American forces from New Orleans occupied Mobile without resistance. The United States never returned West Florida to the Spanish, but ambitions for East Florida had to be deferred to the post-war years.[25]

With the British blockade tightening, American finances in disarray, and widespread disaffection in New England, the United States approached the spring and summer of 1813 with the hope that the increasingly disastrous situation could be redeemed by a successful invasion of Canada. This would not solve the maritime problems, but it would allow the American government to claim some advantage from having fought, and would provide a bargaining counter in any future negotiations with the British. For many Republicans in Congress the original object of invading Canada – to force the British to recognize American neutral rights – had been succeeded by the aim of conquering and retaining Britain's remaining American possession. Unfortunately for American hopes, mobilization and organization for war had not suddenly reached a new level of accomplishment. The armies of 1813 were to be beset by many of the same problems as those of 1812.

25   Robert V. Remini, *Andrew Jackson and the Course of American Empire, 1767–1821* (New York, 1977), pp.170–7.

CHAPTER 15

CRISIS

In 1813 the United States tried to seize control of the Great Lakes, a step that it should have taken before declaring war. Control of the lakes would mean the ability to sever communications to British armies in the West, and would make advancing on land much safer. The lake on which a navy would be of immediate use was Erie. The Americans had been defeated on the Detroit frontier, but in that region the British army and its Indian allies depended on traffic on Lake Erie for their supplies. A naval force on Lake Erie would change the balance of power in the region.

The first step to an organized policy on the lakes was taken in September 1812 when Commodore Isaac Chauncey was given command of all the lakes west of Lake Champlain. He took personal charge of activities on Lake Ontario, establishing his headquarters at Sackett's Harbor. He sent Commander Jesse D. Elliott to establish a navy on Lake Erie. Elliott built two small brigs and bought schooners that could be used as gunboats. He raised American morale when he sailed from Black Rock and attacked two small British vessels anchored near Fort Erie.[1]

In the winter a more ambitious building plan went into operation at Presque Isle (Erie, Pennsylvania). Under the able direction of shipbuilder Noah Brown, two 20-gun brigs, a schooner, and three gunboats began to take shape. There was an additional brig, three schooners, and a sloop at Black Rock. In March 1813 Master Commandant Oliver Hazard Perry arrived at Presque Isle to take command of this new, unfinished fleet, and the ships from Black Rock joined him in June. For the Americans, shipbuilding on the lakes was more feasible than it was for the British, for they had resources that were unavailable to the Canadians. They were also able to send experienced seamen from the Atlantic coast, while the British often had to depend on Canadian landsmen to man their ships.

---

1   William S. Dudley *et al.* (eds), *The Naval War of 1812: A Documentary History* (Washington, DC, 1985–), 1, pp.296–317, 327–33.

Entrance to the harbor at Presque Isle was blocked by a sand bar that prevented incursions by British ships, but also made it difficult for the Americans to leave. In mid-summer, British ships off the port briefly sailed away, and Perry took the opportunity to drag his ships over the bar into the lake. The Americans were now in a strong position on Lake Erie. The British squadron on the lake was under the command of an experienced seaman, Captain Robert Barclay, but it was weaker than the American force. Barclay needed seamen and his ships were ill prepared. He was obliged to seek a battle because the British and the Indians on the Detroit frontier desperately needed more supplies. They could only obtain them by way of Lake Erie. Barclay sailed from Amherstburg on 9 September and met the American squadron at Put-in-Bay in the Bass Islands on the following day. The battle resulted in a complete victory for the Americans, but for a time it was touch and go. In the middle of the battle Perry had to be rowed from his own disabled vessel to take command of another ship. When the battle was over, Perry's fleet commanded Lake Erie.[2]

The importance of naval command of the lakes was demonstrated decisively by Perry's victory. Major-General Henry Procter, the British commander of the forces at Fort Malden and Detroit, immediately decided that he had no choice but to abandon the Detroit frontier region and retreat to the western end of Lake Ontario. This caused considerable confusion at Fort Malden because the Indian commander Tecumseh resisted the move. The Indians were unwilling to accept the argument that because of some distant naval battle they would have to retreat from the region in which they had been victorious. Tecumseh protested in vain, and within two weeks Procter and his army had abandoned Detroit and Fort Malden and retreated eastwards. While many Indians now left the British, Tecumseh and some 500 Indians remained.

The Americans occupied the Detroit region with a force of some 4,500 men, and followed the British as they retreated. Procter conducted an inept and confused withdrawal. On 5 October he was obliged to make a stand against the Americans at the village of Moraviantown on the Thames River. The battle of the Thames was a complete victory for the Americans. Procter and the remnant of his army fled in confusion while Tecumseh was killed on the battlefield. The Americans were again in control of the Detroit frontier region, and had taken Fort Malden, but at the beginning of the war this had

---

2   Ibid., 2, pp.406–11, 479–88, 543–65; David C. Skaggs and Gerard T. Althoff, *A Signal Victory: The Lake Erie Campaign, 1812–1813* (Annapolis, Md, 1997).

simply been an objective to forestall any British–Indian raids on the American frontier. It did nothing to further the conquest of Canada.[3]

The situation on Lake Ontario was far less clear-cut than on Lake Erie.
When Commodore Chauncey took over the American naval forces there
early in the fall of 1812, the British held an advantage in ships. Chauncey
began a shipbuilding program, but the British authorities in Canada also
exerted great efforts. As they did not have the same resources as the
Americans to build new ships, and as ocean-going vessels could not be taken
past Montreal, they even sent frames of ships from England in an effort to
maintain the balance of power. In this they were successful. The shipbuilding race on Lake Ontario resulted in a stand-off, even though by the end of
the war the Americans were constructing a ship of the line. At different times
each side temporarily held the advantage, but there was no decisive shift in
the balance of power.[4]

Lake Ontario loomed large in American plans because Secretary of War
Armstrong realized that an attack on Montreal was impractical in the near
future. In February 1813 the Americans had only some 2,400 men along
Lake Champlain. Armstrong's alternative plan was to capture Kingston and
cut off British communication with all west of that spot. The Americans
would destroy the British ships at Kingston, then attack York (the modern
Toronto), the capital of Upper Canada, before assaulting Fort George and
Fort Erie along the Niagara frontier. The military commander was to be the
cautious Henry Dearborn. Armstrong's plan was ambitious, and ultimately
the most important part of it was abandoned.[5]

At Sackett's Harbor, Dearborn quickly convinced himself that not only
was the attack on Kingston impractical, but that his own base was in danger.
Above all, he wanted to avoid an immediate, risky assault on Kingston. His
solution was to argue that York should be attacked first, the ships there
destroyed, naval command of the lake obtained, the forts on the Niagara
River captured, and finally Kingston attacked. In April Chauncey's ships
took an American force across the lake to York. It was a marauding raid, not
an invasion of Canada. The Americans succeeded in destroying a ship under
construction, along with naval stores and other public property, but the commander of the assault, Brigadier-General Zebulon Pike, was killed with
many of his men when a magazine blew up. Also, American actions at York,

3   John Sugden, *Tecumseh's Last Stand* (Norman, Okla, 1985), has a detailed account of Procter's
    retreat and the battle of the Thames.
4   Reginald Horsman, *The War of 1812* (London, 1969), pp.86–8, 138–40.
5   C. Edward Skeen, *John Armstrong, Jr, 1758–1843: A Biography* (Syracuse, NY, 1981), pp.145–6.

including the burning of the Parliament building, was used by the British as the excuse for their burning of buildings in Washington, DC in the following year.[6]

Dearborn's unwillingness to take risks had frustrated Secretary of War Armstrong's hopes of winning a major victory by an attack on Kingston, but even that victory would only have given the Americans control of Upper Canada. Fighting on the Niagara and Lake Champlain fronts remained indecisive throughout the summer.

Although American forces on the vital Lake Champlain front remained weak, Armstrong was determined that the campaigning season should not pass without an attack on Montreal. Dearborn had been replaced as Commander-in-Chief by Brigadier-General James Wilkinson, a man whose career had survived entanglements with the Spanish and involvement in the Burr conspiracy. He had a remarkable survival ability. His abilities as a general were less remarkable.

Armstrong suggested alternative plans to the new Commander-in-Chief, one of them calling for an assault on Kingston while a diversionary attack was launched on Montreal. The other, which was eventually decided on, was to take an army from Sackett's Harbor, bypass Kingston, and advance down the St Lawrence to attack Montreal in combination with an army advancing north from Lake Champlain. Wilkinson was not enthusiastic for either plan. His own preference was for attacks in the Niagara region, and possibly farther west. Knowing that the chances of conquering Canada were fast disappearing for another year, Secretary of War Armstrong insisted that Wilkinson should move east down the St Lawrence.

On paper, the idea of armies timing their advances in a pincer movement, dividing the British defenses, and uniting before Montreal, looked extremely attractive. But, as the army had encountered the greatest logistical difficulties in performing the simplest advances into Canada, there seemed considerable reason to doubt whether this more ambitious plan could be accomplished. The commanders involved made the whole project even more questionable. Wilkinson, who was in overall charge, and who would lead the armies from Sackett's Harbor, had not wanted to carry out this plan. The general in command on the Lake Champlain front was Wade Hampton, a very rich South Carolina planter. He disliked Wilkinson intensely. When he

---

6   William Wood (ed.), *Select British Documents of the Canadian War of 1812* 4 vols (Toronto, 1920–8), 2, pp.85–96; *ASP, MA*, 1, pp.443–4; CO 42/150, pp.162–3, CO 42/354, pp.107, 109, 132–5, 350–1.

accepted the appointment from Armstrong he had insisted that he would [2 3 9]
receive his orders only from the War Department, and that only in the event
of a combined operation would he accept orders from the Commander-in-
Chief, Wilkinson. That combined operation was now about to take place.[7]

Wilkinson arrived at Sackett's Harbor in August. He hoped to set out in
September. This did not happen. With a naval stand-off on Lake Ontario,
there were difficulties in bringing troops from the Niagara frontier to rein-
force Wilkinson's army. Secretary of War Armstrong was so concerned about
the whole operation that in September he came to Sackett's Harbor, adding
further confusion to the proceedings. The American forces were ill prepared
for amphibious operations, and though the first troops were loaded on the
ships in mid-October it was not until early November that they moved to the
entrance to the St Lawrence (under 20 miles away). The force amounted to
some 8,000 men.

For Hampton's advance north from Lake Champlain it had only been
possible to assemble some 4,000 troops. This theatre of operations, which
should have been the most important one of the war, continued to suffer
greatly from the unwillingness of the New England states to supply militia.
Hampton, still fuming at being under the command of Wilkinson, moved
towards the Canadian border in mid-January. He was to advance down the
Chateauguay River to the St Lawrence. The British had ample notice of what
was happening, and to augment 5,000 regulars had called out some 13,000
militia. Even if the American operation had been more efficiently organized,
they were advancing with too few troops.

The American forces were never to discover whether they could successfully assault Montreal with inferior numbers, because they never got
there. After meeting the first outlying British resistance on the Chateauguay,
and having heard nothing from Wilkinson, Hampton decided to retreat.
Wilkinson entered the St Lawrence early in November. The weather was
deteriorating, the force encountered stubborn resistance from the British and
the Canadian militia, and had supplies for less than a month's campaigning.
In the second week of November, when Wilkinson heard that Hampton was
withdrawing, he abandoned the whole operation. He withdrew to French
Mills on the American side of the boarder, and there, lacking sufficient food,
clothing, or shelter, the American army spent a large part of the winter.[8]

7   Skeen, *Armstrong*, pp.158–61.
8   Horsman, *War of 1812*, pp.117–31; J. Mackay Hitsman, *The Incredible War of 1812* (Toronto,
    1965), pp.160–70.

In the fall, while Wilkinson and Hampton were leading the attempt to take Montreal, the British had won back all they had lost on the Niagara frontier, and the American towns of Lewiston, Black Rock, and Buffalo had been burned to the ground in retaliation for the American destruction of the Canadian village of Newark.[9] Canada was no nearer being conquered at the end of 1813 than it was in June 1812, and there was to be no other opportunity. The campaigning season of 1814 was to bring the invasion of the United States, not the invasion of Canada.

The 13th Congress inherited the daunting task of attempting to finance an unsuccessful war at a time when revenue and American trade were diminishing rapidly. When it was called into a special session in May 1813 the House spent much of its time trying to get Republican agreement on unpopular internal taxes. Some Republicans were extremely reluctant to place taxes on slaves and dwellings, as well as duties on the distillation of spirits and sugar, auctions, and retailers of wines and spirits, but after much debate the measures were approved.[10]

When Congress reassembled in December 1813 the position was worse. The British blockade was now becoming increasingly effective in the area south from New York. New England could still trade, because so much of that trade went to British possessions that the British continued to confine their tight blockade to other areas. As late as August 1814 British governor in chief Prevost said two-thirds of the army in Canada was eating beef provided by American contractors, principally from Vermont and New York. Madison had long wanted to stop this trade with the enemy, but in the special session of Congress his request for an embargo on exports had been rejected by the Senate. The American navy was not in a position to stop the trade because the British blockade had confined their ships to port.[11]

In December Madison again asked Congress to place an embargo on American exports and a ban on imports of British goods. Madison wanted to stop both New England ships aiding the British and the extensive trade across the Canadian border. Although Congress was divided, it acted rapidly. The House passed the bill by a vote of 85 to 57 and the Senate by

9   Horsman, *War of 1812*, pp.134–6; Hitsman, *Incredible War*, pp.172–3.

10 *AC*, 13th Cong., 1st Sess., pp.319–28, 351–83, 387–413, 421–9, 441–65, 468–9; Henry Adams, *History of the United States of America during the Administrations of Thomas Jefferson and James Madison* 9 vols (New York, 1889–91), 7, pp.53–71; Alexander Balinky, *Albert Gallatin: Fiscal Policies and Theories* (New Brunswick, NJ, 1958), pp.198–9.

11 *AC*, 13th Cong., 1st Sess., pp.100–1; J. C. A. Stagg, *Mr Madison's War: Politics, Diplomacy, and Warfare in the Early Republic, 1783–1830* (Chapel Hill, NC, 1983), pp.318–19; CO 42/157, pp.120–1, 157–8 (5, 27 Aug. 1814).

20 to 14. Madison signed it on 17 December. New England's opposition to the war became more intense, although the embargo was repealed in April 1814.[12]

For the coming year the financial position of the government was reaching a crisis point. Even with the new internal taxes, the tighter British blockade meant that revenue was reduced. Gallatin had still not officially resigned from the Treasury, but he had left on a diplomatic mission to Europe. William Jones, the Secretary of the Navy, handled the Treasury until February 1814. He estimated in January that to meet its expenses the government would need to borrow $29,350,000 in the coming year. In March Congress approved $25,000,000 in loans and the issue of $10,000,000 in Treasury notes. But borrowing was becoming increasingly difficult. There was no Bank of the United States to facilitate loans – the Republicans had killed it in 1811 – and New England, the area with the most capital, gave very little support to the government's efforts to raise money.[13]

In February 1814 Gallatin resigned from the Treasury, and George Washington Campbell accepted the thankless task of running it. In the course of the spring and summer the government kept discounting its stock to try and get buyers; eventually it was disposed of at only four-fifths of its face value. The government also had to accept state bank notes instead of specie, and since the banks themselves were experiencing increasing difficulty their bank notes were circulating in a depreciated state. By the end of the summer the government was approaching bankruptcy.[14]

In looking towards the campaigning season of 1814 the United States appeared to face overwhelming problems. Napoleon was nearing defeat. British armies had pushed the French out of the Spanish Peninsula, the Russians were advancing from the East, and in the winter of 1813–14 armies poured into France. In April Napoleon surrendered. Up to this time the war in America had been a sideshow for the British. Their best officers and their best troops were fighting in Europe, but with the war in Europe ending they could now concentrate on bringing an end to the American conflict. They had numerous ships and numerous men available for the American war.

---

12 *AC*, 13th Cong., 2nd Sess., pp.554–61, 2033–54, 2781–8, 2830; Stagg, *Madison's War*, p.384.
13 Balinky, *Gallatin*, pp.204–5.
14 Balinky, *Gallatin*, pp.205–6; Adams, *History*, 7, pp.384–90; David R. Dewey, *Financial History of the United States* 9th edn (New York, 1924), pp.131–4; Edward J. Perkins, *American Public Finance and Financial Services, 1700–1815* (Columbus, Ohio, 1994), pp.334–5.

In November 1813 the British had extended their blockade northwards into Long Island Sound, leaving only New England free to trade. British naval strength for the North American station at Halifax was set in the same month at 10 ships of the line, 20 frigates, and 25 20-gun ships, as well as smaller vessels. There were additional ships on the West India stations. In April 1814 Vice-Admiral Sir Alexander Cochrane assumed command at Halifax. He quickly extended the blockade to the whole New England coastline.[15]

Even before the formal extension of the blockade to New England its coastal residents had begun to feel the effects of the new British determination to end the conflict. In early April a British raiding party entered the Connecticut River at New London and destroyed some 27 ships there. The American traitor who guided the British party was rewarded with the princely sum of $2,000. In the following months the New England coast began to endure the harassment that communities on Chesapeake Bay had been experiencing for over a year.[16]

For the island of Nantucket, 30 miles off the New England coast, the extension of the blockade was a complete disaster. In peacetime they made their living from whaling. The island was so barren that provisions and wood had to be imported. In the winter of 1813–14 Congress had exempted Nantucket from the embargo so that the inhabitants of the island could import food and fuel from the mainland. But when the British blockade was extended to New England the islanders were completely isolated. By August they had only two weeks supply of fuel and food. As a result they were placed in the strange position of signing their own peace agreement with the British navy. In August Nantucket commissioners boarded a British ship and formally declared the island neutral. In the following month they also agreed that they would pay no more taxes to the American government during the war with Great Britain.[17]

Nantucket was an exceptional situation, but in 1814 the British blockade had drastic results. American exports fell to less than $7,000,000. They had amounted to over $108,000,000 in 1807. The lucrative grain trade that the northeastern shippers had carried on to the Spanish Peninsula was brought to an end. Although privateering to some extent offset other losses, those

15 ADM 1/505, pp.277–8 (20 Nov. 1813), ADM 1/506, pp.26, 38–9, 44–5 (25, 28 Apr. 1814).
16 ADM 1/506, pp.47–8, 203, 272–7, 280 (9, 13, 27 Apr., 10 May 1814).
17 Reginald Horsman, 'Nantucket's peace treaty with England in 1814,' *New England Quarterly*, 54 (1981), pp.180–98.

engaged in shipping and its support activities suffered badly in the war. They were joined in their distress by the staple crop producers of the South, who had great difficulty marketing their tobacco and cotton. Manufacturing in the Northeast was given a sizeable boost by the conflict, and surplus maritime capital from earlier years often went into manufacturing rather than into government loans for the Americans. Certain areas, particularly Pennsylvania, New York, and the western states, benefited from the vastly increased levels of government expenditure needed to supply the armies. Western towns boomed. Pittsburgh sold to the military, and was also able to develop vigorous infant industries to fill the gap left by the lack of British imports. As in all wars, some prospered while soldiers suffered. The government sank deeper and deeper into financial crisis.[18]

Even the increased blockades of 1813 and 1814 could not keep American privateers in port. Although there was always a danger of being seized, individual ships were able to make their escape. Over 300 British merchant ships were seized by American privateers in 1813, and even the commitment of far more British ships to the American war in 1814 did not stop their activities. In the House of Commons in December 1814 the members were told that the war had resulted in the seizure of some 1,175 British ships by the Americans. What was particularly galling to the British was that the privateers were operating around the coasts of Britain. In an age with no surveillance from the air, and no radio communication, ships could easily disappear. And if they were lucky with the winds, fast sailing and well-manned American privateers could often escape larger ships even when they were sighted.[19]

Privateering was of no help along the vulnerable American coasts, and could not stop the movement of British troops to Canada in preparation for an invasion of the United States. England was ready to turn to the attack, and impose a peace that would probably result in permanent American losses of territory south of the Maine–New Brunswick border and along the Great Lakes. The British were also planning to invade in the South, but it seemed most likely that any successful British invasion on the Gulf was less likely to lead to enforced cessions there than to bring pressure for cessions in other areas. The British anticipated major victories in 1814. Now that the war in

18 Donald R. Hickey, *The War of 1812: A Forgotten Conflict* (Urbana, Ill, 1989), pp.227–31; Curtis P. Nettels, *The Emergence of a National Economy, 1775–1815* (New York, 1962), pp.331–7; Emory R. Johnson *et al.* (eds), *History of Domestic and Foreign Commerce of the United States* 2 vols (1915; rpr, New York, 1967), 2, p.20.

19 *Hansard*, 1st Ser., 29 (1814–15), pp.649; Adams, *History*, 7, pp.315–21.

[244] Europe was over the British government was determined to win a decisive victory over the Americans.

In the spring of 1814 the British decided to send 10,000 veteran troops to Canada. They began to leave in May. British objectives were detailed in secret instructions sent to governor in chief Prevost in June 1814. The British wished to provide for the long-term security of Canada. Prevost was told to destroy Sackett's Harbor and the American navy on Lake Erie and Lake Champlain, and to recapture Detroit and the whole of Michigan country. The British wanted to keep Fort Niagara, and to erect an Indian barrier state to provide a buffer between the United States and Canada. This had been a dream of the British since the early 1790s. They ignored the fact that it had been made impossible by the large-scale advance of American settlers across the Ohio River in the previous two decades.[20]

For all the veteran reinforcements from Europe, the British were to have as little success as the Americans in achieving their objectives along the Canadian border. The main British success was on the Northeast coast. Making use of their naval superiority, they transported troops to occupy a large part of northern Maine, as far south as the Penobscot River. American resistance was minimal. Far to the West, the British were also successful in retaining control of Fort Mackinac, and they extended their influence in the region by sending a force to capture Prairie du Chien on the Mississippi River. Governor Prevost made no attempt to retake Detroit. The Americans still had naval control of Lake Erie. Although a large part of Maine and what is now the state of Wisconsin were under the control of the British, their retention would depend on the major battles along the Canadian border.[21]

Both on Lake Ontario and on the Niagara front the British were to discover that the Americans had learned from their dismal experiences in 1812 and 1813. There were more experienced American troops, and most of the incompetent officers had been tested and replaced. The supply situation was still poor, but morale was higher. Also, the British missed an opportunity on Lake Ontario. For a time in May, after launching ships of 58 and 44 guns, the British had temporary naval superiority, but they failed to take advantage of it to attack Sackett's Harbor. Soon the naval stand-off was restored by American ship construction, and continued until the end of the war.

20   CO 43/23, pp.150–5 (3 June 1814).

21   For Maine, see ADM 1/506, pp.379–82, 539–40 (12 July, 25 Aug. 1814), ADM 1/507, pp.128–37, 304–6 (3, 9, 11, 14, 27 Sept. 1814). For Wisconsin, see Reginald Horsman, 'Wisconsin and the War of 1812,' *Wisconsin Magazine of History* 46 (1962), pp.3–15.

On the Niagara frontier, the Americans took the initiative. Crossing into Canada in July they took Fort Erie and defeated the British at the battle of Chippawa. The American force under Major-General Jacob Brown surprised the British by their effectiveness in this battle. Military lessons had been learned from the earlier disasters, but they had been learned too late to produce a successful invasion of Canada. Brown eventually had to retreat in the face of superior British forces, but at Lundy's Lane the American troops fought well before withdrawing to Fort Erie. In August they successfully repulsed a British attack. In November they blew up the fort and withdrew to the American side of the river. The Americans had not been able to advance very far into Canada in this effort at Niagara, but on this occasion the British were more disappointed than the Americans. In 1814 they had more to lose from a stand-off than the United States.[22]

Prevost's main effort to carry out his orders from the British government was by invading the United States southwards from Montreal to Lake Champlain. The United States army remained weak on this front in 1814, and there seemed little doubt that it could be swept aside by Prevost's veteran European troops. The key to the British advance, however, was on the lake itself. To advance southwards to New York the British needed control of Lake Champlain for supplies, and to prevent being outflanked. It appeared that naval strength on the lake was fairly evenly balanced.

At the end of August the British were poised to begin their invasion with a force of some 10,000 regulars, most of them veterans of the European wars. At this decisive moment Secretary of War Armstrong ordered Major-General George Izard and 4,000 men to march from Lake Champlain to Sackett's Harbor. Izard had warned him that he expected a British attack, but Armstrong ignored him. Brigadier-General Alexander Macomb, now in command at Plattsburgh, was left with some 3,000 men, of whom only half were effective. If the British overran Plattsburgh, and there was not the slightest reason to suppose they could be stopped, there was nothing to prevent them advancing to take New York City and separating the Northeast from the rest of the Union.[23]

The British marched rapidly southwards. An advantage for the Americans was that the experienced generals from Europe were under the command of governor in chief Prevost, and he was a cautious man. The British army met only token resistance before it reached the outskirts of Plattsburgh on

---

22   Horsman, *War of 1812*, pp.173–9.
23   Ibid., pp.185–7.

[246] 6 September. The American fleet on Lake Champlain was in Plattsburgh Bay under the command of Captain Thomas Macdonough. Prevost decided that he could not continue his advance until any danger from that fleet had been removed, and called on the British Lake Champlain fleet, which was near to Plattsburgh, to engage the Americans.

The British fleet, under the command of Captain George Downie, moved to the attack on 11 September. The British had four vessels; the largest, the *Confiance*, rated at 36 guns, and 12 gunboats. The Americans also had four vessels, but their largest ship, the *Saratoga* was only rated at 26 guns, and they had ten gunboats. The British had the largest ship, but it had only recently been launched. Overall the British had a slight advantage in guns, but the lack of preparation on the *Confiance*, Captain Downie's death early in the engagement, and Captain Macdonough's skill carried the day for the Americans. The battle was a complete victory for the United States. As soon as Prevost knew that his fleet was lost he decided that he could not risk advancing any farther south, and withdrew to Canada.[24] This American victory was to be of decisive importance in the negotiations for peace.

While the Americans were waiting for Prevost and his army at Plattsburgh, the United States was suffering humiliation in the national capital. The American inability to resist any sizeable British naval force had made Chesapeake Bay highly vulnerable throughout the war. In the summers of both 1813 and 1814 British raiding parties had landed on its shores, harassed its inhabitants, and destroyed stores and ships. They also encouraged slaves to flee their masters and join the British forces. In the summer of 1814 a force of several hundred men formed from these slaves took part in the fighting in the Bay.[25] In July and August American resistance was so weak that the British were finding no difficulty in raiding at will. The British commander, Vice-Admiral Sir Alexander Cochrane, argued that his raids were retaliation for the American destruction of property in Upper Canada. The British government reinforced the forces in the Chesapeake in 1814 so that action there could divert American attention from the main British attack from Canada.

In August several thousand troops under Major-General Robert Ross joined the British in the Chesapeake. Having encountered little American resistance the British decided that, after attacking a force of gunboats in

---

24   Allan S. Everest, *The War of 1812* in the Champlain Valley (Syracuse, NY, 1981), pp.179–92.
25   Horsman, *War of 1812*, pp.75–80, 153–7; Frank A. Cassell, 'Slaves of the Chesapeake Bay area in the War of 1812,' *Journal of Negro History*, 57 (1972), pp.144–55.

Patuxent River, they would advance on Washington. American defenses around Washington were very weak, and, in spite of earlier British activity in the Chesapeake region, the capital was unfortified. The American commander in the region, Brigadier-General William H. Winder, had only some 1,000 regulars and less than 2,000 militia, although in theory he could call on thousands more from the surrounding states. On 19 August the British force of some 4,000 men landed at Benedict, Maryland. Once the Americans realized that the British seemed likely to march on Washington desperate attempts were made to raise more militia, but the general scene was one of confusion and near panic. Winder was an inept general, and he was also hindered by interference from Secretary of War Armstrong and other members of the cabinet.

By 24 August, when Winder attempted to make a stand at Bladensburg, the Americans had some 7,000 men in the field, but there were only about 1,000 regulars and the militia were ill prepared. The battle turned into a rout. The British regulars swept through the American force. One of the few strong points of American resistance was provided by several hundred sailors defending gun batteries. Casualties on both sides were low because of the speed with which the American force broke and ran. The British lost 64 killed, the Americans 26. The British marched into Washington. President Madison and American government officials fled. The Navy Yard was destroyed by the retreating Americans, the British burned the president's house, the Capitol, the War Office, and the Treasury, and they destroyed the main bridge over the Potomac. Two other bridges had been destroyed by the Americans.[26] Fortunately for the United States the burning of Washington was not followed by news of a British army sweeping through Plattsburgh and marching on New York City.

The British quickly left Washington. They had met such little resistance that they decided to move against the major port of Baltimore. They were not sure they had the force to take it, but now anything seemed possible. There was a great deal of valuable property in Baltimore, and, knowing what had happened in Washington, militia flocked to its defense. It was a difficult city to attack. The narrow entrance to its bay was guarded by Fort McHenry. When the British army advanced to the vicinity of Baltimore a preliminary skirmish resulted in the death of the British commander, Major-General Robert Ross. More decisive for the attempt on the city was the failure of the

---

26   Horsman, *War of 1812*, pp.194–202; *ASP, MA*, 1, pp.524–99; WO1/141, pp.34–7, 51–2, 57 (30 Aug., 1 Sept. 1814).

[2 4 8] British fleet to enter the bay. Throughout 13 September, and through the night to the morning of the 14th, British ships bombarded Fort McHenry. It did not fall. American lawyer and poet Francis Scott Key, who was on a British ship to arrange the release of a prisoner, watched the bombardment, and wrote 'The Star Spangled Banner.' It was immediately published in a Baltimore newspaper, although it did not become the official American national anthem until the twentieth century. Baltimore had held, and the British decided to retreat.[27] The burning of Washington had been a humiliation for the United States, but the victory on Lake Champlain was far more important for the outcome of the war.

In the late summer the political situation was in confusion. Madison and his Secretary of War Armstrong had clashed throughout the summer. On 4 September Armstrong resigned. A week later Secretary of the Navy William Jones announced that he would leave on 1 December. Monroe took over as Secretary of War, and for the time being also continued as Secretary of State. When Congress assembled in Washington on 20 September its members had to meet in the Post and Patent Office. The financial situation was chaotic. In the aftermath of the burning of Washington banks outside of New England had suspended specie payments, and the government could not raise the loans necessary to pay its obligations. Secretary of the Treasury Campbell reported that the nation needed more than $23,000,000 for the rest of 1814. Congress had to accept increased internal taxes, but they could not solve the immediate problems. Campbell resigned.

The new Secretary of the Treasury, Alexander J. Dallas of Philadelphia, took over in October. There was little he could do to solve the immediate problems. He borrowed what money he could, and the balance was made up by the issue of government Treasury notes. The country was bankrupt, unable to pay the interest on the national debt. Many Republicans were unhappy when Dallas told them that a new national bank was needed. A party that had begun to emerge in opposition to Hamilton's policies, of which the bank was a key element, found it difficult to stomach the idea that Hamilton had been right. The proposal produced vigorous debate in the winter of 1814–15. By 1816 it was to result in the passage of an act to create a Second Bank of the United States.[28]

27 ADM 1/507, pp.172–5 (17 Sept. 1814); WO 1/141, pp.75–84, 95–8 (15, 17 Sept.); Charles G. Muller, *The Darkest Day: The Washington–Baltimore Campaign* (Philadelphia, 1963), pp.173–205.
28 Stagg, *Madison's War*, pp.426–7, 444–52; Adams, *History*, 8, pp.213–15, 240–4; Dewey, *Financial History*, p.139.

The crisis in the fall of 1814 extended far beyond the government's [249] financial problems. In New England there was talk of secession from the Union. In many ways New England had suffered less economically from the war than the South. Although the great profits of the years before 1807 were no longer possible, New England had benefited from trade with the enemy, from privateering, and from the investment of available capital in manufacturing. At a time when there was a financial crisis in other areas of the country New England was still drawing in specie. But New England Federalists thought that the War of 1812 was an incredibly foolish and dangerous war; they believed that the United States should be aiding Britain against Napoleon, not fighting her. Federalists believed that the War of 1812 was a prime example of a southern- and western-dominated government acting totally against America's commercial interests and risking national ruin. Throughout the war traitorous and near-traitorous activity had been common in New England, and Federalist governors had frequently hindered the national war effort. By 1814 there was strong Federalist support for governmental changes that would decrease the power of the South and increase that of the New England states. A minority believed that the only solution was separation from the Union.

Shortly before the outbreak of war Gouverneur Morris of New York had proposed a convention of states north of the Potomac, with the object of eliminating the three-fifths compromise that allowed the South to have extra representation in Congress based on its slaves. This did not occur, but Morris continued to argue for it, and for restrictions on the admission of new states to the Union from the area encompassed by the Louisiana purchase. In 1813 the Massachusetts legislature condemned the Louisiana purchase, and instructed its representatives to attempt to get a repeal of the act admitting Louisiana to the Union.[29]

The crisis of 1814 led the Federalists to believe that the United States faced the risk of successful British invasions and dismemberment, and the Massachusetts legislature decided to invite the other New England states to attend a conference to discuss their common problems. This resulted in the Hartford Convention, which met in Hartford, Connecticut, from mid-December 1814 to early January 1815. Massachusetts sent 12 delegates, Connecticut 7 and Rhode Island 4. New Hampshire and Vermont did not

29 Samuel E. Morison, *The Life and Letters of Harrison Gray Otis, Federalist, 1765–1848* 2 vols (Boston, Mass, 1913), 2, pp.82–3; Anne Cary Morris, *The Diary and Letters of Gouverneur Morris* 2 vols (New York, 1888), 2, pp.549–52; Henry Adams (ed.), *Documents Relating to New-England Federalism, 1800–1815* (Boston, Mass, 1877), pp.388–93.

officially participate, but two unofficial delegates came from New Hampshire, and one from Vermont.

The convention met in secret, but the minority of extremists lost out to those who wished to remain in the Union. The delegates were an elite group, unhappy with Jefferson's whole idea of an 'empire for liberty.' They felt that not only their commercial interests, but also the whole sense of community that had been developed in New England was being overwhelmed by unrestrained growth. The report of the convention listed nine reasons why the Jefferson and Madison administrations had been ruinous to the nation. Most of these reasons concerned the ways in which the delegates believed that the southerners had manipulated the government for their own benefit and against that of the Northeast. To end this situation the convention suggested seven amendments to the Constitution: ending the extra southern representation provided for by the three-fifths compromise; requiring two-thirds votes in Congress for declaring war, passing non-intercourse acts, and admitting new states; limiting embargoes to 60 days; limiting presidents to only one term; prohibiting the election of two presidents in succession from the same state; and excluding naturalized citizens from federal office. The last measure reflected not only Federalist distrust of immigrants, but more particularly their hatred of Albert Gallatin. Late in January two delegates were appointed to go to Washington with the resolutions of the convention. By the time they arrived a peace treaty and a great victory, won after the war was over, had served to make the convention another cause of ruin for the Federalist party.[30]

The process of trying to end the war had begun in its first months. At that time, England had suggested that the repeal of the Orders in Council had made the war unnecessary. For the United States, a concession that would probably have prevented the war starting was not enough to stop it once begun, and they countered with the proposal that both the Orders in Council and impressment had to end. This was not acceptable to the British. In the fall of 1812 the Tsar of Russia, an ally of Great Britain, offered mediation to John Quincy Adams, the American minister in St Petersburg. His offer did not even reach the United States until March 1813. By then the United States was ready to talk, and James A. Bayard (a Federalist), and Secretary of the Treasury Albert Gallatin (who wanted to go) were sent to Europe to join Adams. They discovered that the British did not want

---

30 Hickey, *War of 1812*, pp.255–80; Theodore Dwight, *History of the Hartford Convention* (Boston, Mass, 1833).

mediation, but to avoid offending the Tsar were willing to talk directly to [2 5 1] the Americans. Finally, in January and February 1814, Madison appointed Adams, Bayard, and Gallatin, together with Henry Clay and Jonathan Russell, the American chargé in London, as a commission to negotiate a treaty.

After further delays the negotiations began in August at Ghent, in what was later Belgium. The English sent a far less distinguished team of negotiators than the Americans. They simply referred problems across the Channel to London. At the beginning of the negotiations both sides had strong demands. The Americans wanted no paper blockades, the giving up of impressment, repudiation of the Rule of 1756, a definition of contraband, and, if possible, Canada! The British, expecting big victories, wanted both sides to keep what they had conquered, no yielding on neutral rights, and an Indian buffer state in the Old Northwest. In the fall of 1814 the demands of both sides gradually disappeared. The key for the British was the news that the invasion of the United States from Canada had failed. The key for the Americans was the burning of Washington, and the total crisis of the early fall. The British were also affected by the attitude of the Duke of Wellington. In November, when offered the command in Canada, he replied that he would not take it unless guaranteed naval control of the Great Lakes, and that in his opinion the British had not achieved a position to justify demanding American cessions.

On 24 December 1814 the Treaty of Ghent was signed. There was no mention of the infringements of neutral rights that had driven the United States into war. There was to be a mutual restoration of territory, and four commissions were to be set up to deal with boundary problems dating from the treaty ending the Revolution. Great Britain had been at war since 1793. There was no desire to keep paying for a war in America when the future boundaries of Europe were still to be settled. The United States was happy to get out of a war that had almost resulted in complete disaster.[31]

Peace had been signed, but the way that the United States eventually viewed the War of 1812 was affected as much by a battle that occurred after the signing of the peace as by anything that happened in the war itself. The battle of New Orleans was the greatest American victory of the war, and Andrew Jackson was to set himself on the road to the presidency by his victory there. He had come to the attention of the federal government in his 1813–14 campaign against the Creek Indians. In 1813 part of the Creek

---

31 Bradford Perkins, *Castlereagh and Adams: England and the United States, 1812–1823* (Berkeley, Cal, 1964), pp.39–127; Fred L. Engelman, *The Peace of Christmas Eve* (New York, 1962).

Indian nation had tried to use the American involvement in the War of 1812 as an opportunity to strike back against those settlers who had been taking their lands. In August 1813 many settlers had been killed when the Creeks overran Fort Mims on the Alabama River, not far from Mobile. In the fall of 1813 and the early months of 1814 Andrew Jackson led an army from Tennessee on a ruthless campaign against the Creeks, killing many and destroying their villages. His campaign culminated in the battle of Horseshoe Bend in March 1814, where hundreds of Creek warriors were killed. At the treaty of Fort Jackson, in August 1814, Jackson forced the Creeks to cede a large part of their territory.[32]

In May 1814 Jackson was appointed as a Major-General in the regular army, and given command of the Gulf region. In the fall he acted with great vigor to raise an army and organize the defenses of the region. All of this was soon needed, for the British had decided to launch a major attack against New Orleans, using Jamaica as a point of assembly. There were the usual delays that plagued amphibious operations in the early nineteenth century, but the British arrived in the Gulf of Mexico in December. They had originally hoped to land at Mobile, and go overland to New Orleans, but that plan had been abandoned because of successful American resistance at Mobile. New Orleans itself, well inland from the mouth of the Mississippi, and with water and low-lying land on all sides, presented formidable obstacles. The British might have taken the city if they had attacked as soon as they arrived, but they delayed to bring up more troops, and after various skirmishes did not launch their main attack until 8 January 1815, three weeks after the peace had been signed. News of the peace had not yet reached them.

The British, confident from their victory over the French, and somewhat scornful of what they viewed as amateur American troops, launched a frontal assault on a narrow front with the Mississippi on the left and a swamp on the right. Jackson had well used the time the British had given him. The well-entrenched American forces slaughtered the advancing British troops. Total British casualties were some 2,000 killed, wounded, and missing. The Americans lost less than 100.[33] The victory was of great importance

---

32 Robert V. Remini, *Andrew Jackson and the Course of American Empire, 1767–1821* (New York, 1977), pp.187–233; Frank L. Owsley, *Struggle for the Gulf Borderlands: The Creek War and the Battle of New Orleans, 1812–1815* (Gainesville, Fla, 1981), pp.6–94.

33 Owsley, *Struggle for the Gulf,* pp.95–168; WO 1/141, pp.137–46, 149–56 (26 Dec. 1814, 10 Jan. 1815); ADM 1/508, pp.376–83; Samuel Carter, *Blaze of Glory: The Fight for New Orleans, 1814–1815* (New York, 1971); Charles B. Brooks, *The Siege of New Orleans* (Seattle, Wash, 1961).

for the self-image of the United States. It enabled a country that had almost [2 5 3] been defeated in 1814 to claim a victory. News of the peace of Ghent and Jackson's victory reached the East at almost the same time. Americans forgot the reasons the war had been fought, and the humiliations it had brought, and celebrated the successful termination of the 'second war for independence.'

CONCLUSION

By 1815 the United States had survived the first great testing time in its history. The Constitution had worked, and the new federal government had proved itself capable of exerting its authority and transferring power between opposing parties without national disruption. The country had even emerged triumphantly from its foreign crises. Not only had the nation established its boundaries in the Mississippi Valley, it had also doubled its size and acquired full access to the Gulf of Mexico. The nation had come nearest to disaster in the Jeffersonian response to the crisis at sea. The decision to retaliate against British interference with American trade by declaring war could easily have resulted in a humiliating defeat, a loss of territory, and the discrediting of the federal government. The war was preceded by totally inadequate preparations, and a failure to understand the vulnerability of American trade and the American coastlines to British naval power. Even a successful invasion of Canada would not have changed British maritime policies, and a successful British invasion of the United States was only prevented by Macdonough's naval victory on Lake Champlain. If that battle had been lost, there is every reason to suppose that New York City would have fallen to the British. If that had occurred, the Hartford Convention would have been a much more threatening gathering.

From 1789 to 1815 American history had been dominated by internal and external fears. The great internal fear had been whether republicanism on a large scale would work. By 1815 federal power was well established. Sharp party divisions had developed, but the emergence of separatism in New England had proved only to be the dream of a small, impotent minority. The Constitution, and the new nation, had surmounted its first great challenge. It was not to be endangered again until southern sectionalism became a powerful force.

Externally, the nation had faced major challenges to its territorial integrity from Spain, Great Britain, and France. The territorial and commercial problems created by the presence of Spain on the Gulf of Mexico were well on the way to being solved by the mid-1790s, and the temporary French threat created by the transfer of Louisiana from Spain to France was ended by the Louisiana purchase; only the dangers presented by the continued British occupation of Canada continued throughout this period. Yet, in 1814 and 1815, the way in which the British threat ended gave the Americans a surging new confidence. The repulse of the British invasion from Canada and Jackson's victory at New Orleans allowed the Americans to claim a second victory against Great Britain. It also helped foster the notion that God had made them a chosen people.

In the years from 1815 to 1850 Americans reveled in what they had achieved. Fears of failure were replaced by a deep belief in unbounded national destiny. Rather than the United States fearing the actions of foreign powers, adjacent territories on the American continent were now to be under threat from the United States. A nation that in its first years had been unable to uphold its boundaries in the eastern half of the Mississippi Valley developed ambitions westward to the Pacific, and confidently expected new territorial acquisitions to the north and to the south. Republicanism triumphant not republicanism threatened was the dominant theme of the years to mid-century.

In many respects the nation of 1815 was not the nation that the Founding Fathers had expected to emerge. The balance of power between the states and the federal government had been tipped decisively in favor of the federal government; although how decisively was not to be fully revealed until the Civil War. Although conflict over the correct interpretation of the Constitution had been one of the main factors in the emergence of political parties in the 1790s, the Republican opposition had demonstrated after achieving power that it was willing to accomplish its ends by a broad interpretation of that document. Federalist philosophies of federal power had triumphed, but Federalist elitism was in disarray. Political deference was being replaced by popular politics.

By 1815, however, the first American party system was already in a state of collapse. The Democratic–Republicans had appealed to a broader base than the Federalists while ultimately accepting Federalist notions of federal power. Frustrated by their impotence, the Federalists had pursued policies that allowed them to be attacked as unpatriotic as well as elitist. When the War of 1812 ended on a note of triumph, the Federalist opposition to that conflict left them in disarray. The Hartford Convention seemed totally irrelevant and misguided in the atmosphere of triumph produced by Jackson's victory at New Orleans.

At the end of the War of 1812 the Jeffersonians were governing a nation engaged in phenomenal growth. The 1790 population of some four million had more than doubled by 1815. Five states had joined the original 13, and another six were to be added by 1821. Settlers were poised to flood the eastern half of the Mississippi Valley, adventurous pioneers were crossing the Mississippi, and American fur traders were following the Missouri west to the Rocky Mountains. In less than ten years Congress was to debate the possibility of placing a military post at the mouth of the Columbia River on the Pacific.

The rapid expansion into the Mississippi Valley became increasingly disastrous for the many Indian occupants of that region. In the years after 1815 hopes that expansion would serve the Indians, as well as the nation and the new settlers, evaporated. The inhabitants of the new states of the Mississippi Valley did not want to live with transformed Indians. They wanted the land for themselves. The federal government responded to state and settler pressures by shaping policies to remove the Indians beyond the Mississippi. Eighteenth-century dreams of common humanity were replaced by nineteenth-century beliefs in superior and inferior races.

The economic dislocation produced by the commercial warfare and blockades ended when peace returned to Europe. In the years after 1815 the dramatic territorial expansion on the American continent was matched by a commercial expansion that sent American ships on to the oceans of the world. While Europe continued to attract the bulk of American trade, American traders extended their reach in Latin America and the Pacific, and dreamed of vast new markets.

Economic development over the next half-century was to amaze both Americans and foreign observers, but it was proceeding in a manner very different to that envisaged by the Jeffersonians in the 1790s. In many ways the economy was developing in ways they had feared. They could approve and support the rapid acquisition of western lands and the sale of farm produce in distant markets, but they had hoped to avoid speculators, entrepreneurs, and constantly multiplying banking and business corporations. The rampant commercialism of these years had extended into the areas that the Jeffersonians had hoped to resist, and in their policies of economic coercion they had stimulated the very factory system they feared. The America of 1815 was well on the way to the emergence of an individualistic, capitalistic society.

The great achievements of the years since 1789 were ultimately to be threatened by one great failure. The hopes of many in the revolutionary

generation that the problem of slavery could be solved had not been real- [2 5 7]
ized. Slavery was more firmly entrenched in 1815 than it had been in 1789.
There were two societies in the United States – a white society of European
origin with more political opportunities, religious freedom, and individual
economic opportunity than anywhere in Europe, and a black society of
African origin trapped in a system of slavery. After 1815 the racial implications of the failure to solve the problem of slavery were increasingly reflected
in relations with the American Indians and all non-white peoples. The political implications were to threaten the Union itself.

GUIDE TO FURTHER READING

Chapter 1

There is a perceptive discussion of the changing nature of society in these years in Gordon S. Wood, *The Radicalism of the American Revolution* (New York, 1992). Daily life is depicted in Jack Larkin, *The Reshaping of Everyday Life, 1740–1840* (New York, 1988), and there is a detailed emphasis of one aspect of changing society in William J. Gilmore-Lehne, *Reading Becomes a Necessity of Life: Material and Cultural Life in New England, 1780–1835* (Knoxville, Tenn, 1989). There is an emphasis on the inter-connections of religion with social and political changes in Nathan O. Hatch, *The Democratization of American Christianity* (New Haven, Conn, 1989). Changes brought in American rural life by commercialism are discussed in Christopher Clark, *The Roots of Rural Capitalism: Western Massachusetts, 1780–1860* (Ithaca, NY, 1990). The extensive literature on American women in these years can be approached through Linda Kerber, *Women of the Republic: Intellect and Ideology in Revolutionary America* (Chapel Hill NC, 1980), Mary Beth Norton, *Liberty's Daughters: The Revolutionary Experience of American Women, 1750–1800* (Boston, Mass, 1980), Nancy Cott, *The Bonds of Womanhood: 'Woman's Sphere in New England, 1780–1835'* (New Haven, Conn, 1977), and Joan Jensen, *Loosening the Bonds: Mid-Atlantic Farm Women, 1750–1850* (New Haven, Conn, 1986).

Chapter 2

There is a comprehensive account of the main political and diplomatic history of the Federalist era in Stanley Elkins and Eric McKitrick *The Age of Federalism* (New York, 1993). The origins of the Bill of Rights is discussed in Robert A. Rutland, *The Birth of the Bill of Rights* (Chapel Hill, NC, 1955). The early use and interpretation of the Constitution is considered in David P. Currie, *The Constitution in Congress: The Federalist Period, 1789–1901* (Chicago, 1997). For the presidents and their political roles, see Richard McCormick, *The Presidential Game: The Origin of American Presidential Politics* (New York, 1982) and Ralph Ketcham, *Presidents Above Party: The First American Presidency, 1789–1829* (Chapel Hill, NC, 1984). There is a good brief

account of Washington's years as president in Forrest McDonald *The Presidency*
of George Washington (Lawrence, Kans, 1974). McDonald depicts Hamilton very
favorably in *Alexander Hamilton: A Biography* (New York, 1979). Hamilton's political
role is analyzed in Gerald Stourzh, *Alexander Hamilton and the Idea of Republican
Government* (Stanford, Cal, 1970). The subtle ways in which emerging nationality and internal divisions entwined on the popular level is probed in David
Waldreicher, *In the Midst of Perpetual Fetes: The Making of American Nationalism,
1776–1820* (Chapel Hill, NC, 1997).

Chapter 3

Relations with Great Britain are treated in Charles R. Ritcheson, *Aftermath of Revolution: British Policy Toward the United States, 1783–1795* (Dallas, Tex, 1969) and in
Samuel F. Bemis, *Jay's Treaty: A Study in Commerce and Diplomacy* rev. edn (New Haven,
Conn, 1962). The French alliance and its strains are discussed in Alexander DeConde,
Entangling Alliance: Politics and Diplomacy Under George Washington (Durham, NC,
1958), Albert H. Bowman, *The Struggle for Neutrality: Franco-American Diplomacy dur-
ing the Federalist Era* (Knoxville, Tenn, 1974), and Harry Ammon, *The Genêt Mission*
(New York, 1973). An older work, which is still of use for Spain and the Southwest,
is Arthur P. Whitaker, *The Spanish–American Frontier, 1783–1795* (1927; rpr, Gloucester,
Mass, 1962). There is also much on the Southwest in Thomas P. Abernethy, *The South
in the New Nation, 1783–1819* (Baton Rouge, La, 1961). Samuel F. Bemis, *Pinckney's
Treaty, America's Advantage from Europe's Distress* rev. edn (New Haven, Conn, 1960)
examines Spain in the context of the general American and European situation.

Chapter 4

A good introduction to the political struggles of these years is James R. Sharp,
American Politics in the Early Republic: The New Nation in Crisis (New Haven, Conn,
1993), and there is a perceptive general analysis in Richard Buel, *Securing the
Revolution: Ideology in American Politics, 1789–1815* (Ithaca, NY, 1972). There are dif-
ferent approaches to Republican ideology in Lance Banning, *The Jeffersonian
Persuasion: Evolution of a Party Ideology* (Ithaca, NY, 1978) and Joyce Appleby,
Capitalism and the New Social Order: The Republican Vision of the 1790s (New York,
1984). Statistical methodology is used in John F. Hoadly, *Origins of American
Political Parties, 1789–1803* (Lexington, Ky, 1986). The wider implications of
specific events are discussed in Thomas P. Slaughter, *The Whiskey Rebellion: Frontier
Epilogue to the American Revolution* (New York, 1986) and Jerald A. Combs, *Jay's
Treaty: Political Background of the Founding Fathers* (Berkeley, Cal, 1970). Some of the
best works on political parties deal with specific states or regions. These include
James M. Banner, Jr, *To the Hartford Convention: The Federalists and the Origin of*

Party Politics in Massachusetts, 1789–1815 (New York, 1970), Alfred F. Young, *The Democratic Republicans of New York: The Origins, 1763–1797* (Chapel Hill, NC, 1967), and Ronald P. Formisano, *The Transformation of Political Culture: Massachusetts Parties, 1790s–1840s* (New York, 1983). In Simon Newman, *Parades and Politics of the Street: Festive Culture in the Early American Republic* (Philadelphia, 1997) the emphasis is on popular political participation. The partisan press of the Jeffersonians receives detailed treatment in Donald H. Stewart, *The Opposition Press of the Federalist Period* (Albany, NY, 1969), and there is a general account of the press in Carol S. Humphrey, *The Press of the Young Republic, 1783–1833* (Westport, Conn, 1996).

Chapter 5

Two effective accounts of Adams' presidential years are Ralph A. Brown, *The Presidency of John Adams* (Lawrence, Kans, 1975) and Stephen G. Kurtz, *The Presidency of John Adams: The Collapse of Federalism, 1795–1800* (Philadelphia, 1957). There is an analysis of party allegiance in Manning J. Dauer, *The Adams Federalists* (Baltimore, Md, 1953). The crisis with France and its political implications are treated in detail in Alexander DeConde, *The Quasi-War: The Politics and Diplomacy of the Undeclared War with France, 1797–1801* (New York, 1966), and in William C. Stinchcombe, *The X, Y, Z Affair* (Westport, Conn, 1980). Secretary of State Timothy Pickering is the subject of Gerard H. Clarfield, *Timothy Pickering and American Diplomacy, 1795–1800* (Columbia, Mo, 1969). The implications of the French crisis for military preparations are discussed in Richard H. Kohn, *Eagle and Sword: The Beginnings of the Military Establishment in America, 1783–1802* (New York, 1975) and Craig L. Symonds, *Navalists and Antinavalists: The Naval Policy Debate in the United States, 1785–1827* (Newark, Del, 1980). The naval war against France is the subject of Michael A. Palmer, *Stoddert's War: Naval Operations during the Quasi-War with France, 1798–1801* (Columbia, SC, 1987). Improved relations with England are the theme of Bradford Perkins, *The First Rapprochement: England and the United States, 1795–1805* (Philadelphia, 1955). There is a full discussion of the Alien and Sedition acts and the ensuing prosecutions in James Morton Smith, *Freedom's Fetters: The Alien and Sedition Laws and American Civil Liberties* (Ithaca, NY, 1956). For the radical immigrants from the British Isles, see Michael Durey, *Transatlantic Radicals and the Early American Republic* (Lawrence, Kans, 1997).

Chapter 6

Curtis P. Nettels, *The Emergence of a National Economy, 1775–1815* (New York, 1962) is a sound survey of the period. A more influential interpretative study is Douglass C. North, *The Economic Growth of the United States, 1790–1860* (New York, 1961).

There is a discussion of the literature and problems regarding farming in these [261] years in 'American Agriculture, 1790–1840: A Symposium,' *Agricultural History*, 46 (1972), pp. 1–233. There is a general account of early industrial development in Thomas C. Cochran, *Frontiers of Change: Early Industrialism in America* (New York, 1981). The role of lawyers and the law in contributing to economic growth is treated in Morton J. Horowitz, *The Transformation of American Law, 1780–1860* (Cambridge, Mass, 1977). There is an extensive literature on the changing status of workers in the new commercialism of the early nineteenth century. Among these studies are Sean Wilentz, *Chants Democratic: New York City and the Rise of the American Working Class, 1788–1850* (New York, 1984), Howard B. Rock, *Artisans of the New Republic: The Tradesmen of New York City in the Age of Jefferson* (New York, 1979), and Charles G. Steffen, *The Mechanics of Baltimore: Workers and Politics in the Age of Revolution, 1763–1812* (Urbana, Ill, 1984). There is a collection of essays in Howard B. Rock, Paul A. Gilje and Robert Asher (eds), *American Artisans: Crafting Social Identity, 1750–1850* (Baltimore, Md, 1995). Banking is related to the main context of American history in Bray Hammond, *Banks and Politics in America: From the Revolution to the Civil War* (Princeton, NJ, 1957).

Chapter 7

There is general coverage of expansion westwards in these years in Malcolm J. Rohrbough, *The Trans-Appalachian Frontier: People, Societies, and Institutions, 1775–1850* (New York, 1978) and Reginald Horsman, *The Frontier in the Formative Years, 1783–1815* (New York, 1970). Newer political and social themes are introduced in Andrew L. Cayton, *The Frontier Republic: Ideology and Politics in the Ohio Country, 1780–1825* (Kent, Ohio, 1986). R. Douglas Hurt, *The Ohio Frontier: Crucible of the Old Northwest, 1720–1830* (Bloomington, Ind, 1996) is effective in examining economic change. Western urban development is discussed in Richard C. Wade, *The Urban Frontier: The Rise of Western Cities, 1790–1830* (Cambridge, Mass, 1959). New historical interpretations are embodied in two books by Alan Taylor: *William Cooper's Town: Power and Persuasion on the Frontier of the Early American Republic* (New York, 1995) and *Liberty Men and Great Proprietors: The Revolutionary Settlement on the Maine Frontier, 1760–1820* (Chapel Hill, NC, 1990). There are different approaches to relations with the American Indians in Reginald Horsman, *Expansion and American Indian Policy, 1783–1812* (East Lansing, Mich, 1967), Francis P. Prucha, *American Indian Policy in the Formative Years: The Indian Trade and Intercourse Acts, 1790–1834* (Cambridge, Mass, 1962), and Bernard Sheehan, *Seeds of Extinction: Jeffersonian Philanthropy and the American Indian* (Chapel Hill, NC, 1973). John Sugden, *Tecumseh: A Life* (New York, 1998) is a comprehensive biography.

Chapter 8

For Jefferson, see Noble E. Cunningham, Jr, *In Pursuit of Reason: The Life of Thomas Jefferson* (Baton Rouge, La, 1987), Merrill Peterson, *Thomas Jefferson and the New Nation: A Biography* (New York, 1970), and Joseph Ellis, *American Sphinx: The Character of Thomas Jefferson* (New York, 1997). The important role of his Secretary of the Treasury is discussed in Raymond Walters, Jr, *Albert Gallatin: Jeffersonian Financier and Diplomat* (New York, 1957). The clash with the courts is the theme of Richard E. Ellis, *The Jeffersonian Crisis: Courts and Politics in the Young Republic* (New York, 1971). Leonard Levy, *Jefferson and Civil Liberties: The Darker Side* (Cambridge, Mass, 1971) modifies the traditional view of this subject. Leonard Baker, *John Marshall: A Life in Law* (New York, 1974) is a comprehensive biography. Drew McCoy, *The Elusive Republic: Political Economy in Jeffersonian America* (Chapel Hill, NC, 1980) incorporates ideas on classical republicanism with Jeffersonian interest in territorial and commercial expansion. The details of party organization can be followed in Noble J. Cunningham, *The Jeffersonian Republicans in Power: Party Operations, 1801–1809* (Chapel Hill, NC, 1963). There are sophisticated interpretations of the Federalist opposition in David H. Fischer, *The Revolution of American Conservatism: The Federalist Party in the Era of Jeffersonian Democracy* (New York, 1965) and in Linda K. Kerber, *Federalists in Dissent: Imagery and Ideology in Jeffersonian America* (Ithaca, NY, 1970).

Chapter 9

The essays in Ira Berlin and Ronald Hoffman (eds) *Slavery and Freedom in the Age of the American Revolution* (Charlottesville, Va, 1983) are an excellent introduction to a variety of aspects of African American history in these years. Reginald Horsman, *Race and Manifest Destiny: The Origins of American Racial Anglo-Saxonism* (Cambridge, Mass, 1981) concentrates on the evolution of white racial attitudes. There is comprehensive coverage in Winthrop D. Jordan, *White Over Black: American Attitudes toward the Negro, 1550–1812* (Chapel Hill, NC, 1968), and David Brion Davis, *The Problem of Slavery in the Age of Revolution, 1770–1823* (Ithaca, NY, 1975). Duncan J. MacLeod, *Slavery, Race, and the American Revolution* (London, 1974) emphasizes racial implications of the continuation of slavery in these years. Black societies in the South are given extensive treatment in Philip D. Morgan, *Slave Counterpoint: Black Culture in the Eighteenth-Century Chesapeake and Lowcountry* (Chapel Hill, NC, 1998), and both white and African American change are considered in Allan Kulikoff, *Tobacco and Slaves: The Development of Southern Cultures in the Chesapeake, 1680–1800* (Chapel Hill, NC, 1986). A basic work on the Afro-American family is Herbert Gutman, *The Black Family in Slavery and Freedom, 1750–1825.* Slave resistance is the theme in Douglas R. Egerton, *Gabriel's Rebellion: The Virginia Slave Conspiracies of*

1800 and 1802 (Chapel Hill, NC, 1993). The last section of Sylvia R. Frey, *Water*
from the Rock: Black Resistance in a Revolutionary Age (Princeton, NJ, 1991) emphasizes
African American religious experience in the post-revolutionary period. For free
African Americans in the North see Leonard P. Curry, *The Free Black in Urban
America, 1800–1850: The Shadow of the Dream* (Chicago, Ill, 1981) and James Oliver
Horton and Lois E. Horton, *In the Hope of Liberty: Culture, Community and Protest
Among Northern Free Blacks, 1700–1860* (New York, 1997).

Chapter 10

Jeffersonian foreign policy is regarded critically in Robert W. Tucker and David
C. Hendrickson, *Empire of Liberty: The Statecraft of Thomas Jefferson* (New York,
1990). Abraham S. Sofaer, *War, Foreign Affairs, and Constitutional Power: The Origins*
(Cambridge, Mass, 1976) examines the constitutional problems in territorial acquisi-
tions. The Louisiana crisis is covered comprehensively in Alexander DeConde,
This Affair of Louisiana (New York, 1976). The French position is examined in
E. Wilson Lyon, *Louisiana in French Diplomacy, 1759–1804* (Norman, Okla, 1934),
and the importance of the issue to the West in Arthur P. Whitaker, *The Mississippi
Question, 1795–1803: A Study in Trade, Politics, and Diplomacy* (1934; rpr, Gloucester,
Mass, 1962). Jefferson's relations with France are treated more generally in
Lawrence S. Kaplan, *Jefferson and France: An Essay on Politics and Political Ideas* (New
Haven, Conn, 1967), and the role of Monroe is effectively dealt with in Harry
Ammon, *James Monroe: The Quest for National Identity* (New York, 1971). Ray W.
Irwin, *The Diplomatic Relations of the United States with the Barbary Powers, 1776–1816*
(Chapel Hill, NC, 1931) is still of use. For Burr and his conspiracy, see Milton
Lomask, *Aaron Burr* 2 vols (New York, 1979) and Thomas P. Abernethy, *The Burr
Conspiracy* (New York, 1954).

Chapter 11

The increasing crisis in relations with Great Britain is the theme of Bradford
Perkins, *Prologue to War: England and the United States, 1805–1812* (Berkeley, Cal,
1961), and the French complications are dealt with in Clifford Egan, *Neither Peace
Nor War: Franco-American Relations, 1803–1812* (Baton Rouge, La, 1983) and in
C. Edward Skeen, *John Armstrong, Jr, 1758–1843: A Biography* (Syracuse, NY, 1981).
The *Chesapeake* affair is treated comprehensively in Spencer Tucker and Frank T.
Reuter, *Injured Honor: The Chesapeake–Leopard Affair, June 22, 1807* (Annapolis, Md,
1996). Jefferson's reactions to the European crisis can be followed in Reginald
Stuart, *The Half-War Pacifist: Thomas Jefferson's View of War* (Toronto, 1978). His
foreign policy is challenged in Doron S. Ben-Atar, *The Origins of Jeffersonian*

Commercial Policy and Diplomacy (New York, 1993). Problems posed by the commercial policies of the European belligerents, and the solutions sought by American shippers, can be seen in detail in Alfred W. Crosby, *America, Russia, Hemp, and Napoleon: American Trade with Russia and the Baltic, 1783–1812* (Columbus, Ohio, 1965).

Chapter 12

Jefferson's motives in urging the embargo are considered in Burton Spivak, *Jefferson's English Crisis: Commerce, Embargo, and the Republic Revolution* (Charlottesville, Va, 1979). The older and more descriptive Louis M. Sears, *Jefferson and the Embargo* (Durham, NC, 1927) is still useful for the economic impact of the measure. J. C. A. Stagg, *Mr Madison's War: Politics, Diplomacy, and Warfare in the Early Republic, 1783–1830* (Princeton, NJ, 1983) is essential for an understanding of the Republican inability to prepare adequately for war. For James Madison, see Robert A. Rutland, *The Presidency of James Madison* (Lawrence, Kans, 1990), Ralph L. Ketcham, *James Madison: A Biography* (New York, 1971), and Drew R. McCoy, *The Last of the Fathers: James Madison and the Republican Legacy* (New York, 1989). Republican dissidents are the subject of Norman K. Risjord, *The Old Republicans: Southern Conservatism in the Age of Jefferson* (New York, 1965) and Robert E. Shalhope, *John Taylor of Caroline: Pastoral Republican* (Columbia, SC, 1980).

Chapter 13

The background and immediate causation of the War of 1812 are covered in Reginald Horsman, *The Causes of the War of 1812* (Philadelphia, Pa, 1962) and Bradford Perkins, *Prologue to War: England and the United States, 1805–1812* (Berkeley, Cal, 1961). Roger H. Brown, *The Republic in Peril: 1812* (New York, 1964) places Congressional reaction in 1811–12 in the context of fears for republicanism. Ronald L. Hatzenbuehler and Robert L. Ivie, *Congress Declares War: Rhetoric, Leadership, and Partisanship in the Early Republic* (Kent, Ohio, 1983) make a detailed analysis of voting and rhetoric. The major part played by Henry Clay is effectively discussed in Bernard Mayo, *Henry Clay: Spokesman of the New West* (Boston, 1937), and Madison's part is viewed favorably in Irving Brant, *James Madison: The President, 1809–1812* (Indianapolis, 1956). The difficulties in raising military forces are considered in Lawrence D. Cress, *Citizens in Arms: The Army and the Militia in American Society to the War of 1812* (Chapel Hill, NC, 1982), James R. Jacobs, *The Beginning of the US Army, 1783–1812* (Princeton, NJ, 1947), and Craig L. Symonds, *Navalists and Antinavalists: The Naval Policy Debate in the United States, 1785–1827* (Newark, Del. 1980).

Chapter 14

Donald R. Hickey, *The War of 1812: A Forgotten Conflict* (Urbana, Ill, 1989) is a sound general account, Reginald Horsman, *The War of 1812* (London, 1969) makes use of British archives, and John K. Mahon, *The War of 1812* (Gainesville, Fla, 1972) has a full description of American military operations. J. Mackay Hitsman, *The Incredible War of 1812: A Military History* (Toronto, 1965) effectively depicts the military reaction from Canada. Two regional studies – Allan S. Everest, *The War of 1812 in the Champlain Valley* (Syracuse, NY, 1981), and Alec R. Gilpin, *The War of 1812 in the Old Northwest* (East Lansing, Mich, 1958) – are of use for the operations on the Canadian border. The problems experienced in waging war are discussed in J. C. A. Stagg, *Mr Madison's War: Politics, Diplomacy, and Warfare in the Early Republic, 1783–1830* (Princeton, NJ, 1983), and there is a favorable view of how Madison led the nation in Irving Brant, *James Madison: Commander in Chief* (Indianapolis, 1961). American privateering and its economic advantages are considered in Jerome R. Garitee, *The Republic's Private Navy: The American Privateering Business as Practised by Baltimore During the War of 1812* (Middletown, Conn, 1977). Steven Watts, *The Republic Reborn: War and the Making of Liberal America, 1790–1820* (Baltimore, 1987) considers the role of the war in the transformation to a nineteenth-century commercial society.

Chapter 15

David C. Skaggs, *A Signal Victory: The Lake Erie Campaign, 1812–1813* (Annapolis, Md, 1997) and John Sugden, *Tecumseh's Last Stand* (Norman, Okla, 1985) describe operations in the western region of the war. C. Edward Skeen, *John Armstrong, Jr, 1745–1843: A Biography* (Syracuse, NY, 1981) is a sound biography of a controversial Secretary of War. For the British operations in the Chesapeake, and the burning of Washington, see Charles C. Muller, *The Darkest Day: 1814, The Washington–Baltimore Campaign* (Philadelphia, Pa, 1963). The campaigns in the Southwest and on the Gulf are the subject of Frank Owsley, *Struggle for the Gulf Borderlands: The Creek War and the Battle of New Orleans, 1812–1815* (Gainesville, Fla, 1981) and Wilburt S. Brown, *The Amphibious Campaigns for West Florida and Louisiana, 1814–1815: A Critical Review of Strategy and Tactics* (University, Ala, 1969). Andrew Jackson's part in these events is effectively depicted in Robert V. Remini, *Andrew Jackson and the Course of American Empire, 1767–1821* (New York, 1977). The negotiations at Ghent are comprehensively covered in Bradford Perkins, *Castlereagh and Adams: England and the United States, 1812–1823* (Berkeley, Cal, 1964) and Fred L. Engelman, *The Peace of Christmas Eve* (New York, 1962).

INDEX